Studies in Folklore

STITH THOMPSON

IN HONOR OF

DISTINGUISHED

SERVICE

PROFESSOR

Stith Thompson

Studies
in
Folklore

EDITED BY

W. Edson Richmond

BLOOMINGTON 1957   INDIANA UNIVERSITY PRESS

INDIANA UNIVERSITY PUBLICATIONS

FOLKLORE SERIES NO. 9

Indiana University, Bloomington, Indiana

Publication Committee

W. Edson Richmond, EDITOR
John W. Ashton, ASSISTANT EDITOR
David Bidney, ASSISTANT EDITOR

The Indiana University Publications, Folklore Series, was founded in 1939 for the publication of occasional papers and monographs in the field of folklore.

FOREWORD

The seventeen articles which appear in this volume represent only a portion of the material which was offered to honor Professor Stith Thompson. When the book was first planned, requests to participate in it came from scholars all over the world. It thus became unhappily obvious at the very first that the editor would have to exercise some power of limitation if the collection were to be fitted into the size of a normal book. This was indeed a difficult task, for all of the many who wished to contribute were scholars of considerable worth, all could claim friendship with Professor Thompson, and more than a few expressed such affection and such a sense of obligation for the help which he had given them at one time or another that to reject their articles called for a constant realization that the number of pages had to be restricted.

A specific attempt was therefore made to include papers by individuals associated with each major phase of Stith Thompson's career: his European colleagues, his American colleagues (especially those at Indiana University), and his students. Three of the seventeen articles were written by scholars living in Denmark, Norway, and Ireland, and the others by American scholars in various states (Pennsylvania, California, Indiana, Michigan, Ohio, and Kentucky) of the U.S. A further attempt was made to diversify the contents sufficiently so that Professor Thompson's wide interests and learning would be adequately represented. Accordingly, such varied aspects of folklore as folklore scholarship and methodology, folklore in literature, the folksong and folktale, and folk belief, superstition and festival have been included.

Since retiring from his Distinguished Service Professorship in English and Folklore at Indiana University at the end of the academic year of 1954-55, when he was seventy, Stith Thompson has continued his career of teaching and writing. The further details of his life and work are given in the biographical sketch which follows, so it remains only to add that this volume is presented with deep affection and thanks from folklorists all over the world (both from those who participated in the making of the book and from those who wished to but could not because of space limitations) to the man who made their own scholarship possible.

W. Edson Richmond

INDIANA UNIVERSITY
February, 1956

CONTENTS

STITH THOMPSON

It is customary when beginning the biographical sketch of a scholar to speak of his crowning scholarly achievement; in the case of Indiana University's Distinguished Service Professor Stith Thompson, this is very difficult. Does one in such an instance write of his compendious *Motif-Index of Folk-Literature* or of his translation, revision, and enlargement of Antti Aarne's *The Types of the Folktale*? Or does one write first of his *European Tales Among the North American Indians* and work one's way through a mass of definitive publications in article, monograph, and book form beginning with "The Ideal of Social Reconstruction in Tolstoy's 'What Shall We Do Then'" to conclude with a mention of *The Folktale*? It is a difficult decision, for each of these works might well serve as the crowning achievement of a lesser scholar. And, of course, to mention only publications is to neglect the very real measure of any scholar: the influence that he has had upon the scholarship in his own and related fields and the students whom he has inspired. Suffice it to say that among his colleagues Professor Thompson is known as "the Dean of American Folklorists" and that this informally acknowledged title has chronological as well as spatial depth.

Stith Thompson was born on March 7, 1885, in Bloomfield, Kentucky, to John Warden and Eliza McClaskey Thompson, who shortly thereafter moved to a farm near Springfield, Kentucky. Beginning his schooling with a three-year stint in a two-room country school at Pleasant Grove, Kentucky, he continued his elementary education in the somewhat larger schools of Springfield. He did his high-school work at Manual Training in Indianapolis, Indiana, where his family had moved when he was twelve, and subsequently began his college career in Indianapolis, at Butler University. At the same time he worked as an office boy for the Bobbs-Merrill Publishing Company, where he came in contact with and received inspiration from the foremost authors of the day including, he fondly recollects, James Whitcomb Riley. To travel today with Stith Thompson through the Bloomfield, Bardstown, Springfield triangle of Kentucky or through Indianapolis and its outskirts is to see these areas as they were at the turn of the century and to realize the reciprocated affection which the Thompson family felt for their neighbors and the country in which they lived.

On the foundation of a pleasant and stimulating youth and early manhood was set a whole series of significant associations. After two years at Butler and two more years of high-school teaching in his boyhood home town of Springfield, Stith Thompson went on to complete his college undergraduate education at the University of Wisconsin, where he received his A.B. degree in 1909. Here he came under the influence of Professor Arthur Beatty, who introduced him to the possibility of doing work in folklore and to the oral literature of the North American Indians.

Because he felt that a well-educated person should know as

much of his country as possible, Stith Thompson spent his next two years in Oregon, teaching English at Lincoln High School, in Portland, and working in a lumber camp in eastern Oregon during the summers. Here he learned to speak Norwegian from the recently emigrated lumberjacks, learned it well enough to act as a translator for the men.

In the immediately following years, he completed his formal education, first as University Fellow at the University of California, where he was influenced by Professor Charles Mills Gayley and where he received his A.M. in 1912; then as the Bonnheim Research Fellow from the University of California at Harvard University. Here he wrote his dissertation, "A Study of the European Tales Among the North American Indians," under the guidance of Professor George Lyman Kittredge. It was here, too, that he met Archer Taylor, then a fellow graduate student, with whom he spent the summer of 1913 in Europe. In the spring of 1914, he received his Ph.D. from Harvard University.

Still intent upon extending his acquaintance with the world around him, Stith Thompson taught as an Instructor in English at the University of Texas from 1914 to 1918, as Professor of English at Colorado College from 1918 to 1920, and as Associate Professor of English at the University of Maine for the academic year of 1920. Kentucky, Indiana, Wisconsin, Oregon, California, Massachusetts, Europe, Texas, Colorado, and Maine—and during these travels he met Louise Faust, a student at the University of Texas, whom he married on June 14, 1918.

Despite his desire for travel, Stith Thompson has always been strongly attracted to his Kentucky-Indiana heritage. In 1921, therefore, he accepted an associate professorship in the Department of English at Indiana University, a position which carried with it the problems of directing the composition program. And to Indiana University he remained attached until the day of his retirement in June, 1955. During this period his two daughters—Dorothy Cosette (now Mrs. Robert L. Letsinger) and Marguerite Frances (now Mrs. David Glenn Hays)—were born.

Dr. Thompson was promoted first to Professor of English and Folklore in 1939 and later, in 1953, to Distinguished Service

Professor; and from 1947 to 1950 he served as Dean of the Graduate School. By his industrious scholarship he brought international fame to Indiana University, which has become a world center for folklore. Indeed, throughout Western and Northern Europe, *Indiana University* and *folklore* are nearly synonymous. In Latin America, too, where the concept of folklore is somewhat different from what is understood by the word as it is used in Europe and North America, Stith Thompson is the man and Indiana University is the place most frequently identified with folklore studies.

Such fame is due not only to Professor Thompson's careful scholarship but also to his personal magnetism. This can, perhaps, best be illustrated by the fact that when he visited Europe in the academic year of 1926-27 he was persuaded by the great Finnish folklorist Kaarle Krohn to stop work on *The Motif-Index of Folk-Literature*, which was in the early stages of preparation, and to revise and enlarge Antti Aarne's *Verzeichnis der Märchentypen*, for, said Krohn, Stith Thompson was obviously the man to carry on Aarne's work. And Stith Thompson has ever since borne this distinction with such ease that his right to it has never been questioned.

Recognition of Professor Thompson's pre-eminence in the academic world has fortunately carried honors with it, both in his own country and in the world at large. In 1946 he was awarded the degree of Doctor of Letters by the University of North Carolina, and in 1953 he received the degree of Doctor of Humane Letters from Indiana Central College. In addition, he has accepted memberships in the American Philosophical Society, the Gustav Adolphs Akademi für Folklivsforskning, the Societé fin-no-ougrienne, Det Norske Videnskaps-Akademi i Oslo, Det kongelige danske Videnskabernes Selskab, the Finnish Society of Letters, the Asociacion Folklorica Argentina, the Sociedade Brasiliera de Folk-lore, the Instituto de Investigaciones Folkloricas de las Universidad de Chile, the Servicio de Investigaciones Folkloricas Nacionales of Venezuela: all societies difficult of attainment, each the crown of achievement within its own geographical area. Stith Thompson has also been President of the

American Folklore Society (1937-40) and Vice-President of CIAP and is a member of the Modern Language Association, Folklore of the Americas, the Folklore societies of Ireland, Peru, and Mexico, and the Medieval Academy of America. In 1947 he served as technical advisor in folklore to the Ministry of Education of Venezuela, where he set up a folklore program that is still carried on despite several changes in government since that time; in 1951-52 he was a Fulbright Professor in Norway; and in 1956-57 he held a Guggenheim Fellowship.

Though he officially retired from his duties at Indiana University in June, 1955, at the age of seventy, he very shortly thereafter saw in print the first volume of his tremendously revised second edition of *The Motif-Index of Folk-Literature,* finished the final mechanical details for the subsequent volumes, and completed his circle of university teaching by accepting a visiting professorship at the University of Texas for the spring semester of 1956.

From October, 1956, until August, 1957, Stith Thompson was in Europe, where he renewed his friendship with his European colleagues and revised his first major publication, the Aarne-Thompson *Types of the Folktale.*

W. Edson Richmond

Laurits Bødker

DANSK FOLKEMINDESAMLING

COPENHAGEN, DENMARK

The Brave Tailor in Danish Tradition

The story of "The Brave Tailor" (AT 1640)[1] is known in Denmark in fifteen oral variants taken down between 1854 and 1933. In addition there are two printed versions, both of which seem to have influenced the tradition. The older of these, which is denoted as var. 1abc, is a metrical text, of which three editions are extant:

1a. En Ny / Selsom og meget lystig / Historie / Om / En Skomager-Svend / i Rysz-Land, / Og / Hvorledis hand for sin usæd-vanlige Tapperheds Skyld, er bleven til en stoer Herre og Regen-tere der udi Landet, og hvad videre mand af Historien haver at fornemme. / Tilsammenskrevet af en Rysk *Historicus* i Finland./ Trykt Aar der dette skeede.

1b. En ny / selsom og meget lystig / Historie / om en Skomager-svend / i Rusland; / hvorledes han for sin usædvanlige Tapperheds

Skyld er bleven til en stor Herre og Regent der i Landet, men hvad videre, man af denne Historie vil fornemme. / Sammenskreven af en Russisk Historikus i Finland./ Kiøbenhavn.

1c. En ny / meget lystig og selsom / Historie / om / en vidtberejst / Skomagersvend / i Rusland, / der omsider, efter mange overstandne Farer, ved sin usædvanlige Tapperhed og store Mod blev en mægtig Herre og Regent der i Kajserdømmet./ Kjøbenhavn./ Tilkjøbs i store Helliggejststræde No 150 og 151.

The three editions are undated, but seem to date from the end of the 18th century, and are here arranged in the order which seems the most likely from typographical and orthographical criteria. Var. 1c must have been printed between 1797 and 1808 by Joh. Rud. Thiele, who, according to Copenhagen directories, in that period had his office at 150–151 Helliggejststræde, whereas from 1808 on he resided at No. 159 in the same street. The Swedish forms of words in var. 1a—*Ryszland,* and *Rysk*—combined with the statement that the story was written by a Russian historian in Finland, would seem to indicate that the story is a translation from a Swedish one, possibly deriving from Finland, which country was under the Swedish Crown until 1809. On the other hand it must be mentioned that it has not been possible, so far, to discover any such edition, and for the present the possibility cannot be ignored that the statements on the title page may be fictitious, with a view to gaining credence for the truthfulness of the story.

A fourth edition of the same text was printed in 1855 by Fr. D. Beyer at Bergen. This edition, however, is probably derived from the Danish texts[2] and is, therefore, of no use in determining the country of origin of the text. But a summary[3] of the four editions which have the same contents gives a new clue, by which we may get nearer the solution.

SECTION I

Three times on end a shoemaker in Russia kills fifteen flies swarming round spilt food on the table. Proud of his feat he considers himself a warrior of ancient warrior's stock, and makes up his mind to go to the King's court, where he feels sure to become a lord. He puts lettering on his buff coat to say that he kills fifteen at every blow and issues handbills with the same assertion. The rumor of his courage is heard even by the Russian Emperor, who sets off with a numerous retinue to find the stalwart warrior and prevail upon him to enter his service. At the same time the shoemaker is on his way to the Emperor, whose men find him sleeping by the way. None of them dares to waken the great hero. While they are debating how to tackle the matter, the shoemaker awakes and is no less frightened than they are; but he bluffs successfully, enters the Emperor's service, and rises even higher in their esteem by declaring that he considers his sword a straw, and will kill everything with his hands.

SECTION III

The shoemaker's courage is put to the test when the Emperor asks him to kill a wild boar who has wounded and killed many people with his tusk. The shoemaker declares himself ready to kill the dangerous beast as he would a bullock, or scare him away. He turns down the Emperor's offer of men, because he intends to flee as soon as he is left alone. In his flight he has the bad luck to encounter the boar, who pursues him with gaping jaws. The shoemaker seeks rescue in a tree, the soporific fruits of which he throws down to the boar, who eats them and soon goes off to sleep, after which the shoemaker climbs down, kills the beast with his knife, and returns to tell the Emperor that the dangerous beast was like a pig (IIIb).

Next he is to kill a unicorn of whom all are afraid. Again he tries to flee, but encounters the unicorn, who butts at him with its horn. He seeks safety up a tree, and the beast, following hard on his heels, runs its horn into the same tree, where it is caught so tightly that the unicorn cannot disengage it. The shoemaker kills the unicorn and returns to say that it was like a calf and, but for its horn, might have been used as a horse (IIIc).

After some years the shoemaker's courage is put to the test

again, when he is to kill a white bear who kills everybody and
drinks the blood of his victims. As usual, the shoemaker begins
fleeing, but in the end, pursued by the bear, he seeks shelter in
a tile kiln. The bear follows, but the shoemaker succeeds in getting out and shuts the door on the bear, after which he returns to
tell the Emperor that the bear can now be killed by his men as
if he were a rat, a wildcat, or a fox, apart from his tail's being so
short. The shoemaker's fame rises even higher when it appears
that the Emperor's men can kill the captive beast only with the
utmost difficulty (IIId).

SECTION IV

Next the country is invaded by many enemies, Turks and
other heathen as well. The shoemaker is made a general, supplied with armor and a sword, and given the Emperor's charger
to ride on. He tries to ride away from the company, the horse
bolts, the shoemaker catches hold of a signpost to halt the speed,
but the signpost is pulled up and trailed along, and the wild ride
goes on toward the enemy, who are frightened and flee across a
bridge. The bridge is broken, and all are drowned in the stream
(IVa).

After this great feat the shoemaker is knighted and given a
castle and stronghold for his own. After a great banquet at the
Emperor's court the newly knighted shoemaker is sent to recover
a town which was captured by the enemy a long time ago. The
shoemaker is followed by all the forces and best men of the
realm, who are to be taught warfare on this occasion. He realizes
that this time flight will be impossible, and that his incompe-
tence will be disclosed to everybody. So he makes up his mind
to pretend having lost his reason, tears off everything but his
shirt, and approaches the town to be killed by the enemy. The
army, however, have been ordered to imitate the shoemaker:
They follow in their shirts, each like him taking a torch, and run
up toward the town. The enemy, thinking themselves seeing a
host of angels, open the gates, crying: "God's angel dear, take me
the first." When the shoemaker gets through the gate, he knocks

them on the head with his torch; his army do likewise, and all of the enemy are killed (IVb).

SECTION VI

After that feat the Emperor gives him his daughter as wife and promises him his whole empire after his death.

Section IV, "The Hero at War," is peculiar to this version of the story, the printed texts as well as the oral variants in Jutland and Norway. If we now follow the old path of traditions from Jutland down into the European Continent, we find Episode IVa, but apparently not Motif IVb in the rich tradition of Holstein,[4] which until 1864 was a duchy under the Danish Crown, and which, together with the Duchy of Schleswig (also under Danish rule until 1864), has been a link between Danish (Scandinavian) and Dutch (Flemish) tradition. The same episode is found in a Dutch chapbook, *"Het wonderlyck en niet min kluchtig Leven van kleyn Kobisje sonder Onderzaten,"* etc.,[5] and in oral variants from the Netherlands, Flanders, and Luxemburg.[6] On the other hand, this episode seems to be rare or unknown in the Northern German material immediately south of Holstein.

With our present knowledge of the cultural relations between the Netherlands and Denmark, it would seem natural to assume that the Danish text is either an adaptation of a Dutch (Flemish) chapbook, or maybe a local, enlarged versification of a Jutlandish tradition which ultimately derives from that area.

This explanation must, of course, be considered as a hypothesis until it is confirmed or invalidated by a comprehensive regional investigation which is in progress and of which only the Danish section has been included in this paper.

Much space has been given to this survey of the printed version of "The Shoemaker of Russia," because by a curious accident it is exactly Section IV, "The Hero at War," that has not gotten into Johannes Bolte's summary of the Danish version.[7] Bolte, who did not know the texts printed in Denmark, nor the Norwegian printed text, has used the short summary in R. Nyerup's old survey of Danish and Norwegian chapbooks,[8] which includes only Sections I, III, and VI. Bolte was therefore not aware of the above-mentioned connection with the Western European material.

To make up for the elaborateness of this account, the other printed version will be dealt with only briefly; it is the version found in the Danish translations of *Grimm No. 20,* "Das tapfere Schneiderlein," in the enlarged and revised 2nd edition of the *Kinder– und Hausmärchen,* 1819:

Var. 2a Folke-Eventyr samlede af Brødrene Grimm. Oversatte af Johan Frederik Lindencrone. *Gjennemseete og udgivne efter anden forøgede og forbedrede Udgave.* (Kiøbenhavn: 1821), p. 97, No. 20. This translation was reprinted in 1823, 1839, 1853, 1857, 1869, 1875, 1881, etc., and in all editions "The Brave Tailor" is found. It has accordingly had ample opportunity to be read and known.
Var. 2b. C. Molbech, *Udvalgte Eventyr og Fortællinger* (Kiøbenhavn: 1843), p. 59, No. 16. New editions 1854, 1873, and 1882, which likewise contain "The Brave Tailor."

Both variants follow the German text rather closely; Lindencrone is somewhat wordy, and Molbech's translation is more succinct, without omitting any essentials. The only point of distinction between the two texts is in Section I (see below): In 2a the tailor buys honey from a farmer's wife, whereas in 2b he buys butter. This diversity is also found in the oral variants.

The Grimm Version is so well-known that it need not be summarized. Suffice it to refer to the motif-survey below and point to the fact that this text does not contain Section IV, "The Hero at War," nor Section V, "Tailor (Bear) and Lion." A special feature of this version is Section II, "Lucky Successes," and Section III, "The Wedding," which are not found in the story of "The Shoemaker of Russia." The two versions have Section III, "Lucky Hunter," in common.

The Grimm brothers themselves have pointed to the fact that "The Brave Tailor" is pieced together from oral tales now classified as Group AT 1060 ff., "Contest between Man and Ogre," and a literary story in Montanus' *Wegkürzer:* "Von einem könig, schneyder, rysen, einhorn und wilden schwein," which, as indicated by the title, contains Section II, "The Lucky Hunter," and Section VII, "The Wedding."[9]

Of particular interest from a Danish point of view is the fact that the story in Montanus was printed as a chapbook in Sweden, and that it is found also in the short Low German edition of *Wegekörter* (1592),[10] which may have influenced the tradition in Holstein, a Low German cultural area, which, as mentioned above, belonged to the Danish Crown until 1864. From this area the version may have spread to Denmark.

THE MOTIFS

I. *Boastful fly-killer:* "seven (fifteen, etc.) at a blow" (K1951.1)

II. *Lucky Successes*
    a: Contest in squeezing water from a stone (K62)
    b: Throwing contest: bird substituted for stone (K18.3)
    c: Deceptive contest in carrying a tree: riding (K71)
    d: Contest: jumping over a cherry tree (cf. K17)
    e: Deceptive eating contest: food in coat (K81.1)
    f: Substituted object left in bed while intended victim escapes (K525.1)

III. *Lucky Hunter*
    a: Ogres (giants) duped into fighting each other (K1082)
    b: Wild boar caught by eating soporific fruits (K776)
    c: Unicorn (wild boar) tricked into running horn into tree (K771)
    d: Wild boar (etc.) captured in chapel (tile kiln, etc.) (K731)
    e. Tiger caught in cleft of tree (cf. K1111)

IV. *The Hero at War*
    a: Runaway cavalry hero (K1951.2)
    b: Enemy frightened by army in white shirts carrying torches in their hands

V. *Tailor and Bear (Lion)*
    a: Contest in biting nuts: the bear (lion) bites a stone (K63)
    b: Bear (lion) wishing to learn to play the fiddle has his claws caught in vise (cf. K1111.0.1)
    c: Bear (lion) terrified by naked woman (cf. K1755)

VI. *Rewards*
    a: Lowly hero marries princess (L161)
    b: Half a kingdom as reward (Q112)
    c: Knighthood as reward (Q113)
    d: Riches as reward (Q111)

VII. *The Wedding*

   a: Tailor married to princess betrays trade by talking in his sleep, scolding a journeyman tailor (cf. H38.2.1)

   b: Attempt to kill hero (H1510)

   c: Overheard human conversation (N455)

   d: Sham warrior intimidates soldiers with his boasting (K1951.3)

THE VARIANTS[11]

1abc. "The Shoemaker of Russia": I   IIIbcd   IVab   VIa

2ab. "The Brave Tailor" (*Grimm* No. 20): I   IIabcdf   IIIacd   VIab VIIabcd

  3. ETKr 1765; coll. 1894 at Hørve /342/: I   IIIc(d)   VIa

  4. DFS 1906/14: J. P. Kuhre; coll. 1933 at Østermarie /763/. Printed J. P. Kuhre: *Borrinjholmska Sansåger* (1938), 86, No. 8: I   IIIc   VId

  5. Gg 94a; coll. 1854 at Fureby /1248/: I   IVa   VId

  6. ETKr 1892; coll. 1895 at Sim /1529/: I   IIb(d)   IIIa(c)d   VIa VIIbd

  7. ETKr 1673; coll. 1894 at Egå /2048/: I   IIbad   III(c)   VIa

  8. ETKr 1656; coll. 1894 at Todbjærg /2049/. Printed E. T. Kristensen, *Jyske Folkeminder*, XII (1895), 139, No. 29: AT 1612 + AT 1611 + AT 1640: I   IVb(a)   IIIed   VId

  9. Gg 94b; coll. 1883 at Lisbjerg /2076/: I   IIIcd   IIedb   VIa VIIabcd

 10. ETKr 2426; coll. 1905 at Vinding /2362/: I   IIIcd   IVa

 11. ETKr 1487; coll. 1890 at Gudun /2422/: I   IIIadc   VIa   VIIabd

 12. ETKr 646; coll. 1874 at Tvis /2481/: I   IIIdc   IVb   VI(b)

13a. ETKr 269; coll. 1872 at Herning[12] /2494/: I   IVb   VabVIaVc

13b. ETKr 2079; coll. 1898 at Gellerup /2489/: I   IVb   VabVIaVc

 14. ETKr 41; coll. 1871 at Gellerup /2489/: I   IVb   VabVIaVc

 15. Db 635; coll. 1873 at Gellerup /2489/: I

 16. ETKr 135b; coll. 1871 at Ikast /2492/: I   V(ab)

This survey seems to show that the material may be broadly classified into three versions: *A* ("The Brave Tailor"; *Grimm* No. 20); *B* ("The Shoemaker of Russia"); and *C* with the following sections:

Version A:	I	II	III		VI	VII	Var. 2ab, 6, 7, 9, 11, 15
Version B:	I		III	IV	VI		Var. 1abc, 3, 4, 5, 8, 10, 12
Version C:	I			IV	V VI		Var. 13ab, 14, 16

The relationship between the variants and their relation to the printed texts will appear from the following analysis.

SECTION I: The Boastful Fly-killer

Version A. A tailor (2ab, 6, 7, 9, 11, 15) buys honey (2a, 6, 11, 15) or butter (2b, 7, 9) and spreads it on bread, which attracts flies, seven of which he kills at a blow (2ab, 6, 7, 9, 11, 15); he puts inscription on belt (2ab, 6, 7, 9, 11) and goes out into the world, bringing with him cheese (2ab, 7), bird (2ab), sparrow (6, 7). He encounters giant (2ab, 6, 7), then goes to King, or is taken into King's service directly (9, 11).

The oral variants follow the printed text fairly closely. The variation between "butter" and "honey" may be due to the difference between Lindencrone's and Molbech's translations, which have both been known everywhere in Denmark. It would seem, in other words, that "butter" was borrowed from one and "honey" from the other. Var. 15 is a fragment which ends in the tailor's killing seven flies and resolving to make the feat known to the whole town. This variant was narrated by a schoolboy; it is possible, however, that he merely reproduces the printed text, which he may have read or heard at school. The other variants of this group (6, 7, 9, 11) show the widespread inclination to modify or "amend." Var. 6, 7, and 9 contain the throwing contest (IIb), and in 6 and 7 the bird has become a sparrow, which may be taken as another instance of the general and well-known inclination to concretize which is so pronounced in Danish tradition. In 9, Section II has been placed after the fight with the unicorn and wild boar (IIIcd), and this also reacts on the opening in that the tailor does not bring a bird with him from home —indeed, it would not have survived if the hero had carried it in his pocket during the violent fights with the two wild beasts. The squeezing contest (IIa) is found in 7 only, and the economy of the narrative is influenced thereby, for only in this variant does the tailor bring a cheese with him from home, as if anticipating his encounter with a giant.

Version B. Shoemaker (1abc, 10, 12) or tailor (3, 4, 5, 8) is disturbed by flies (1abc, 3, 4, 5, 8, 10, 12) eating food (1abc, 4, 8, 12). He kills fifteen flies at a blow (1abc, 3, 4, 8, 12), or 5/10/20 (5), or 30

(10). He has inscription made on clothes (1abc, 4, 10, 12), on belt (8), or tin sheet (3), or label (5). Next he enters the service of Russian Emperor (1abc, 4), of King (3, 5, 10), more particularly of the (Danish) King in Copenhagen (8, 12).

Compared with *Version A,* this version shows a distinctive character of its own, which may be described negatively: Honey/butter is never mentioned; it is never seven flies that are killed; in one case only (8) is the inscription placed on the belt; the hero does not encounter a giant before entering the Emperor's (King's) service. Besides, some variants (1abc, 4, 8, 12) have a localization which is not found in the first version.

An examination of the variants of *Version B* show the group to be rather heterogeneous. The two variants from Eastern Denmark (3, 4) take an intermediate position between the two versions. In both tales the hero is a tailor who kills fifteen flies which enter by a window (3) or light on a cabbage (4); next follows the unicorn episode (IIIc), which is found in both versions and for that reason is of no avail in determining the classification of the two variants in one or the other version. Var. 4 is localized to a definite farmstead called Vejdemandsgård, in the native parish of the narrator, Østermarie, in the island of Bornholm, in the Baltic. This tale has so many particular features that it must rather be considered a local mutation: The hero is called Per Syv ("Seven"), which by the way is the name of one of the earliest Danish folklorists, Peder Syv (1631–1701). The killing episode takes place while the people at the farm are having their midday meal, cabbage, and takes the form of a killing contest, which is won by the tailor, who kills fifteen flies with the palm of his hand. Next the farm people all go to the barn to have the after-dinner nap, but the tailor snores so loudly that the others cannot sleep. To make fun of him, they write the well-known inscription in chalk on his belt. In the afternoon, when Per Syv is out felling trees, he is met by the Russian Emperor, who just now comes walking from Paris and, seeing the inscription, takes the tailor into his service. This episode shows association with *Version B.*

Two variants have a particular opening: 5 has an episode between the tailor and a butcher, and in 8 the tailor becomes a mate on board a ship bound from Aarhus to Kalundborg, the ancient route between Jutland and Zealand. On the way he is thrown overboard by the sailors, hangs on to a rope trailing after the ship, and on his arrival at Kalundborg declares that he has swum four Danish miles (twenty English miles). Next follow the contest in swimming (AT 1612; K 1761) and the contest in climbing the mast (AT 1611; K 1762), after which the Brave Tailor makes for Copenhagen, kills fifteen flies at an inn, etc. The hero of 12 likewise goes to Copenhagen after killing fifteen flies that cannot keep away from his gruel.

Version C. Tailor (13ab, 14, 16) is disturbed by flies eating leavings on table (14). He kills fifteen at a blow (13ab, 14), puts inscription on silver or gold plate (3ab, 14), goes out into the world, and enters the service of the King (13ab, 14).

In this group the hero is always a tailor who kills fifteen flies, the same combination as found in three variants (3, 5, 8) of *Version B,* which seems to be, also in other particulars, closely connected with *C.* (Cf. Section IV.)

SECTION II: Lucky Successes

Version A. The tailor's encounter with the giant is not found in 11, which all the same is reckoned in this group on the ground of its containing Section IV, "The Hero at War." The other three oral variants (6, 7, 9) contain the throwing contest (IIb), but all of them are without the tree-carrying episode (IIc) and the attempt to murder the hero (IIf); further, the squeezing contest is found only in (7). As no direct connection has been established between the three variants, the three narrators, or previous narrators, must be supposed to have independently dropped the several episodes, which otherwise are generally found in Danish popular tradition. It would seem, then, to be a conscious deviation from the printed text. Such economy in dealing with given material need not be attributed to "forgetfulness," but may be due to a critical, selective attitude toward the many parallel episodes in Grimm's conglomerate.

In the printed text (2ab), the jumping contest (IId) opens with the giant and the tailor picking cherries; the bough which is hauled down to the tailor by the giant whips up and throws the tailor over the tree, after which he explains that he wanted to get over the tree to avoid the hunter's shot. The three oral variants have retained this episode, but in a somewhat different form: In 7 and 9 the giant does not try to jump over the cherry tree; in 6 the cherry tree incident is lacking, and the tailor wins the jumping contest by bending a young mountain ash and jumping over it.

The greatest deviation from the printed text is found in 9, in which the whole of this section is not told till after the tailor's encounter with the unicorn and the wild boar (Section III). In this variant, the deceptive contest in eating (IIe) has been added, forming a sort of framework story: The giant eats eight dishes of porridge while the tailor pretends to eat nine, actually putting the porridge into his leather coat; next follow the cherry tree episode and the throwing contest, after which the tailor takes out his knife and cuts a hole in his coat, letting the porridge pour out. The giant, too, wishes to relieve himself of the porridge, but he cuts his belly and dies.

This section of the story is not found in *Versions B* and *C*.

SECTION III: Lucky Hunter

Version A. The tailor makes two giants kill each other (2ab, 6, 11). Next he is to kill or catch a unicorn (2ab, 6, 9, 11), or wild boar (7), who is tricked into running his horn into a tree (2ab, 7, 9, 11), or is so slow as to be easily killed by the tailor with a sabre (6). The third task is to catch or kill one wild boar (2ab, 9, 11), or two (6), who are decoyed into a chapel (2ab), or summerhouse (9), or cottage in the wood (11), or into a gateway in the King's castle (6).

In this section also the usual individual divergences between the several variants are found. The fast-running unicorn, for example, has in 6 been changed into a slow animal covered with scales through which nobody has been able to stab until the tailor arrives. The greatest alteration is found in 7, which has only one episode; but then this one has been amplified with motifs derived from quite another group of stories: after the encounter with the giant the tailor goes to a King whose daughter has been promised to an ogre with two heads; the ogre, in the shape of a wild beast, is to fetch her in a wood. The tailor goes into the wood, where by decoy calls he tricks the beast, a unicorn, into coming out; the beast is killed in the usual way.

In the third episode, the fight with the wild boar, all oral variants have divergences from the printed text, in which the beast is caught in a chapel. These alterations were certainly not made for religious reasons; they must be accounted for by the fact that there are no chapels in Danish woods; and such a place for the capture has therefore been felt as an alien feature by the Danish narrators, each of whom has given his own substitute. It is worth noticing that none have used the tile kiln, which is invariably found in *Version B*. This exclusive attitude is found also in Section I, where we have noted that the hero nearly always is a tailor who kills seven flies.

Version B. Hero is to kill wild boar (1abc), who is tricked into eating soporific fruits (1abc), and/or unicorn (1abc, 3, 4, 10, 12), who runs his horn into tree, or tiger (8), who gets his head caught in cleft of tree. Besides, the hero is to catch a bear (1abc, 12), a lion (8), or a *To-horn* (10), who is enticed into a tile kiln (1abc, 8, 10, 12).

In Section III, too, independence of the printed text is noticeable, in that none of the oral variants have included the fight with the wild boar.[13] This episode, incidentally, bears a strong resemblance to the story of *Aper,* which does not occur in popular tradition either, although *The Seven Sages,* in which the story is found, is known in not less than eighteen editions between about 1571 and 1859.

Var. 8, which in Section I showed great divergences from the ordinary pattern, also has an independent form of this section, in that the unicorn has become a tiger who, having no horn, must be killed by another method. The scene is laid in the *Dyrehaven,* an animal park north of Copenhagen, and the whole of this section has been placed after Section IV, "The Hero at War." In Var. 5 the whole of this section is missing, and 3 has made a conglomeration of the two episodes: Unicorn runs horn into tree standing just in front of tile kiln where tailor is hiding. The narrator of 10 has invented a quite novel animal, a *"To-horn"* (Two-horn) after the analogy of *En-horn* (One-horn), the ordinary vernacular form of unicorn.

In the printed text (1abc) the shoemaker is a coward who is always frightened and has no other thought than flight when sent to catch or kill the wild boar, the unicorn, the bear, or the Turkish army. Also in the oral variants (3, 8, 10, 12) we find that the shoemaker is a coward. In Var. 10 and 12 he even demands board allowance, so as not to starve on his homeward flight.

A comparison with *Version A,* where it is not the tailor but the King and his warriors as well that are frightened, shows that the two printed versions take different views of the hero's character, and this variance is reflected in the oral tradition.

Section III is not found in *Version C.*

SECTION IV: The Hero at War

Version B. The hero is to free the country of Turks and other heathen (1abc), of Swedes (8), a host of enemies (10), or a giant (5). He is put on a horse who bolts, and in his speed he catches hold of a signpost (1abc, 10) or a field gate (8) or has a doorframe hanging on his shoulder (5). The enemy flee, frightened at the strange spectacle. The hero is to relieve a town (1abc) or a province (12). He makes his army advance riding in their shirts, carrying torches in their hands; the enemy, thinking them to be angels (1abc), or the Lord and angels (12), surrender.

Section IV is missing in 3; the other variants have one episode only; 8, as usual, has an individual form, a conglomeration of the two episodes: the tailor advances on the Swedish army, riding at the head of the hussars; on his way he loses his shako and his tunic; and the hussars divest themselves of the same articles of uniform. The tailor, still leading the way on his bolting horse, arrives at a field gate across the road. The horse rushes onward, the gate round his neck; and the enemy are frightened. The narrator of 12 has given a very vivid description of this episode: The shoemaker is in the service of the King in Copenhagen, who has lost a province some years before, which the hero is now to reconquer. When the inhabitants of the occupied province see the shoemaker and his army in white shirts, torches in their hands, "they advance on them. And they sang and were glad of them, thinking them to be the Lord and the angels coming. They sang a tune opening with the words: 'Christ is coming with trumpets in his hands.' But the shoemaker got angry at that; and he said: 'If I am Christ, I shall'—and here he made an oath—'christen you.' And then he dealt one of them a blow on the head which made him tumble over; and all his men did likewise. They went on doing so until the rest surrendered." After this the shoemaker takes possession of the country, and writes home to his wife and family, who next come to join him.

Section IV is not found in *Version A*.

Version C. The tailor is to free the country of enemies: He makes his men put on white shirts and furnishes them with torches. The attack takes place at night; thinking them to be angels, the enemy flee (13ab, 14). In 14 there are some clues suggesting that the enemy are Swedes, though this is not plainly stated: They are coming across "the Sound" on a floating bridge and have camped in a valley near the coast.

This episode is known only in a limited region of Central Jutland. Var. 13ab and 14 and Var. 12 of *Version B* have all been collected in the parishes around the place where the town of Herning is now situated. Var. 8, containing a conglomeration of the two episodes, was taken down about sixty kilometers farther southeast.

SECTION V: Tailor and Bear (Lion)

Version C. The tailor is to spend a night with a bear (13ab) or a lion (14) living in a tower (14). He brings nuts, pebbles, and a violin with him, and sits down to play (13ab, 14), taking out a nut from time to time, and cracking it with his teeth. The beast also wants some nuts, but instead gets pebbles, which he cannot crush. He is thus inspired with great awe of tailor with strong teeth (13b, 14). Bear (lion) will also be taught to play, but the tailor asserts that bear (lion) cannot keep his foot quiet (13b, 14) and that his claws are too long (13ab, 14). The beast is tricked into putting his foot in a vise, which is tightened until he is caught, and tailor cuts off the animal's foot (13ab, 14) almost to the knee (13ab). Next, the tailor lies down to sleep; and when the guard arrives in the morning, the beast says, "Softly, softly! My master is sleeping." (14, 16).

The tailor is given the Princess as wife and drives away with her in a carriage, but they are pursued by bear (lion). The hero makes the carriage stop, the Princess undresses and lies down like a corpse, and the tailor pretends to scrape her with knife (13ab) or lies down across her. Bear (lion) takes fright and runs home to the King.

This section is not found in the other two versions and is probably a local *oikotype* which was taken down in the three parishes of Herning, Gellerup, and Ikast in Central Jutland. On the other hand, we must not forget that exactly these three parishes belong to the small area in which E. Tang Kristensen, while he was the schoolmaster in Gellerup (1868–75), visited practically every house and talked to everybody with the purpose of collecting folklore. Such thorough collecting has not been undertaken in the rest of Denmark; and there is a possibility, therefore, that this version of AT 1640 has been known, though not taken down, elsewhere.

Two variants of this group (14, 16) have a metrical passage, which seems to derive from the chapbook:

Var. 14, 16	Var. 1abc
Alt Sværd og gevær	Alt gevær jeg agter som straa
det agter jeg for en pennings værd	Med mine hænder og stolte mod
med min' raske hænder og stolte mod	Haver jeg mangen fældet forfod'.
slår jeg til døde femten for fod.	

Such reminiscences of the printed text (1abc) are not found in the oral variants of *Version B,* which thus at this point shows more independence than does *C.*[14] The verse in 14 and 16 is an independent modeling of the printed text and may derive from another printed text which is now unknown.

SECTION VI: Rewards

Version A. The tailor is married to a Princess (2ab, 6, 7, 9, 11) and is given half of the Kingdom (2ab).

Version B. The hero is married to a Princess (1abc, 3), and is given half of the kingdom (3), or succeeds to the throne on the death of the King (1abc) "and their children go about selling buttermilk by the yard" (3). He is made a Count (Knight) and is given a County (1abc, 8), or is made King of the conquered country and takes his wife and family to him (12). In two variants (4, 5) he is given a reward, and in 10 he stays at the King's court in high esteem.

Version C. Tailor is married to Princess (13ab, 14), and "they build children and beget houses" (13a).

SECTION VII: The Wedding

Version A. After the wedding the tailor, in his sleep, reveals his trade by scolding a lazy tailor's apprentice (2ab, 9, 11). The Princess, wishing to get rid of her low-born husband (2abc, 6, 11), tells her father (2ab, 9, 11) that she is married to a tailor. The King (2ab, 9, 11) or Princess (6) places sentry outside the door intending to kill the tailor while he is sleeping (2ab, 6, 9, 11). This plot is disclosed by a servant (2ab, 9, 11), and the tailor scares the sentry by pretending to talk in his sleep, boasting of his former feats (2ab, 6 9, 11). This section is not found in 7, where it would indeed be an anticlimax, the tailor having proved a true hero by rescuing Princess from ogre with two heads.

This section is not found in *Version B. Version C* has put Episode Vc, "The Bear (Lion) and the Naked Princess," after the wedding, for which reason this episode should possibly have been placed in Section VII. On the other hand, the whole of Section V is so well-knit that the three episodes with the bear (lion) must more naturally be considered as a whole with the wedding as a link to the latter episode.

The varying view of the hero's character and the King's attitude to him is reflected in Sections VI and VII. In the printed text (2ab) of *Version A* the King's warriors are afraid of the brave tailor and ask their discharge. The King does not wish to lose them; but he fears that the tailor, if dismissed, will get furious, kill the King, and make himself ruler of the country. The King, to get out of the dilemma, asks the tailor to kill the two giants, etc., hoping thus to have the tailor killed. He makes the tasks the more attractive by promising the tailor both the Princess and half of the Kingdom. When the tailor successfully performs the tasks, the King is forced to keep his promise. Thus a logical link to Section VII is obtained, in which section also the Princess tries to have the tailor killed, and the latter escapes as usual. The fear motif is not found in the oral traditions, but Var. 6, 9, 11 have nevertheless retained Section VII, often with the emphasis on the discontent felt by the noble Princess at being married to such a mean-born fellow (6, 11).

In *Version B* the hero succeeds in bluffing; nobody finds out about his cowardice, nobody tries to get rid of him, and it is universally agreed that he deserves his reward, be it the Princess, half of the Kingdom, a County, a Kingdom, or money.

Version C has made the hero a clever man who has, with cunning and shrewdness, done the tasks that were set him, whereas the King has become rather a dubious character. The King promises the tailor both the Princess and half of the Kingdom if he can free the country of enemies. The hero performs the task by a thoroughly thought-out scheme, with soldiers in their shirts carrying torches, which is a deliberate embodiment of the same episode in the printed text (1abc). On his return the King asserts that the tailor has been victorious by cunning; and he demands a test of manliness before giving the reward. When the hero has spent the night with the bear (lion), acting, in this case, too, on a deliberate plan (having collected pebbles and nuts in advance and having brought his violin), the King is forced to let him have the Princess. But he does not scruple to send the bear after them when the tailor and the Princess drive away. Once more the tailor's cunning is put to the test, the bear slinks home, and the Princess accompanies her husband to live long and happily with him, away from the old scheming King.

Conclusion. It has been pointed out in the opening that the Danish tradition cannot be placed in the proper European context until a complete survey of the episodes and motifs of all the material is provided. But also within the Danish region of tradition it is difficult to determine the paths of diffusion. One thing only seems to be certain: Both of the printed texts were printed in Copenhagen, and that town must accordingly be considered as the center of diffusion for these texts and the oral tradition inspired by them. But the migrations and alterations of the material from the printed text to the individual oral variant cannot be traced. All intermediate links between the two ends are missing, and an endeavor to trace these links cannot give more than, at best, probability. Take for an example *Version A:* With the knowledge we have of the Danish, more particularly the Jutlandish, peasant culture in the period 1821 to about 1870, it may be asserted with some certainty that reading for recreation was rather unknown in those poor parts of Denmark where "The Brave Tailor" was taken down as popular tradition. Peasants, living like those in the period here dealt with in a self-supplying, bartering civilization, neither have the desire nor can afford to buy such a big and expensive book as the collected edition of Grimm's folktales. Conditions were somewhat different in Sweden, for instance, where, among other tales, "The Brave Tailor" was printed separately in a cheap popular edition.

If in spite of what has been said "The Brave Tailor" has got into the oral tradition, the explanation may be found in the fact that since 1814 there has been seven years' compulsory school attendance for all Danish children and that the story has been transmitted through the schools, either by the children's own reading or by the schoolmaster's reading aloud. One instance of this form of transmission is probably found in Var. 15, which, as mentioned above, is a fragment told by a schoolboy, following the printed text fairly closely.

On the other hand, it is also possible that there was an oral transmission from Germany. We know, for instance, that Kjeld Rasmussen, who narrated Var. 11 of *Version A,* lived in the German-speaking part of Schleswig or in Holstein, which, as already noted, were under the Danish crown until 1864.

The story of the shoemaker of Russia, *Version B,* was printed in rather cheap editions, but the diffusion of this text must be supposed to have been somewhat hampered by the fact that it is in verse. Danish peasants have had no interest in printed verse unless the texts were fit for singing, which at any rate is not the case with the text here dealt with.

There seem, then, to be certain difficulties in elucidating the path of the printed texts into oral tradition. Nor does it become easier if we try to solve the problem by investigating the combinations of episodes and motifs in the tradition, and their relation to the printed texts. If we try to do so, we shall fall out of the frying pan into the fire, for such an investigation will take us into a quite different set of problems, which cannot be solved either.

In "The Brave Tailor" (Shoemaker) the central episode is told at the beginning: Tailor (shoemaker) kills 7 (15, etc.) flies at a blow, and then proclaims himself a hero, while the rest of the story consists of a number of paratactic episodes dealing with the adventures into which the hero is led by his boasting, until in the end he wins the Princess, half of the Kingdom, or another appropriate reward.[15] This random composition gives ample scope for invention and appeals to the ingenuity and powers of combination in the individual narrator. Thus the Grimm brothers have deliberately amplified the old story with new episodes and motifs. The unknown narrator of the Danish chapbook has probably followed the same method: we cannot otherwise account for the insertion of Motif IIb with the soporific fruits, which may be an individual form of the well-known story of *Aper* (K 836).

In those variants which are dependent on the printed texts, we meet the same inclination to remodel the material, by re-arranging, altering, or eliminating the original episodes and motifs, and to replace them with others. Indeed, the foregoing survey has become as comprehensive as it is exactly because these tendencies are so pronounced in the story dealt with. This tendency is particularly evident in the short local *Version C*, an *oikotype* which to a certain extent builds on the printed chap-book, used by an unknown creative artist as a starting point for a new version, with the addition of other well-known motifs, which have been so altered as to fit into the new context. In like manner the printed Var. 8 has enlarged the opening with new motifs.

These tendencies have been in action for rather a long period of time. The story of the shoemaker of Russia has been known in Denmark at any rate since the end of the 18th century; "The Brave Tailor" has been read in Denmark since 1821; and the recorded oral tradition dates from the period 1854 to 1933.[16] Both printed texts have therefore had ample time for influencing popular tradition; and we must suppose that Grimm's text at any rate has exerted its influence on every generation since 1821. Such influence may either create new popular tradition (cf. the discussion on Var. 15), or it may remodel a tradition already in existence, i.e., by assimilating it to the printed text. This com-plicated interaction between the printed texts and the oral tra-dition can be only guessed at; it cannot be analyzed because we miss the countless uncollected variants underlying each of those that have been taken down. Those variants that are not derived from, or influenced by, the printed texts present the same prob-lem in respect of derivation and migration, but to a still greater extent.

Add to this a third problem which makes the whole of the discussion of literary influence and paths of tradition even more complicated. The material that has been collected is so varying and contains so many individual traits that the known narrators, and their unknown predecessors, cannot be considered simply as more or less good preservers of more or less unknown arche-

types. First and foremost, the narrators have been creative art-
ists, good or bad, whose existence and reputation as narrators
are dependent on their powers to recount familiar material in
such a manner that their audience will feel like listening to them.

Notes

1. AT denotes *Type* in Aarne-Thompson, *The Types of the Folk-Tale* (Helsinki: FFC No. 74, 1928).

2. Professor Reidar Th. Christiansen has, with his usual friendliness, given me
information about this point. The Norwegian edition (perhaps the Danish editions) also has been of some importance to the Norwegian tradition in that not less
than four variants contain Section IV (see below), which seems to be a particular
feature of this version; cf. Reidar Th. Christiansen, *Norske Eventyr* (Kristiania:
1921), Type 1640, Var. Nos. 4, 8, 10 (Motif IIF and IIG), and K. Strompedal, *Ga-
malt frå Helgeland* (Oslo: 1938), pp. 25 ff. All Danish variants of this group were
taken down in Jutland; accordingly, there is a possibility that we have here another instance of the close traditional relationship between Jutland and Norway
which has been demonstrated by Professor Christiansen in a number of well-
known publications.

3. The division into sections and episodes is not found in the original texts.
The summary given in the chapbook is complete, but in this arrangement of
the survey of episodes and motifs (pp. 2–5) the numbers assigned to the sections are
I, III, IV, and VI. Sections II and V occur only in the Grimm version.

4. Cf. W. Wisser, "Das Märchen vom tapfern Schneiderlein in Ostholstein,"
Zeitschrift des Vereins für Volkskunde, XXII (1912), 166–79.

5. Cf. Johannes Bolte and Georg Polívka, *Anmerkungen zu den Kinder und
Hausmärchen der Brüder Grimm*, I (1913), pp. 152 ff., in particular, p. 153. *See also*
Witteryck-Stalpaert, *Oude Westvlaamsche Volksvertelsels* (1941), pp. 281 ff.

6. A list of printed variants is found in Bolte-Polívka, *op. cit.*, I, 162¹ which
must be supplemented with more recent material in the local, national type indices.

7. Bolte-Polívka, *op. cit.*, I, 155.

8. R. Nyerup, *Almindelig Morskabslæsning i Danmark og Norge* (Kjøbenhavn:
1816), p. 241.

9. *Kinder und Hausmärchen, zweite vermehrte und verbesserte Aufl.*, III (1822),
pp. 30 ff.; cf. Bolte-Polívka, *op. cit.*, I, 148 ff. Montanus' text has been printed in
Martin Montanus, *Schwänkbücher (1557–66)*, hrsg. von Johannes Bolte (Tübingen:
1899), chap. 5, p. 19.

10. Cf. *Jahrbuch des Vereins für niederdeutsche Sprachforschung*, XX (1895),
No. 1, p. 135.

11. Only the material in the southern Scandinavian part of Denmark has been
considered in this survey. The Faroes and Greenland are not included. The vari-

ants have been arranged chronologically according to parishes and given the parish numbers in italic type. These parish numbers are printed also in the *Festskrift til H. F. Feilberg* (1911), 477–88. Var. 3 derives from Zealand; Var. 4 from Bornholm; and the others from Jutland. The following abbreviations have been used: *Gg:* Svend Grundtvig Collection; *ETKr:* E. T. Kristensen Collection; *DFS:* New Collection (Nyere Samling) in the Danish Folklore Archives (*DFG:* Dansk Folkemindesamling). *Db* refers to E. T. Kristensen's original collections in his diaries (*Dagbøger*).

12. Vars. 13a and 13b were taken down from the same narrator, who moved from Gellerup to Herning sometime between 1872 and 1898.

13. As is mentioned, the printed text is also known in Norway, and this episode is included in the oral variants; cf. Reidar Th. Christiansen, *op. cit.*, Type 1640, Vars. 6, 7, 8, 10: Motif IIB1.

14. At least one Norwegian variant has retained metrical vestiges of the printed text; cf. Reidar Th. Christiansen, *op. cit.*, Var. 10.

15. The converse technique of composition is found, e.g., in AT 852, in which the hero forces the princess to say, "That is a lie." In that type the central episode is placed as the ending of a long series of parallel and paratactic extravagant fictional episodes; these, in turn, may be introduced by other episodes relating to the strange birth of the hero, his great hunting and/or fishing before meeting the princess. Cf. the survey of the Danish material in *Danske Studier* (1954), pp. 109 ff.

16. In the mock-heroic epic *Lars von Larsen eller den jydske Ulysses,* by S. Lycke (Copenhagen: 1782), the hero starts his career in his boyhood by organizing an army of boys and waging war on the flies which have alighted on his bread and sugar; this is the oldest known instance of the appearance of the motif in Denmark proper.

Reidar Th. Christiansen

NORSK FOLKEMINNESAMLING

OSLO, NORWAY

The Sisters and the Troll:
Notes to a Folktale

Students of folktales will un-doubtedly agree that Stith Thompson's *The Folktale* is a most valuable and indispensable guide, and, even more emphatically, that without his revised and enlarged *Types of the Folktale* and his stupendous *Motif-Index of Folk Literature* it would be hopeless to seek a way through the overwhelming and ever-increasing mass of collections, variants, and studies of folktales. It may, therefore, not seem irrelevant when a fellow student of his selects a passage from his text and piles around it some notes and further comments founded upon materials less easily accessible, keeping, however, to a definite, smaller regional area. My chosen text is his comment upon the tale "Rescue by their sister"—Type 311. The statement, quoted from page 36 of *The Folktale* (New York: 1947), reads as follows:

The story has never been thoroughly studied, but a cursory examination of the variants suggests Norway as at least an important center of dissemination of this tale, if not its original home. [*The Folktale,* p. 36]

Having no ambition to attempt "a thorough study," I have restricted my notes to the tradition of the Scandinavian countries in an attempt to ascertain whether, on closer examination, the conclusion just quoted is confirmed.

The tale was evidently rather popular in Norwegian tradition, and some fifty-four variants were recorded.[1] Moreover, their geographical distribution within the country presents some features that have a certain interest. Briefly, six fairly distinct areas may be identified in Norwegian traditional lore. These vary in size and overlap to a certain extent. The first area (I) consists of Eastern Norway with its long valleys (six counties); the second area (II) is Telemark (one county only); the third (III) is Southern Norway (two counties); the fourth (IV) is the West of Norway (four counties); the fifth area (V) consists of Trøndelag and Central Norway (two counties); and the sixth area (VI) is the North (two counties). Because Telemark was the first area visited by collectors and because it has been probed more extensively than any other area, it shows for every folktale a greater number of variants than are found in other districts; as a result, it is here treated as a group in itself. If one examines the variants of the tale in question, one finds that they are distributed among the various areas in this manner: I, three variants; II, twenty-four variants; III, nine variants; IV, thirteen variants; V, two variants; and VI, two variants. The provenance of two variants is unknown. With respect to age, the oldest variant (GN 2) takes us back as far as about 1830; three or four may be dated before 1850 and some between 1870 and 1880; of the rest, about fifty per cent were recorded after the year 1900.

Thus it will be noted that the tale was principally known in Southern Norway, but the special conditions just referred to are, in this case, not a sufficient explanation of the large number of variants from Telemark. Moreover, no one should conclude from this superiority in numbers that the tale was composed in Telemark, for it is an international tale found in many European countries. However, in studying the Norwegian variants, the second group (II) may serve as a convenient point of departure, and within this group there is a still narrower circle, the seven variants taken down between 1878 and 1880 in a single parish, Bøherad, in eastern Telemark.[2] In three closely related variants the title is given as "The Golden Magpie"; and the others either have no title (twice) or are entitled "The Widow and her Three Daughters" (in one instance "The Widow and her Two Daughters").

The pattern of the tale is very simple. It has two principal motifs: the forbidden room and the rescue of the girls. The explanation of how they were captured varies. Five of these variants introduce a man at work in the wood who is brought his dinner by each of his three daughters in turn (A). They have been led astray by a golden magpie (A1) or by a troll altering the bits of straw laid out to show them what road to take (A2). In one variant (8) a widow has a hen which is inclined to go astray; the widow sends each of her three daughters in turn to find out where the hen used to lay its eggs; they try to find out by tying a piece of string to the hen's foot (B).[3] These two types of introduction (cf. the titles given to the story) seem to indicate two distinct redactions which are also traceable in the sequel. Both groups, however, agree that the girls met a troll, a giant, who, using a set formula, asks each of them to be his wife.[4] According to one redaction (A), the first two refuse and are instantly killed; the other redaction, on the other hand, says that all three consent at first and that two are later killed for failing to avoid entering the forbidden room.

A further difference between A and B is that according to the former the third sister, when left alone in the house, found two kinds of ointment and, by experimenting upon her own finger, found out which to use.[5] When, in A5, she is given a key and an apple, the key may have been introduced according to the formula used by the troll, but the motif (the apple being stained and the stain being removed by using the ointment) seems to presuppose the forbidden room; this motif is, however, found only in the B redaction. All seven versions, however, agree that she restores her sisters to life and also that the troll carries them (hidden in sacks or chests) back to their parents, while she pretends that she has been watching him all the time to prevent him from examining the contents.[6] The final episode—involving the rag doll and the returning master's failure to get an answer—is alike in all variants except in GN 9; here, the troll accompanies her home, and she makes him stay so long that he is caught by the rising sun and killed. Thus, within this small group, six variants represent one redaction, a single variant another.

This brief survey of the variants from Bøherad indicates the regular pattern of the story, but one should also see their relationship to the other variants from Telemark. The A redaction is the best known, and it is represented by a couple of variants from further east which differ in explaining who discovered the ointment.[7] In Central Telemark, one notes a slightly different arrangement of the introductory episode: the girls are herding cows, and the magpie leads them on to the pastures of the troll (A3). Only once, in GN 13, is the hidden room mentioned; the girl is forbidden to look into a cauldron behind the door. Other versions from adjacent parishes have the characteristic features of the A redaction. In one instance (GN 16) a cat shows her the jar with the ointment. The herding (A3) recurs in a version taken down in the 1860's,[8] while a contemporary variant from a neighboring parish says that she was forbidden to look into a certain corner—also an echo of the forbidden-room motif. At the end, the angry troll "flew into flints," i.e., splinters. Accordingly, the A redaction appears to be dominant in Telemark tradition, for only once is a full version of the B redaction found, though such motifs as the forbidden room and the apple with stains point to the influence of the B pattern.

Further south (III), six variants were recorded in Setesdal. Though one of these (27) was recorded as early as 1850, it is known only as a brief summary; another one (28), however, was recorded at a later date from the same parish, and it is virtually identical. It contains a reminiscence of the forbidden-room episode: the girl is expressly forbidden to go down into the cellar; she discovers the use of the ointment by seeing a cat use it to replace the head of a cock (a motif which is widely known);[9] and a cat has occasionally replaced the animal—the goat—killed by the troll and revived to please the girl (31). Two collectors took down the tale from the same storyteller, though an interval of twenty years elapsed between the recordings; and the records illustrate the fact that a practised storyteller has his own definite style and manner and will faithfully stick to it with very few alterations. Accordingly, these Setesdal variants follow the same pattern as those from Telemark without any important varia-tions,[10] and the A redaction can be traced further south (46), while the other redaction (B) is represented by a variant still further south—collected about 1880—with all the characteristic incidents of this pattern and yet so different that it could hardly have had the printed version as its source.

In the East (I) the story seems to have been less widely known, and only two variants are on record—curiously few even if one remembers that less collecting was done here than in Telemark.

The earliest version was recorded around 1830 and is from a district not far from Oslo, the capital; it follows the B redaction. The girls follow the hen and end by tumbling down into the house of the troll, who himself later proposes to carry a load to their home when one of the girls becomes sad and dejected at not being allowed to return. She smuggles gold and silver into the load—probably to explain why he had to be prevented from looking into the sack. Later she discovers the use of the ointment when a goat who comes tumbling down is killed and then re-vived at her request.[11] The third girl flees, and the troll who goes in pursuit is killed by the rising sun.

There are several features common to this story and the Tele-mark versions: the goat and the ointment, the ending (9), and the apple (5). Moreover, there is no mention of the forbidden room, and the first two sisters are not put to the test but are killed on their refusal to marry the troll. These missing features are included, however, in another variant (50) which has the same redaction; here, too, the third girl takes precautions to cover her own escape. (She warns the troll that she will be busy and should not be disturbed.) The story was collected in 1924 in a parish close to the Swedish frontier. A third variant (GN 1) was written down in the capital in 1889 from the telling of a schoolboy, and it has obvious Danish affinities. From such a distribution of the variants, the conclusion seems to be that the characteristic Telemark (A) redaction could not have been introduced from the East.

The Western Norway group (IV) covers a much wider area, and the variation in stories and tales is far greater than in Telemark and Southern Norway. Variants have been recorded from most western districts. A version from the far South, recorded in 1880 (33), has localized the tale to a certain hill, and from a parish not far away (34) comes a variant with the A pattern better preserved. Further west, a good version of the B redaction has preserved most of the features, and it is curiously like the one just referred to from the frontier parish (50). For example, in both versions the strange room is called "the red room." Since, however, the western version was not printed until 1928 and the other was taken down in 1924, a connection between them seems hardly possible. A close parallel is further offered by a variant from Hardanger, where, however, the room is said to be blue, so that such designations by color may be purely accidental. Other versions from the Hardanger district are curiously simplified, and in one from a place further along the west coast we have the A redaction. Here one may note that at the end the angry troll "flew into flints," the bits being extant to this very day (36). Sometimes the sisters are not killed at all, but locked up in a room (37).

The parishes along the deeply indented coast of Sognefjord had an old and well-established overland route to the valleys of Eastern Norway, and the B redaction is represented by several variants (38, 39), as also in one recorded from an earlier date (40). Versions from further north also have the B redaction; once the girls are caught when trying to catch "a cat with a silver chain tied to its tail."[12] Again the forbidden room is called "the red room." In Trøndelag (V) and further north (VI), the few variants follow the pattern of B, and a single Lapp variant is altered and abridged to such an extent that it is impossible to determine from what source it came. The ogre is Stallo, a special Lapp species of troll.[13]

From the distribution of the Norwegian variants of the tale, it might be concluded that the center and possible origin of the tradition was Telemark; but the circulation of the story is by no means restricted to Norway. It is accordingly necessary to examine the relationship between the Norwegian versions and those from the neighboring countries, especially from Denmark, where evidently the tale was at least as popular as it has been in Norway.

In Denmark, thirty-seven variants have been recorded, mostly from the peninsula of Jutland, and only eleven variants come from the islands.[14] Some were collected in the 1860's and 1870's, but the greater part around the year 1900. In briefly examining the variants, we will note only the characteristic features, for the general pattern is already sufficiently familiar from the survey of the Norwegian materials.

Some thirty per cent of the Danish versions endow the girls with personal names, e.g., Karen, Maren, and Mette; this can probably be explained by the fact that it is far easier to tell a story well when the acting persons can be referred to by names. Only a single Norwegian version (GN 1) employs names; this is the one which also has other Danish affinities, especially the special introductory incident found in about half of the Danish variants. A strange animal appears in the garden, and when the girls are sent in turn to drive it away, they are somehow captured and carried off. Less common is the opening familiar from the Norwegian (B) redaction, the hen that goes astray. There are, moreover, other conventional ways of beginning the story: cf. the Norwegian C, in which the girls have to herd sheep, or are sent to gather firewood, or simply leave home and look for a job. Another way to introduce the situation (F) is to say that a troll, "a man from the hill," is living close to the girls' home and simply captures them so that his wife may have servants. An echo from the Bluebeard story is seen (18) when a strange gentleman comes as a suitor. He has a bristling beard, sharp as needles. However, the introduction from the A redaction—the girls bringing dinner, etc.—is found only in a single Danish variant (36).[15]

All of these situations, of course, lead to the encounter with the troll. As in some Norwegian tales, the first two girls refuse outright to marry him and are killed or, when some informants think the procedure too brutal, are shut up in separate rooms (cf. GN 37). Most Danish versions, however, agree that all of the girls submitted to the test. That the test originally had a connection with the forbidden room is further corroborated by the fact that twenty-one Danish versions employ it. The other tests sometimes suggested do not fit into the pattern at all and are borrowed from other stories.[16]

It is probable that the apple, too, like the room, was originally a part of the pattern, and substitutes for it are rare (as, e.g., a key [8, 10]). The apple seems to have had magical powers, and a difficulty arises in explaining how the third sister escapes detection when she enters the room. She sometimes hides the apple, although this is not always sufficient.[17] The best solution, and the one generally adopted, is that the apple also is stained, but, thanks to the ointment, she is able to remove the stain. How, then, did she discover the precious ointment?[18] The mere statement that she found it was for some storytellers not sufficient, and they added that the jar had a label indicating its use, or, as in a Norwegian variant, that she tested the contents upon her finger, or that she imitated the behavior of a mouse that had killed another one (cf. GN 30). The grateful animals may tell her, or an old woman may give her the information—these she finds somehow in one of the rooms (29, 30). But, it should be noted, the mere statement that she found the jar is also acceptable.

The second half of the story—the rescue and the carrying of the sacks—is, as a rule, very constant, perhaps because it is the most dramatic part. Aside from the few versions that are wholly divergent,[19] it is rendered in the same way by most storytellers. An obvious difficulty, however, is felt by many informants: how did she get herself away? One might, of course, say, "She put herself into the sack," and let it go at that; but the realistic sense of both reciter and audience could hardly fail to ask how. One expedient was to say that she pretended to be ill, or, better still, that she had hurt her hand,[20] thus leaving the sack for him to tie up, but it was still easier to let her run away, perhaps dressed in tar and feathers, or as a beggar woman in case she should meet the troll on the road. The troll finally "burst into flints," with the aetiological verificative touch that this explains the many flint stones found everywhere.

Compared with the Danish tradition, the small number of Swedish variants on record is surprising. Only four versions seem to be known,[21] to which may be added another four from Swedish speakers in Finland. Of the Swedish versions, one (GS 2), taken down in 1924 in central Sweden, was obviously derived from the classic Norwegian collection of tales by Asbjørnsen and Moe, a book very popular in Sweden and translated several times; the individual stories, moreover, were also published separately as cheap booklets. The title given to the Swedish story is "The Hen that Walked in the Mountain"; this offers a further clue to its derivation from Asbjørsen and Moe, for this title was substituted in the Norwegian versions, beginning in 1899, for the more elaborate, and rather clumsy "The Three Sisters that Were Taken into the Mountain."[22]

There is another variant from the South—from Skåne—but it is only distantly related, as a summary will indicate. A troll in the shape of a golden cat carried away the daughters of a king; a test is employed in the form of an order not to touch a golden apple in the troll's garden. Further north, near the Norwegian frontier, a fairly complete version of the B redaction[23] was recorded with the usual motifs: the straying hen, the string tied to its feet, etc.; in most particulars, in other words, this is like the versions from Eastern Norway (S GN 2, 50). A fourth variant—from Värmland—has distinct traces of the influence of the Grimm version in the *Household Tales*. The versions from Finland present few new departures. One is a well-told version of the B redaction, and this has a novel addition: when the troll comes in pursuit of the girls, with the intention of punishing them, he is kept outside by the expedient of nailing to the door a bit of paper containing the names of the Trinity.

The distribution of the variants within the Scandinavian countries (and we have no other indication of their migration) points to the conclusion that this folktale belongs to a Western-Nordic traditional group which was never to any great extent accepted by Swedish storytellers. The principal interest, therefore, centers upon the relationship between the Norwegian and the Danish variants. These have many features in common, the most interesting being the B redaction (the hen, etc.) which in Denmark is represented in variants from Jutland as well as from the islands. Other parallels occur with individual incidents: e.g., the girl testing the ointment upon her own fingers (GD 10) or discovering the virtues of the ointment when the troll brings back to life a goat with a broken neck (GD 24), and the expression that the troll "flew into flints." These parallels may well be accidental. Finally there is also the recurrence of the introduction to the A redaction in a single Danish version 36, but this is hardly an indication of some special connection, for the same incident occurs in versions from countries far away.[24]

It thus seems probable that the B redaction was at some period and by some storyteller—not through a book—carried to Norway to be accepted and retold in southern and eastern districts and sporadically along the western coast. In favor of its coming from the South is the fact that another redaction was far more popular in Norway. Furthermore, the general trend of international folktales is to pass from Denmark and the Continent toward Norway which, as a rule, together with Lapp folktales, marks the northern limit of their circulation.

It is generally admitted that in folktales the introductory passages are those most exposed to alterations; these, therefore, could hardly be taken as indications of some special redaction. When, however, the pattern is as simple as it is in this story—essentially a children's tale—and when the main episodes are so constant, the incidents offering the opening explanation—and their number is also limited—may be expected to be connected with some special sequel. In this tale the two main incidents—the test (the forbidden chamber in nearly every case at least in the north) and the rescue by being carried away—were hardly ever altered except in the case of a version which diverged into a wholly different story. As may be seen from the summaries given in Heckman's study, these incidents reappear wherever the tale is told.

The dominant Norwegian type—redaction A—might be explained as a purely local invention, but it is also found in a small group of variants from Iceland and the Faroe Islands.[25] In all these the third girl is rescued by being carried away, and there are at least reminiscences of the room. There is also an explanation of the fact that the troll gets hold of the girls: their father has promised them to a troll, and in order to expose them he has sent them on some errand (to fetch something he has forgotten), and then the troll—in the shape of a bird—carries them away. They see a strange bird, follow it, and are captured.

The motif—the enforced promise—is found in a great number of folktales and may serve as an introduction to various stories, but even if its occurrence in this tale is no definite indication of its being an original part of this particular redaction, one must admit that such a reasonable explanation of the appearance of the strange bird is not superfluous. The golden magpie might easily appear in a folktale without exciting further comment— for every listener would recognize that it was no ordinary bird —but, after all, an explanation, and one of a kind usually associated with such happenings, seems a natural introduction. The variants from the Faroe Islands and Iceland had no similarity with those collected in Denmark, and they may well, together with the representatives of the same redaction preserved in isolated inland districts in Norway, represent an earlier way of rendering the story which in these districts had retained its popularity. One may also note that neither in Telemark nor in Iceland and the Faroe Islands does the motif almost invariably connected with the tale, that of the forbidden room, occur, even if some slight touch might seem to presuppose a knowledge of it.

These notes in no way intend to trace the further migration of the tale, for they are restricted to the situation in northern countries only. It may, however, be stressed that the German variants, as may be seen from the summaries in Heckman's study, had none of the introductions found in the northern countries. One may also note the absence of versions of this tale in Schleswig and Holstein, districts that in many cases seem to have been important links in the transmission of folklore from the Continent to the North.[26] At the same time, however, the main pattern of the German variants is the same as in the North.

The ultimate home of this tale was probably somewhere in the Near East, in Greece or in Turkey, where the many records show that the story was well known.[27] These variants, as well as those of most other countries, agree that the being who captured the girls was some species of demon who in every new country is described in correspondence with local conceptions of such beings. The strange gentleman, coming as a suitor, and having some striking personal feature, is a more recent substitute, owing partly to the influence of the Bluebeard story as told by Perrault and partly to contamination with another distantly related folktale ("The Vampire," MT 363).

When S. Hartland, who published a series of notes on the hidden-chamber motif, wrote that "probably none of these variations in the mode in which the ogre acquired possession of the heroine is important,"[28] he was only partly right, for the trick used is somehow connected with the type of ogre and, as was noted above, the main incidents of the tale admit of only a few variations, as is easily seen from the summaries given by Heckman. Such incidents are the test (forbidden chamber) and the rescue of the third girl by carrying her away. In comparing the various incidents and combinations, one must also take another factor into consideration: the contribution of the individual storyteller in arranging his story. He took his plot from oral tradition, but he also had occasion to use his own artistic sense, and every pattern, however simple and constant, contained several technically difficult points. A good storyteller was keenly aware of the necessity of preserving the logical, realistic coloring in his rendering. He was, of course, allowed wide license in the use of "unrealistic" motifs (enchantment, magic, shape-shifting, etc.), but they had to be fitted logically and convincingly together, and the plot could not be overloaded with such incidents. The ethics of folktales seem to require that even if villain and hero be equally free to use magic, only the hero can come out victorious in the end.

Some such technically difficult points were mentioned in connection with the Danish variants, as, for example, how to explain how the third girl managed to have herself carried away. The solution that she profited by the ogre's absence and ran away would naturally occur to storytellers everywhere, and its appearance in several versions does not imply any special connection. Similarly it is easily seen how such an arrangement could be enlarged and serve to introduce another tense dramatic situation, e.g., when she fled in a disguise of tar and feathers[29] to avoid the returning ogre.

A similar individual effort of storytellers to arrange their motifs can be observed in connection with the various types of introduction. The three main types—the Danish form as well as the A and B redactions—indicate that some animal played a part in what happened. When the animal was the ogre in disguise, he did not adopt the shape of a bird; more frequently he came as a pig, a steer, or a horse. When he once was a bird (GD 26), the introduction was altered, and the girls were simply looking for a job and were engaged by a starling who retained his bird shape throughout the story.

When the bird was part of the scheme, on the other hand, it was more usually sent by the ogre to lead the sisters astray (cf. the A redaction). Less happy was the solution adopted by the B redaction, for it did not seem natural that such excessive care should be taken of a hen. It was hardly ever done in actual daily life; as a result, several storytellers felt the need of explaining why it was done. The hen laid golden eggs (GD 9), or fifteen or sixteen eggs every day (GD 7, 22), or, in fact, so many eggs that the hen was the main support of the family (GSF 3). The editor of the Norwegian classic story, Jørgen Moe, chose another explanation by ascribing the inordinate fondness for her hen to the silliness of the old widow: "She loved it like the apple of her eye, and she fussed over it and petted it from morning to night."

From an *artistic* point of view, i.e., in consideration of how it fits into the story pattern, the B redaction seems to me to be inferior. One would be inclined to consider it a later arrangement, an adaptation chosen as a folktale particularly suitable for a juvenile audience. To such listeners, the statement that the hen started to lay her eggs in some hidden place would appear a perfectly natural excuse for sending the girls out to find them. But, once such an introduction had been adopted, the more serious aspects of the original plot would tend to get lost, and this aspect was a variation of a motif, easily the most popular in Northern tradition from very early days and used in *fornaldarsagas,* in ballads, and in folktales: a motif of young women caught by giants and trolls and saved by intrepid heroes or by their own ingenuity. If, then, this was the original Northern conception of the tale, the conclusion hinted at above—that the B redaction is a later innovation than the A redaction—seems to be confirmed. In Norway it never did attain such a popularity that it ousted the older type from the repertoire of the storytellers.

Notes

1. Cf. the catalogue in *Norske Eventyr: En systematisk fortegnelse* (Kristiania: 1921), Type 311, Nos. GN 1–44. To this should be added Nos. 44–49 in the *Qvigstad Festskrift* (1928); No. 50 in A. B. Larsen, Jr., NFS (Norwegian Folklore Institute), VIII, 127 (from Solør); No. 51 from *Norske Folkekultur*, XVI, 102 (from Hardanger); No. 52 from *Norsk Folkeminnelag*, LIV, 37 (from Trøndelag); No. 53 in Moltke Moe, NFS, CXVI, 41; and No. 54, Moltke Moe, NFS, CXVII, 9. (These last two are both from Agder.)

2. *Norske Eventyr*, Type 311, Nos. 4–9.

3. A 1: 1·3·6. A 2: 7·9·B·8.

4. "What would you like, to be my bride or to carry my keys?" In 6: "to be my bride or to lose your life?"

5. 3·6·7.

6. "Your daughter sent it, your son-in-law carried it. Shame upon you, but it was heavy."

7. a.: An animal, a goat or a horse, strayed into the precincts of the troll, who killed it by breaking its neck. On the girl's complaint, he restored it to life by using the ointment: GN 10.11. Cf. 2.

8. GN 17.18.

9. *See* Johannes Bolte and Georg Polívka, *Anmerkungen zu den Kinder und Häusmärchen der Brüder Grimm*, I, 26; IV, 114.

10. One version (No. 32) was probably influenced by the story of the children and the ogre: MT 327. Four little boys were captured by a troll and saved by their mother in the same way that the girl saved her sisters.

11. The troll saying, as the goat came tumbling down: "What brought you here, your ragged beast?" In the end she got a man with a gun to accompany her, and he fired a shot to frighten the troll away.

12. Some particulars may be noted: (33) Troll killed by the rising sun. (54) The golden magpie, the formula on delivering the sacks. (47) The hen with a string tied to its leg, all three sisters tested, the willingness of the troll to carry the loads explained by his infatuation for the girl. (35) Only two sisters caught; the one was to marry the troll, the other to be fattened for the wedding dinner; the latter saved in the usual way, and her sister ran away while the troll was killed by the wedding guests, who were infuriated because there was no dinner. (36) The introduction was that the father sent the girl to fetch a coat he had left in the wood; cf. a realistic introduction, in 41, where the girls have in turn to stay at home on three successive Sundays to have dinner ready for the other people coming from church, and the third girl flees disguised as a beggar woman.

13. Qvigstad, *Lapp eventyr og sagn*, II, No. 23, recorded in 1883.

14. GD Nos. 1–7: the Svend Grundtvig MS No. 49 a-h; a and b were published in Grundtvig's *Gamle Danske Minder*, III, No. 8, and II, p. 312. For full titles, see the Bolte-Polívka volumes for their bibliography, No. 8: Madsen *Handved*, p. 7. Nos. 9–10: K. Berntsen, *Folkeæventyr*. No. 11: E. T. Kristensen, *Dansk Folkeæventyr*, No. 7. No. 12: *Jyske Folkeminder*, GV, p. 277. No. 13: *Efterslat Skattegr.*, No. 28. No. 14: *Fra Bindestue*, I, 57. Nos. 15–33: E. T. Kristensen's MS Collection, Nos. 39, 164, 515, 534, 666, 748, 879, 1152, 1363, 1457, 1809, 1810, 1819, 2032, 2125, 2197, 2460. No. 34: Dansk Folkemindesamling, 1906, Christensen. Nos. 35–36: J. Kamp, Dansk Folkemindesamling. No. 37: *Aarbøger fra Holbæk amt*. From Fyen: Nos. 9, 26, 27, 35. Sjælland: Nos. 1, 5, 30, and 37. From Falster: 11, Bogø (a small island south of Sjælland), 36. No. 28a was recorded in the U.S.A. from a Danish immigrant.

15. The animal in the garden was a pig, a steer, a hare, and once also a golden wheel (10·29·36) or a golden apple; cf. a later incident (11). Introduction B: the hen in seven variants; C: herd sheep (24, 33); fetch firewood (19,28); look for a job (5, 17, 25); F: 23, 31, 32. Once they are looking for a job and are engaged by a bird, a starling, and have to manage his household. He behaves in the usual way but carries the sacks in his bill. This version is incomplete and trails off in some kind of jingle.

16. Other tests: a series of questions ("Did you ever . . . ?" Cf. MT 425 C). Carry water in a sieve; birds giving advice, from MT 480; but the birds as well as some grateful animals who are neglected by the two sisters are befriended by a third sister and are sure to give valuable advice as to the ointment and the way of escape.

17. She hid the apple in a cupboard but heard it bump against the walls in an effort to get out (1). A rather lame conclusion consists of her throwing the apple away, then pretending to have lost it. The troll lets the matter pass.

18. Instead of the ointment, a reviving flute is used (4·7·22).

19. She simply left her dead sisters in the bed (9). No. 19 is modelled upon the tale of the boy and the ogre (MT 327 C). Cf. the Bluebeard story, 18.

20. Nos. 8, 15, 16, 20, 25, 31, 33, 35; cf. GN 50.

21. Swedish versions :GS(1) Skåne, *Svenska Landsmål*, V:1, p. 34; (2) Ostergötland Folkminnesarkivet i Lund; (3) Tanum Bohuslen, *Folkeminnen och Folktankar*, X:4; (4) Värmland, Liungman, *Sv. samtl. Folks.*, I; cf. Vol. III; from Finland: *Finlands sv. folkd. Sagor*, cf. collection number 46, p. 58.

22. Swedish translation in 1868; a new one in 1927; in both, the story has the original title. The new story is from the revised edition of 1899.

23. Cf., e.g., the key instead of the apple; also her pretending to watch him carrying the sack from her window. Grimm: "Ich schaue durch mein Fensterlein," o.s.v.

24. For example, in Northern Russia, quoted from the study by E. Heckman Blaubart, *Ein Beitrag zur vergleichenden Märchenforschung* (1930), p. 56. The three daughters of a peasant had to carry pancakes to their father, who was cutting wood in the forest, and the wood shavings scattered to show them the way were changed by a bear so as to lead the daughters to its lair.

25. Jakobsen, *Færøiske Folkesagn og Æventyr*, p. 254. E. O. Sveinsson, FFC 83 to Type 311.

26. *Zeitschrift für Volkskunde* [Niederd], IX, 200.

27. Cf. Eberhard and Borotav, *Typen türkischer Volksmärchen* (Wiesbaden: 1953), Type 157.

28. *Folklore Journal*, III, 121.

29. Cf. Grimm, "Fitchers Vogel."

MacEdward Leach

UNIVERSITY OF PENNSYLVANIA

PHILADELPHIA, PENNSYLVANIA

Celtic Tales from Cape Breton

Crossing the straits from Cape Breton to Newfoundland, one passes from one stage in a folk culture to another. In the outports of Newfoundland songs are sung and stories told by people of all ages—boys in their teens, burly fishermen, gaffers in the warm corner. The old time songs and stories are a part of living culture. A middle-aged woman— the local midwife near Salmonier—sang for me the song and told the story of the "Rose of Branch." It is the account of a local fishing schooner rammed and sunk by a larger vessel with the loss of all hands. Halfway through, tears came to her eyes and she announced that she could not go on. I was eager to get the story and song and after a time persuaded her to continue. She finally finished it. I asked her if a member of her family had been aboard. "Oh, no," she said. "It happened a hundred years ago, but I always think of the mothers and wives of those poor men." This is not survival but living lore. There is no dredging out of the dim memory of an octogenarian to come up with scraps and fragments. In such a region as Newfoundland the folklorist finds the pattern intact, preserved by economic, geographical, and social barriers.

The contrast between the folk culture of Newfoundland and that of Cape Breton is everywhere discernible. In Cape Breton the task of the collector is much more difficult. It is the old who know the old songs and the old tales, and even they are seldom permitted to recall them. And when they do, the collector must often be content with fragments, with the half-recalled tale.

But every folklorist knows the value of a bit of a tale or a snatch of song, if a snatch is all that is forthcoming. Shards often tell the story of the pot. Folklore should not be a study of survivals but the study of a chain of being.

Cape Breton was settled by a superior people, a people who came from a rich cultural background of story, poetry, and song. The beauty, the imaginative power, the dramatic quality, the richness of detail of the old Celtic lore is unsurpassed in western Europe. Many studies have traced this material into the culture of the present, but the account is not yet complete. How much of this culture did the Breton take with him to Brittany from Wales and Cornwall and there keep alive? How much did the Highlander settlers take to Scotland and thence to Cape Breton? Often on the periphery of a culture the most archaic elements are found. It is conceivable that older stories and songs might be found in Cape Breton than in Scotland or Ireland. With this in mind I went to Cape Breton in 1950 expressly to search out evidence. I secured in Gaelic and English a large store of material: songs, beliefs, stories. Very little of it is a part of living culture; rather it is recalled from the past by the very old. The significant part is that these "fragments" show how widespread must have been Celtic story material and song material in the formative years of modern culture. I have selected several of the tales for study and illustration.

i

Hector Campbell, age *ca.* 70, told this tale. He lived alone in a small house in the mountains behind Judique. He was a piper and a singer as well as a storyteller. He could remember the tales only in Gaelic, though he spoke English. He said that he never tells these tales any more but that he often thinks of them to himself.

A king and his army went to the mountains to the place where the giants lived, and he was after the wife of the Chief of the Giants and a certain dog that was a wonderful dog. The wife, she changed color; in part of the year she was white and part of the year she was green. The dog could see in the night; it had red eyes that looked like fire. The king had a thousand boats. When the Chief of the Giants heard of this, he said he would never give up his wife and dog. The giants met them halfway. First thing, the Chief of the Giants caught the King and tied him up. But when they saw how big and noble the King's people were, they retreated, taking the King with them. The King lived with the Giants and became their king when the Chief of the Giants died. These were the Finns; they were an able tribe of people.

Comment. A number of informants had heard of Finn Mac-Cumhail, but none had detailed stories. The standard sources tell of several encounters between the Fenians and giants and gods, but none for reasons indicated here, nor is there a story of the capture of Finn. Usually the giant is defeated in folk story (F. 628.2.3),[1] but here the giant wins and conquers the king (*F 531.1.2). Other motifs are: dog with red eyes that looked like fire (B 15.4.2; cf. F 541.1.1); person changes colors, white to green (*D 57.2). This certainly seems like a vegetation myth. Strange that it is associated with a woman.

ii

One Sunday early I was driving down the narrow dirt road toward Benacadie Pond. As I approached one of the few houses on the road, I saw an old man leaning on the gate. I stopped, and we talked. He said that his name was Patterson and that he was 93. He had never heard of Cuchulain or Conchobar or Deirdre, but he had known "stories of the Finns and other old stories." Standing there he told a story that most certainly goes back to the ancient Mythological Cycle, for it is a story of Balor of the Evil Eye. Balor was one of the Fomorians, huge deformed giants. He had one eye whose glance was so powerful that it killed every living thing that came within the range of its vision. Balor was wheeled into battle, eye shut; then his eye-lid was raised by a hook and the opposing army destroyed through its glance. Balor was killed by Lugh, the sun god, who struck Balor's eye out with a magic stone.[2] The following story was told in English.

In the old days there was a great creature that lived in the sea off Cape Breton. He had only one eye, but that eye was so strong that anything it looked upon was instantly killed. For that reason the eye had to be kept closed by a heavy lid lest sight from it destroy the creature's own people. Frequently it would come out of the sea and kill people and cattle. Finally, the giants from the hills came down and fought with the creature and his people. They killed all his people by turning him around and making him look at them with his powerful eye; then they cut him to pieces, and there was so much blood that the water was red and the sands were made red.

Comment. It is interesting to note that Balor and the Fomorians were sea dwellers. *Motifs:* creature with one eye (F 512.1.1); one eye deals death (*F 512.1.2). See A. H. Krappe, *Balor . . . Eye, Studies in Celtic and French Literature* (New York: 1927).

iii

The second tale Mr. Patterson told is a portion of the Diarmaid and Grainne story, a part of the Finn cycle. Mr. Patterson did not know the names Diarmaid and Grainne, nor did he associate the story with Finn. He told this one also in English.

This man was running away with his uncle's wife, and she was a mighty pretty woman. The King almost caught them, but they got loose and climbed up through a hollow tree and sat in the leaves. And the King sat under the tree and began to play a chess game. The King was about to win, but the nephew saw what the other fellow had to do, and he dropped a nut from the tree right down on the spot where the fellow should move the piece. And he won the game. But the King knew it, but he didn't let on, and the nephew and the girl got away, but I think they were finally killed.

Comment. Mr. Patterson said that he had known more of this story, that he had had it from his grandfather, who had come from Skye. *Motifs:* forest as refuge for eloping lovers (R 312); nephew elopes with uncle's wife (*P 297.1); clever way of giving information (*J 1674) by dropping nut on spot on chess board (*J 1674.1).

iv

The following fragment was told by Angus MacEachern, age 65, Port Hood. The informant said that it is very old, that he had heard it from an old *seanachaidh* when he was a boy. Can this possibly be a remnant of the story of the wrestling match between Cuchlainn and Aoife? If so, it should end with the birth of the child (after the man leaves) and with the man later fighting with the boy (without recognizing him) and killing him. The story was told in Gaelic.

One night a man was walking through the forest. It was dark and foggy, but finally he saw a light, and there was a house. He went to the door and opened it, and an old woman was sitting by the fireplace. When she saw him, she said, "You get out of here." He refused, and then she said, "If you don't leave, there is someone coming who will throw you out." At that moment who comes in but a young woman; she's a very big girl, and she has a dead heifer on her shoulders. She asks him who he is, and he tells her that he is a traveller and that he is looking for a place to stay. "Well, you can't stay here." "I think I'll stay here till someone puts me out," he says. "Well, I'll do that." She rushes at him and forces him to his knees, but he is a great strong man, and after they have wrestled a long time, he gets the better of her and throws her. Then she says he can stay the night. He sleeps with her, and finally a child is born to the two of them.

Motif: This may be a suitor contest (H 331.6.1).

v

Mr. MacEachern told another story which had come to him from the same storyteller. He told this one in English.

When the world was new, there was this boy whose father was dead, and his mother and some more women brought him up. When he was a man, he told his mother that he was going out to see the world. She said, "Go to your father's people, and they will give you gold and horses, for they are all kings." And she gave him a ring so his uncle would know him. She told him never to sleep in the same place twice, or to sleep in a place where he had eaten. And she told him never to cross arms with another until he had been welcomed by his father's brother. He went for many days over steep mountains and rough land, and he came to a lake. The next morning there were one thousand men there, and the leader challenged him to fight, but he would not. Then they treated him well. After they they led him up the mountain, and at the top was a door made of some kind of metal. It opened, and they all went in. It was a big room. And there was a fire on the floor and four pillars around it. On each of the pillars were hung a thousand shields. The shields belonged to the men who had brought him there. His uncle knew him by the ring. Then the uncle gave him a sword and a javelin and a shield. Then the men carried in a great fine kettle. And was it not full of all kind of food, meat and bread, and other food. And the thousand men and the uncle and the boy all sat around it, and they were just enough. (Mr. MacEachern explained that they sat in a circle and just surrounded the kettle). And everyone ate, and if you took out one piece of meat, another was there, and if you took out one sup, another was there, and when they were filled, the kettle was the same as before. And the boy lived in this place, and when the uncle died, he owned the cave and the kettle and all the warriors.

Comment. I have found no exact parallel to this story. Probably elements have dropped out. The motif of the ever-full cauldron (D 1472.1.12.) and the motif of the widow's son are widely found. Both motifs occur in the Grail stories, though the cauldron here is rather different from the Grail vessel as we know it in twelfth-century story. (See De Jubainville, *Le Cycle . . .* ; Chrestien's *Perceval;* Roger S. Loomis, *Arthurian Tradition and Chrestien de Troyes.*)

vi

The next stories are *Märchen.* As one would expect, they are more plentiful and more complete. This one was told in Gaelic by Ronald Smith, age *ca.* 75, of Inverness. He had it from the "old folks."

Cornu lived at the king's palace with his three sons. The king also had three sons. One day the king's sons got in a fight with Cornu's sons, and one of the king's sons was killed. That evening the king said to Cornu, "All three of your boys came home tonight, but only two of mine returned. For this reason, I am going to have you and your three sons put to death, unless you go to the king who owns it and bring back to me the famous mare." Cornu and his sons set out at once. On the way they stopped at a grist mill and asked the owner how they could get into the palace. He suggested that they get into grain bags and so be smuggled into the palace. Each of them crawled into a bag, and the porters unsuspectingly carried them into the palace. That night they slipped out and began to put the bridle on the mare, but she neighed loudly, and they had to hide again in the bags. The king, hearing the neigh, called to his soldiers to look at the horse. The soldiers could find nothing amiss. After they had departed, Cornu and his sons crawled forth again and again essayed to put the bridle on the mare, but again she neighed and again the king sent out the soldiers, but they found nothing since Cornu and his sons had got safely back in the bags. They tried it a third time and this time the king himself went, and he discovered the intruders. When they stood before him, the king said to Cornu, "Have you ever been closer to death than you are at this moment? If you have and can prove it by a story, I will let one of your sons go free." "Yes," said Cornu, "I have been closer to death. Once I was milking cows when twelve great cats came, and one of them began to purr very loudly, and I asked him what he'd take for the purr, and he said one cow. I agreed, and then all the cats began to swallow the cows, and I climbed to the top of a tree, but the tree began to bend, and the cats were about to devour me when a man came and shot the cats." (The story is confused.) The king agreed that Cornu had proved his point and released one of the boys. Then the king said, "If you have been closer to death a second time than you are now and can prove it with a story, I'll release a second son." "Well," said Cornu, "I used to sail, and one day as I was sailing along the shore, I saw a giant in a cave about to kill a girl. I shouted at him, but he refused to let her alone. He killed her and then turned on me. He had only one good eye. I told him I'd cure his eye, and he agreed to let me try. I mixed up some hot medicine and poured it into his eye, and it blinded him. The giant tried to catch me, but he could not because he was blind, and I hid among the goats in the cave. Then the giant told his son to open the gate and let the goats out. He stood in the doorway feeling each goat as it went out. There was a little goat at the end of the line; I took it on my back and slipped out between the giant's legs. When I got outside, I called, 'Catch me if you can.' The giant answered, 'Since you are so clever, take this ring.' Then he threw a ring to me. 'Have you the ring on your finger?' 'Yes,' I answered. Then the giant shouted, 'Ring come here, come close.' The ring began to drag me toward the giant, but I escaped by cutting off my finger." The king agreed that Cornu had fulfilled the condition, and so he set the second son free. Then the king said, "If you have been closer to death a third time than you are now, I'll release your third son." Whereupon Cornu told the third story. "One time I was at the sea shore when a beautiful ship came in. I went on board, and it sailed away to a house in the ocean. There was a woman there raising a poker to a child. When I asked her what she was doing, she replied that she was going to kill the child for the dinner of the giant who lived there. I told her to hide the child and so she did. I went up the stairs and lay down among the dead men there. The giant came home and made a great feast of the dead men and then went to sleep. Then I killed the giant and saved that baby. And that baby was you." When the king heard this he released the man and all his sons.

Motifs: formulistic framework for tales, tale to avert execution (*Z 18); quest assigned to punish man for sons' fault (*H 1216.1); man (and sons) hiding in bag in order to be carried into palace (*K 1892.2); execution escaped by telling stories (J 1185); father tells stories to save sons and himself (*J 1185.1; cf. R 153.3.3); speaking animal (B 211.8)—all the foregoing of type 545. Great cats swallow cows (*B 871.6); tigers swallow cows (B 871.6.1); panthers swallow cows (B 871.6.2)—cf. extraordinary swallowings (F 911); cat swallows animal (*F 911.2.1). Giant with only one eye (F 512.1.1); giant's eye destroyed by hot medicine (*S 165.2); escape from giant's cave by hiding under goat (*K 603.1); magic ring adheres to finger (*D 2171.1); cutting off finger to save one's life (*S 161.1); escape by shamming death (K 522).

vii

Told by Hector Campbell in Gaelic.

Once upon a time a man cut his hay and made it into a stack. Then the wind came and blew the stack away. When the man saw this he went to the God of the Winds and told him that he would have to pay for the hay he had destroyed. "That is only fair," said the God of the Winds, and he gave the man a duck. "Now," he said, "whenever you want money, just squeeze the duck and a gold piece will drop out." The man took the duck and departed. On the way home he stopped for the night at an inn. There he told the keeper about the duck. In the morning the duck was gone. He was told that it had flown away during the night. Back home the man thought again about his hay; thinking that he had not been paid for it, he set out a second time for the home of the God of the Winds. When he explained about the loss of the duck, the God of the Winds said, "Yes, your hay is not paid for; here is a mill; just turn the handle when you want money, and the mill will grind out gold." The man stopped at the same inn, and the same thing happened, for when he awoke in the morning, the mill was gone. He then made a third trip to the God of the Winds. When he told the God of the Winds about the loss of the mill, the God of the Winds asked him where he had stayed the night. When he told him, the God of the Winds said, "Those people have stolen the duck and the mill. Now you take this sod, and when they ask you what you do with it, tell them that you say, 'Wrap me up, wrap me up.' " So the man took the sod and departed. That night he stopped at the inn. And when they asked him about the sod, he said, "I say to it, 'Wrap me up, wrap me up.' " After he was sound asleep, the people at the inn stole the sod and, thinking it would produce gold like the duck and mill, said to it, "Wrap me up, wrap me up." Instantly the sod began to wrap up everything on the place, the furniture, the wagons, the sheep and cattle, even the people themselves. Whereupon they cried out and woke the man, who, after they had restored his duck and mill, rescued them from the sod. Taking the duck and mill he went home.

Comment. This tale is especially interesting because the mill that grinds without ceasing is not the climax, as is usual in such stories, and also because of the unique motif of the sod. *Motifs:* Magic object stolen at inn (D 861.1)—type 563. Gold-producing duck (*B 101.2.1). Self-grinding gold mill (*D 1601.21.2). Sod wraps up enemy (*D 1401.4).

viii

Angus ("The Ridge") MacDonald, age 73, Lake Katrine, sang a number of songs, recounted tales of the MacDonalds, and finally was prevailed upon to tell several *sgeulachdan*, of which the following is typical. He told it in Gaelic.

A man had an only son. As the boy grew in years, he also grew in body. Finally one day he said to his father, "I'll go out in the world to seek my fortune." He told his father to go to the forge and get a stick made of the best wood the blacksmith had. The father did as requested, and the boy set out with the stick. After walking a long time, he came to a house. The woman there said, "You must be hungry. Come in and eat. We have plenty; my husband just killed a deer." After eating, the boy went on his way toward the king's palace. Presently he met a terrified bull, made crazy by the people who were going to kill it. Making it crazy, they thought, would make the meat tender. Watt killed the bull with one blow. Then he asked the gatekeeper to allow him to see the king. The king met him and greeted him with the words, "You are the strongest man I've ever seen." Watt asked for a job as shepherd. The king replied, "Many have gone out as herdsmen, but they have lost many cattle; however, I'll give you a try." Watt took the cattle to pasture, and there he climbed a tall tree to watch. As he was eating his lunch there in the tree, he saw a giant coming. When the giant saw him, he shouted, "Come down and I'll kill you." Watt replied, "Wait till I have my dinner." When he had finished his lunch, he came down from the tree and killed the giant. That evening he came back to the castle with all the cattle. The king was very pleased. The next day Watt took the cattle again to pasture, and as he was eating his lunch, the giant's mate appeared. When she asked him to come down from the tree, he told her to wait until he had finished his lunch. When he had finished, he came down and fought with the giantess and finally overcame her. He asked her where she lived. She answered, "Where I live is a house of gold, and inside is a mare, a cloak, and a white sword of light which will cut ninety-nine forward and ninety-nine backward." Watt then cut off the giantess's head, and then he found the house and all the things therein as she had told him. That night he took the cows home, and the king was very pleased. The next day the king went to fight the Danes. Watt went out to the pasture with the cows as usual, but when he got there, he took the horse, the sword, and the cloak and went to the battle. With his magic sword he cut down ninety-nine forward and ninety-nine backward, and soon he had put the battle to one side. The king and queen and all the princesses saw these deeds. When the battle was over, Watt took the king to the pasture and showed him the dead giants and the house of the giants. Then he told him to get a new cowherd. Then he took the king's daughter as his wife.

Comment. It is extraordinary that this tale contains reference to the Danes as enemies, for the Danes had ceased to be a factor in the history of Scotland and even the Islands by the twelfth century. *Motifs:* strong man kills giant (F 628.2.3), kills giantess (*F 628.2.4); magic objects taken from giant's house (*838.3);

magic cloak (D 1053)—probably it was a cloak of invisibility; magic sword (D 1081)—types 328; 665. Formulistic number: sword cuts ninety-nine forward and ninety-nine backward (Z 71.6).

ix

This story, told by Angus MacIsaac, age *ca.* 70, of Antigonish, shows how neatly a well-known *Märchen* can be localized. The two hammers at each place for use in defense against the mice, and the mice peering cautiously from their holes after the cat appears, are delightful details. This story was told in Gaelic.

Some people were fitting out a ship to go to a strange country. Many people brought things to send on the ship to trade in the foreign port. They got a lot of stuff and expected great returns from that foreign king. When they had the vessel pretty well loaded, who should come along but an old woman and what in the world did she have but a cat. And she said she would send the cat, and all made fun of her. But they took the cat on the voyage. When they arrived, they went to the palace, and there was a great reception. And the king said, "Before you go, you will have to dine with me." They did. When they went to the table, the first thing they saw were little hammers, two at each place. The first course, wasn't that all taken by the mice that came swarming out of every hole and crack in the walls and floor. They tried to keep the mice away by hitting them with the hammers, but there were so many that no one got more than a mouthful of that first course. Then came the second course, and that was just as bad. They had to wait for the third course before they got anything to eat. Then the captain of the ship said, "We have something that will frighten the life out of these pests." And he sent for the cat. The king and his people had never seen the like of a cat before. They brought on another course, and soon the cat had half of the mice killed with his paws and the rest so frightened that all they could do was sit in their holes and peer out at the cat. So they brought on another course, and all ate in peace. The king asked for the cat, and they gave it to him. The king in return sent the old woman enough property and money to last her a lifetime. And they got more money for the cat than anything else they brought.

Comment. Motifs: Cat in mouse-infested land sold for fortune (N 411.1)—types 1650, 1651.

x

Most of the older storytellers have a good store of fairy lore. There are, however, few long tales of the fairy and no fairy mistress or lover tales. Michael MacMullen, age 80, Sydney, was very serious about the fairy folk. When asked about the fairy, he told me:

"My grandmother and twenty-two other girls were lost in the fairy den, and they came back months later. My grandmother told me it was a glorious and splendid place. She thought she had been there only a few minutes."

One morning a week later, when we had become better acquainted, he said, "I'm going to show you something I have never shown anyone else. You don't laugh at these things." Then he extricated from the bottom of a trunk in the room a newspaper bundle and carefully unwrapped it, finally revealing a brown stone. It appeared to be sandstone; it was three inches long, half an inch wide, and a quarter of an inch thick. "That's a fairy stone," he said. "When my grandmother came from the fairy den, she had this in her hand, and she passed it on to my mother and my mother to me." When questioned about its powers, he said, "This stone protects you from the fairy; they'll not snatch any of your folk when you have this or do anything else wrong." He scorned my suggestion that the stone be given to a folklore museum. "No, it's too personal; I'm the last of my people, and it's going to be put in my coffin." So the old and the new mingle: the fairy stone below and the cross above. He should rest in peace.

Comment. The only other reference to a fairy stone that I have found is in E. S. Hartland's *The Science of Fairy Tales* (New York: 1891), p. 61. Here the stone is not from a fairy den but is just a magic stone which, placed on the eyes, enables one to see the fairy. *Motif:* D 931; or perhaps extraordinary stone protects from fairies (*F 808).

xi

Mr. MacMullen told another fairy story:

There was this woman. She put the baby outside for fresh air. All of a sudden there was a dream melody in her ears. Such a charming melody she had never heard. Someone must be charming the baby. God knows it must be the fairy. She jumped and the baby was there, but the sweet melody had stopped. But she always remembered that melody. Consider what a memory she had.

xii

Mrs. Dave Patterson, Benacadie Pond, age *ca.* 75, told a male Cinderella story with a fairy addition, in English.

This is a true story; it happened to my grandfather. Now his father was a poor man, and when his wife died, leaving him with one son, he married a widow woman who was well-off, and she had two sons. She was mean to his son; she made him eat in the kitchen and made him set there and not come into the parlor with the rest. Her sons played the pipes fine. She brought them two sets of pipes, and she paid a lot for them, and all his son had was a little old chanter. He couldn't play very well. One day he was out in the hills herding the cows and trying to play on his little chanter when who should he see but one of the little fairy men, and this one said to him, "Do you want to play as well as your brothers?" And he said he did. "Well," said the little man, "put your fingers in my mouth, don't be afraid." He put his fingers in the little man's mouth, and then he picked up the chanter and played such marvellous music that he charmed the fishes out of the water and the little birds from their nests and milk from maidens' breasts. When he went home, he did not say anything about it, but sat in the kitchen as usual. The next day a man came there to hire one of the brothers to play the pipes on his steamer to entertain the people. He had heard that these two boys were good pipers. He asked them to play so he could choose. When they had finished, he said to the wife,

"Who is that fellow I see out there in the kitchen?"

"Oh, he's just the boy that tends the cows," she replied.

"Well I see he has a chanter," said the man. "Let's hear him play."

"Oh, you don't want to hear him. He can't play. All he makes is noises on his wretched chanter."

"Let me hear him anyway," insisted the man. So the boy was called in and given the pipes, and he played so wonderfully that even the stepmother had to admit that he was better than her own sons. And he got the job, and became the piper on the steamer. One day when the steamer was eighteen miles off shore, it began to leak. The captain did not know what to do. Then the boy said to him, "If you warm my fingers, I'll play distress music so loud that they will hear it on shore." So they warmed his fingers, and he went up on the upper deck, and he played distress music so loud that they heard him on shore and sent out another boat and rescued all the passengers. After that the boy came ashore and settled in this valley, and all his sons were great pipers after him because they learned from him. And that is why this valley is called Piper's Glen.

Comment. The male Cinderella is a common enough story, but the combination here found with the fairy helper is unique. This uses stock motifs at the beginning: cruel stepmother (S 31); male Cinderella (L 101); widower's son as hero (L 111.5). The motifs building up the remainder of the story are rare: boy learns to play pipes by putting his fingers in fairy's mouth (*D 262.2.1); magic music charms birds from nest, fish from sea, milk from maidens' breasts (*D 1275.2.1).

Notes

1. Numbers refer to the classification according to motifs in Stith Thompson, *Motif-Index of Folk-Literature* (Bloomington, Indiana: 1933).

2. See Whitley Stokes, *Revue Celtique,* XII; H. d'Arbois de Jubainville, *Le Cycle Mythologique Irlandais et la Mythologie Celtique* (Paris: 1884).

Joseph Szövérffy

OTTAWA UNIVERSITY

OTTAWA, CANADA

A Medieval Story and Its
Irish Version

In his index of Spanish tales[1]
R. S. Boggs refers to a story taken from the 13th-century collection of Alfonso El Sabio: "Boy offers bread to statue of Christ or
Virgin. Statue answers: 'I shall give you some of my bread.' Boy
dies."

This story, which is given by Boggs the number *767, is recorded in the motif-index of Professor Stith Thompson as No.
Q 172.1 under religious motifs.[2] I know, however, no other volume in the series of F. F. C. where the tale would be listed under
this or any other number. A particularly striking fact is that the
story is not referred to by Tom Peete Cross in his *Motif Index to
Early Irish Literature*,[3] where he deals with features of both
medieval Irish literature and modern Irish folklore, mostly
drawn from collections published in *Béaloideas*.[4]

The story is known also in modern and Irish folklore. A recent collection of Irish religious folktales published by Seán Ó Súilleabháin,[5] Archivist of the Irish Folklore Commission, contains an Irish version of this story that is here translated into English. Its title is *The Straight Road.*

There was a poor woman, and she was on her way [*literally*, was walking ahead]. A little lad was with her, and he was not very big. They were at Mass one day, and the priest said in the sermon that anyone who keeps the straight road has nothing to fear. There was a village, and a short path led toward it, and the mother wanted to go the short cut, but the boy would not go except the straight road. As they were arguing together, who should come toward them but the priest, who was probably returning home after saying Mass.

"What is wrong with you, at all," said the priest to the old woman.

[It is probable that she was not a very old woman as she had this little boy with her.]

"This little blagard would not come along with me," said she.

"Why would you not go with your mother?" said the priest to the boy; "do what she wishes."

"Certainly I will go with her," said the boy, "if she will go the straight road."

"Is it not all the same to you?" said the priest.

"And why did you say in the sermon today," asked the boy, "that anyone who would keep the straight road had nothing to fear?"

The priest did not speak for a while, and then he asked the old woman if she would let the boy go along with himself and he would take him.

"Well, you'll be able to do nothing else, Father, surely, but mind him," said she.

"Don't bother about that," said the priest; "let him come with me and I will take him."

"By my word, I will let him go, indeed, Father," said she, "and my blessing with him."

He placed the boy on the horse, either on a saddle or coach, I don't know which. He then ordered the housekeeper to give food to the boy, to bring it to him when it had been prepared. There was a picture of Our Saviour, may He ever be praised, on the way as the boy went into the room, like a hall or something similar. The boy never passed it but he left a piece of the food for the Child who was in the [picture]. On Christmas Eve, the Child asked the boy, who was carrying food to the priest, would he go to spend the Christmas with Him. The boy said he would go if the priest would allow him.

"You may go to the priest," said the Child, "and if he lets you come with me, we will go to celebrate Christmas together tonight."

He went to the priest and asked would he allow him to spend Christmas with the little Boy who was outside.

"Who is the boy?" said the priest.

"A Boy is outside here on the wall, in the picture," he said.

"Was he talking to you?" asked the priest.

"He was asking me," said he, "if I would spend the Christmas with Him."

"What connection have you with that Boy?" asked the priest.

"We had no connection at all," said he, "but when I brought food in for you, I [always] left a piece for Him."

"And did He eat it?" asked the priest.

"I do not know whether He did or not," said the boy, "as I did not delay except to leave it with Him, but none of the food was there when I went out from you."

"Go out to Him, so," said the priest, "and tell Him that I will allow you if He lets myself go with you."

He went out and said that [the priest] would allow him to go if he also could go. He returned to the priest, then, and he told him that he might go with them.

"When you are going to sleep tonight, come in to me," said the priest.

He went in, and the priest told him to come to the other side of the bed, and he did so. On Christmas morning then, people were waiting a very long time for the priest to get up to celebrate Mass and they went to him at the end. It happened that the priest and the boy were dead in the bed, and they had received an invitation to Christmas.

The main peculiarities of this text can be summed up in a few words:

(1) This is a genuine Irish folk story taken down by Seosamh Ó Dálaigh from Muiris Ó Conchubhair, age 77, at Baile Uí

Bhoithín, parish of Márthan, County Kerry, at Christmas, 1947.[6]

(2) It exactly corresponds in all essential points to the German version recorded by the Brothers Grimm.[7]

(3) The story can be divided into two main parts: (a) The first part contains the episode of the priest's sermon and the boy's reaction to this, taking the word literally; (b) the second part tells of the boy offering food to a (holy) statue (or picture) and being invited by it to come to celebrate Christmas or to take food (etc.), according to the different versions.

(4) The text published by Seán Ó Súilleabháin reflects many of the characteristics of short religious tales still circulating in Ireland among country people. In many cases these stories contain some didactic end or aetiological "point." Although this story is, beyond doubt, of non-Irish origin, its "setting" is nevertheless as typically Irish as if it were a product of the Irish countryside. The simple, undecorated, and straightforward style, the slowly developed conversation between the priest, the old woman, and the boy (which occupies a large portion of the story) and the repetition of words and phrases already used reflect the well-known type of everyday conversation of the Irish country people. (One must stress here that this type of story has a completely different character from that of the Irish hero tales and the tales of magic that are described and analyzed by Professor Séamus Ó Duilearga in his "Gaelic Story-teller."[8] In the latter, which represent a quite different orientation in story-telling, we find traditional, often ancient, phrases and an artistic rendering—sometimes a rhythmical structure—and a romantic atmosphere full of magic, marvels, and adventures.)

This story is only one version of the tale. There are many more collected by the Irish Folklore Commission and catalogued under the heading "Religious Tales" in the card index of the Commission in Dublin. According to Seán Ó Súilleabháin, the tale enjoys a great popularity in Ireland.[9] As already stated, the version translated here was recorded quite recently.

In the Middle Ages the story was quite popular, and countless versions of it are preserved in medieval manuscripts. Apart from the source referred to by Boggs, there are several other sources listed in the great reference work by Bolte and Polívka;[10] among others, Latin collections such as the *Speculum exemplorum*,[11] Dutch versions incorporated in Vooys' collection,[12] and French-Picard poems such as that edited by Reinhard. (See also his bibliography of miracles).[13] Taking into account the additional fact that the Brothers Grimm were able to collect current versions in Germany nearly a hundred and fifty years ago and that it is still current in Ireland, we must admire the tenacity of this simple story. From these facts we can recognize beyond doubt that it appealed and still appeals to the taste and feelings of the listeners and thus shows that human feelings and attitudes have changed but little in certain spheres of life since the Middle Ages.

We turn now to certain features which can be used to illustrate briefly the development of this story. As it is not our aim to follow its development from start to finish, only a few medieval and later versions will be compared with the Irish story provided by Seán Ó Súilleabháin.

The most extensive bibliography found was in the *Anmerkungen*, by Bolte and Polívka, under No. 209 ("Die himmlische Hochzeit"), including some extracts from medieval versions.[14] The authors quote from *De pignoribus sanctorum*, by Guibert of Nogent, where an altar boy (*acolytus puer*) offers bread to the Crucifix, which answers as in the version quoted by Boggs: "I shall give you soon my bread" (12th century).[15]

A number of later medieval stories echo this type with certain changes: e.g., the text from the *Speculum exemplorum*, where a young monk (*parvus monachus*) offers food to the statue and, when in turn invited by the statue, asks the abbot for permission. The latter wants to go with the monk. Permission is granted, and both die at Pentecost.[16] (In this text the word *"nuptiae"* occurs as in the German text of the Brothers Grimm; cf. "Die himmlische Hochzeit.") The medieval Dutch texts published by C. G. N. de Vooys mostly follow this latter pattern with certain motifs added or narrated with minute details,[17] and some of them show a further development: instead of giving food to the statue, the young monk plays with Christ, the Child.[18]

In addition to this type of medieval narrative, we find, as early as the 13th century, or late in the 12th century, that a second version of the story has been recorded by Gautier de Cluny[19] and that this also occurs in the French-Picard version edited by J. R. Reinhard.[20] According to this, a mother comes to the Church to pray with her son. The child offers food to the statue and starts to cry; the statue then says: "In three days time I will eat with you." The priest (or priests) comes to the mother and warns her to take care of the child, who dies on the third day. This version is also found in the collection of miracles by Johannes Herolt,[21] where—as in several other texts[22]—Speyer, on the Rhine, is the locale. The version of Herolt is taken from Vincentius Bellovacensis' *Speculum Historiale*.

These are the two main types of the medieval versions, with a secondary development (the young monk playing with Christ, taking his apple, etc., as indicated above in connection with Dutch-Flemish texts).

The writer has also collated two Italian versions with the text printed by the Brothers Grimm. One of them was originally published by Pitrè[23] and dealt with by Crane.[24] The other is in a German translation in the collection of Laura Gonzenbach.[25] They show a similar treatment of the larger part of the story but differ somewhat, mainly in the introduction and at the end.

The Pitrè version, from Sicily, seems to preserve the introduction best. This story begins with the motif of the "straight road": a simple youth asks the priest about the way to Paradise. Then he comes (see also the Grimm version) to the church of a convent. He thinks he is in Heaven, wants to stay, gets food, asks the Lord on the Crucifix why He was crucified, and then conveys the warning of the Lord to the convent's superior, to sell their property and to repent. This is done, and the monks all repent and die.

The version in Gonzenbach's collection tells of a foundling who accompanies his foster father to Catania. He goes to the church and talks to the Crucifix, which nods its head in answer. The boy gets food and drink and offers them to the Crucifix. He then dies, is buried in the church, and venerated as a saint.

In the Grimm version, the priest preaches of the straight road that is taken literally by the simple boy. He finds a church and believes that he is in Heaven. The priest takes him into his service. The boy offers food to the statue of the Madonna with the Child, and it is accepted. When he recovers after an illness, the priest watches him and hears that the boy has been invited to a (heavenly) wedding on the following Sunday.[26] (Cf. above and also the text of the *Speculum exemplorum*.) The priest sends the boy to ask permission for the priest to attend the wedding also, but this is refused. Next Sunday at communion the boy dies. (From Mecklenburg, but according to the records it was also known in Münster.)

There are other versions of this story from the Heanzenland, a German-speaking district of Western Hungary, as well as Flemish, Rumanian, Serbian and Croatian, Czech and Slovak, and Polish versions.[27]

If we compare the versions, we find certain important features common to all as well as minor degrees of similarity. *The Straight Road* reminds us, in its introduction, of the medieval type represented by (among other variants) the story of Gautier of Cluny and the Picard-French version edited by Reinhard. The Irish tale, however, follows the Grimm type in all important features, except at the end, where the priest is allowed to join the boy. (In this point, the Irish story corresponds to the versions found in the *Speculum exemplorum* and in several Dutch texts.) Christmas is mentioned in the Irish story and in some of the medieval Dutch versions,[28] but the Grimm text has Sunday, and the version of the *Speculum exemplorum* Pentecost. In most variants there is no fixed date at all.

The Grimm story preserved the motif of the young boy's illness, which also occurs in some Dutch versions. The Grimm tale, the Sicilian story edited by Pitrè, and the Irish text published by Seán Ó Súilleabháin all correspond to one another in one important point: the introduction of the "straight road," a motif that is lost in the other Italian version published in Gonzenbach's collection. On the other hand, we may note that both Italian versions seem to be completed by additional elements that are not to be found either in Grimm or in the Irish variants.

These are, of course, only a few of the features of these variants; space does not permit a detailed discussion.

How have the types developed? On the basis of this comparatively brief sketch, we may note that two main types (with some
variations in the details) can be established: (*a*) the medieval
type, in which—generally speaking—only one episode (the offering of food followed by an invitation to come and take part in
the heavenly feast) can be found, apart from some incidental elements, particularly in Dutch versions; (*b*) the bi-episodic modern
folklore versions, with two parts: on the one hand, the "straight-
road" motif, on the other, the offering of food, etc. In this connection I note that Seán Ó Súilleabháin suggests that the first
part of his Irish story (the "straight-road" motif) is basically identical with type Aa.-Th. 1696, although it has not the humorous
character of the latter.

In the medieval type we find a further bifurcation: the older
type seems to be the story of the altar boy (or young monk), expanded by the addition of new details (see some of the texts
printed by de Vooys),[29] and a slightly later type, a mother visiting
a church with her child. A side development is the episode of
the young monk playing with Christ, in the Dutch versions.

The modern folklore versions are normally based on the bi-
episodic type (Irish, Sicilian, German verisons) although the
introductory episode may be dropped, as in the Gonzenbach
version, or enlarged by incidental elements, as in the conversion
of the monks in Pitrè's Sicilian story.

In certain cases, however, the single-episodic type seems to
have survived, as in the Rumanian story collected by Pauline
Schullerus:

There were a man and a woman, and they had a son who con-
stantly asked his mother for "punje" [bread or cake]; she gave it him
and still, he was permanently hungry. The mother, amazed at
this, watched him, in order to find out what he did with the "punje."
The boy ran to a picture of Christ and called out: "Take, cousin,
[this] 'punje.' " Christ stepped out from the picture, took the piece,

and returned again into the frame. When the child asked again for
"punje," his mother said: "Go now and ask the Lord Christ for some
food to eat." He ran to the picture and began to cry: "Cousin, my
mother will not give me 'punje' any more; she sent me to you; you
should give it to me this time."

Then the Lord Christ came down once more, took some meat from
the one side and wonderful, soft "punje" and money from the other
and gave the whole to the boy. When the mother saw this, she also
went and asked for money. But the Lord Christ gave her nothing and
never left the picture again.[30]

Though the character of this story is sometimes strongly transformed by local adaptation, it still shows the main characteristics
of the older, medieval, single-episodic type. In this connection,
we may note that the story seems to be particularly suitable for
local adaptations and that it easily absorbs the features of *couleur
locale,* as the Grimm story, the Irish variant, and the Rumanian
tale show.

As indicated above, the standard work of references by Bolte
and Polívka refers to several Slavonic versions. On the other
hand, the fact that this work has also German and Irish versions
in addition to the Flemish ones shows that the story was told over
a large part of Western Europe. Thus, its extent is by no means
limited, and we may presume that several other versions must
exist which are not listed either by Bolte and Polívka or elsewhere in the volumes of F. F. C., etc. No explanation can be
given as to why no Hungarian version of this story is listed nor
as to what versions can be found between the German and Irish
area. We certainly know little of the exact history and spread of
this little tale, and a full-scale investigation would probably
throw light on many questions not dealt with in this fragmentary
note.

Finally, I wish to suggest that the entry in Boggs's Spanish index should be accepted as an international reference number for
this story,[31] which is certainly known in many European countries and which, irrespective of its origin in medieval legend, is
to be regarded as a folklore story in its later, bi-episodic form.
Thus, this story must take its place in the future revised edition

of Aarne-Thompson in a form that corresponds to both the Grimm story and the Irish tale alike.[32]

Notes

1. R. S. Boggs, *Index of Spanish Folktales* (Helsinki: 1930), p. 90.

2. Stith Thompson, *Motif-Index of Folk-Literature* (Helsinki: 1935), V, 149. "Child taken to heaven; offers food to crucifix."

3. Tom Peete Cross, *Motif-Index of Early Irish Literature* (Bloomington, Indiana: 1952).

4. *Béaloideas—The Journal of the Folklore of Ireland Society*, ed. by Séamus Ó Duilearga (Dublin: 1927–28; in progress).

5. Seán Ó Súilleabháin, *Scéalta Cráibhtheacha* (Baile Átha Cliath, 1952), pp. 231–33 (summary in English, p. 333); cf. Béaloideas, XXI, and *A Handbook of Irish Folklore* (Dublin: 1942), p. 629.

6. *Scéalta Cráibhtheacha*, p. 300.

7. Fr. Panzer, *Die Kinder- und Hausmärchen der Brüder Grimm in ihrer Urgestalt* (Munich: 1913), II, 190–92, "Die himmlische Hochzeit"; cf. *ibid.*, II, 344 (Notes), and Margaret Hunt, *Grimm's Household Tales* (London: 1884), II, 370–71, 466.

8. J. H. Delargy, "The Gaelic Story-Teller," *Proceedings of the British Academy*, XXXI, The Sir John Rhŷs Memorial Lecture, British Academy, 1945, *passim*; cf. p. 34, etc.

9. According to him, more than fifty variants are listed in the present "Interim-Catalogue" of the Commission.

10. Johannes Bolte and Georg Polívka, *Ammerkungen zu den Kinder- und Hausmärchen der Brüder Grimm* (Leipzig: 1918), III, 474–77; and *ibid.*, IV, 464 (in a division of the Grimm tales according to Fr. von der Leyen; this tale is included in the section called "Ritterliche Dichtung des Mittelalters") and 472 (among the "Kindergeschichten," on the list of Berendsohn). I refer here to the fact that a parallel from India is listed in the reference work by Bolte and Polívka (III, 476) and is also mentioned in the notes of the Grimms (see Hunt, II, 466).

11. I used the following edition: *Speculum Exemplorum* (Haguenau: 1480), IX, chap. lxxviii.

12. C. G. N. de Vooys, *Middelnederlandse Marialegenden* (Leiden: n.d.), I, 143, 140; II, 185, 221, 222, *passim*.

13. J. R. Reinhard, "Bread Offered to the Child-Christ," *PMLA*, XL (1925), 93–95; bibliography, 96–97; cf. A. Poncelet, *Miraculorum BMV quae saec.*, VI-XV. *Latine conscripta sunt Index, Analecta Bollandiana*, XXI (1902), 241–360, in two groups: (*A*) Nos. 29, 1252, 1532, 1668, 1671, 1672; (*B*) Nos. 111, 954, 1253, 1320, 1510, and No. 10 ("Puer porrigit panem [pomum, etc.] Christo"). Cf. H. L. D. Ward, *Catalogue of Romances in the Dept. of MSS in the British Museum* (London: 1893), II, 623, 627, 694, 695 (= Group *A*); and II, 668, No. 19 (*B*). A. Mussafia, "Studien zu den ma. Marienlegenden," *Sitszungsber. der Kaiserl. Akad. d. Wiss. H. Ph. Kl. I*,

1886 (v. 113), 917–94; 1887 (v. 115), 5–95; 1889 (Abt. ix), 1 ff.; 1890 (Abt. viii), 1–85; 1898 (v. 139, Abt. viii), 1–74. Cf. Reinhard, p. 95: "For possible Latin sources or analogues see Mussafia. . . ." For an English version, not collated by me, see R. Tryon, "Miracles of Our Lady," *PMLA*, XXXVIII (1923), 308 ff.

14. Bolte-Polívka, III, 474-75.

15. *Ibid.*, 474.

16. Cf. *supra*, No. 11.

17. De Vooys, I, 140–42 (No. 75); II, 185–94 (No. 331), and II, 222–25 (No. 347).

18. *Ibid.*, I, 143 (No. 76), and II, 221–22 (No. 346).

19. Bolte-Polívka, III, 474.

20. *PMLA*, XL (1925), 93–95. Cf. de Vooys, II, 185 (No. 330).

21. C. C. Swinton Bland, *Miracles of the Blessed Virgin Mary* [by] *Johannes Herolt Called Discipulus* (London: 1928), p. 34.

22. Bolte-Polívka, III, 475.

23. Giuseppe Pitrè, *Fiabe, Novelle e Racconti Popolari Siciliani* (Torino-Palermo: 1875) III, 6–11 (No. 112).

24. Th. Fr. Crane, *Italian Popular Tales* (London: 1885), p. 211; cf. p. 366 (notes).

25. Laura Gonzenbach, *Sicilianische Märchen* (Leipzig: 1870), ed. by Otto Hartwig, II, 163–65.

26. Panzer, II, 190–92; Hunt, II, 370; different parallels, etc. See L. Mackensen, *Handwörterbuch des deutschen Märchens* (Leipzig: 1930–40) *passim;* cf. *Index*, I, 658; II, 697.

27. Bolte-Polívka, III, 476. In this connection I must draw attention to the fact that this story is closely related in its origin to several others recorded in the Middle Ages concerning the statues of the Blessed Virgin (see the bibliography compiled by Reinhard, *supra*, No. 13 and the surveys by Mussafia) and preserved also in later tales and stories (cf. *Marienlegenden* in the *Index* of Bolte-Polívka, V, 286 and versions of the St. Kümmernis legend: III, 241–44; and see III, 127).

28. De Vooys, II, 188 ff. (No. 331).

29. Cf. especially de Vooys: I, 140–42; II, 185–94; II, 222–25, etc.

30. Pauline Schullerus, *Rumänische Volksmärchen aus dem mittleren Harbachtal: Im Anhang: aus dem Alttal* (Hermannstadt: 1907), p. 233 (No. 109: "Nimm, Vetter, Punje," told by Ana Folobă, of Leschkirch).

31. I used the copy of Gonzenbach's collection that once belonged to the late Professor C. W. von Sydow, who annotated it in several places. As a curious thing, I mention that he added to the Sicilian story (Aa 775) dealt with above.

32. At the end, I must add a Lithuanian version that is recorded in the *Motif-Index* by Jonas Balys: "A Poor Shepherd Boy Feeds a Crucifix. Following the words of a preacher, the shepherd boy always carries about with him a crucifix and nourishes it; the miraculous death," etc.; cf. J. Balys, *Motif-Index of Lithuanian Narrative Folk-Lore* (Kaunas: 1936), p. 249 (No. 3727).

Erminie Wheeler-Voegelin

and Remedios W. Moore

INDIANA UNIVERSITY

BLOOMINGTON, INDIANA

The Emergence Myth in
Native North America

In native North American mythology the emergence myth commands attention for a variety of reasons. First among these is the distribution of the myth, which is continental. Some fifty native groups (see map facing p. 68) account for their presence on the earth by a myth relating, either in simple or elaborate form, how their forebears ascended from underground to the top of the earth. The importance of the myth in tribal mythologies is attested by the fact that, for the sixty or so groups having it, a total of some 120 versions have been recorded.[1] It is on these 120 versions that we base the present study.

Distributionally speaking, we are not dealing with a closed corpus in this paper.[2] Hence we are unable to offer any suggestions regarding a possible point of origin or the probable age of the myth.[3] There are various indications that in North America north of Mexico the myth may have traveled from a Southwestern center of diffusion to California-Plateau, Plains, Southeastern, and Woodlands groups. Independent invention of the myth several times over in the same subareas that have just been mentioned seems improbable.

Linkage between the emergence myth and migration tales is a notable feature of the North American material; over half of our versions exhibit such a linkage. In some groups the linked emergence-migration accounts consist of a detailed emergence myth and a detailed migration tale;[4] in others the emergence myth may be simple in form, amounting to a bald statement, and the account of migration detailed.[5] In still other accounts a detailed emergence myth may be coupled with a simple migration tale;[6] finally, some accounts combine a simple emergence and a simple migration story.[7]

Those emergence myths not linked with migration accounts have either a simple form of the myth[8] or a detailed account of emergence with no account of migration.[9]

Linkage variation and lack of linkage may be expressed thus:

$$DE^{10} + DM^{11}$$
$$DE \ \ + SM^{12}$$
$$SE^{13} + DM$$
$$SE \ \ + SM$$
$$DE \ \ - M^{14}$$
$$SE \ \ - M$$

In the North American material all the formulaic combinations given above are present and, what is more interesting, are often localized in two or more adjacent groups.

I FUNCTIONAL ASPECTS

Turning to a brief consideration of the myth as a document authenticating various beliefs and practices, we find that for many groups the emergence myth, especially in its detailed forms, is of great significance. The various accounts embody, among other religious beliefs, a series of concepts relating to the nature of the universe, the characteristics and deeds of important deities and other supernaturals, and the nature of life after death. The belief in origin from the underworld is strongly connected with belief in return to the underworld after death. How this return is effected varies. The worthy dead among the Mandans, for example, reach the ancient village beneath the ground by means of a lake, which the burden of the sins of the wicked will not enable them to cross.[15] The Navaho believe that the soul wanders over a gloomy marsh for four days before it can

KEY TO MAP SYMBOLS

Numbers used in the map on the facing page refer to the following tribes and groups:

1. Northern Tiwa—Taos, Picuris	24. Creek
2. Tewa	25. Alibamu
3. Keresan (Eastern)—Cochiti, Santa Fe, Santa Ana, Sia	26. Choctaw
	27. Chickasaw
4. Keresan (Western)—Acoma, Laguna	28. Tunica
	29. Avoyelle
5. Zuñi	30. Atakapa
6. Mohave	31. Tonkawa
7. Yuma	32. Caddo
8. Thompson	33. Wichita
9. Tinlineh (Yokuts)	34. Lipan Apache
10. Hopi	35. Kiowa
11. Mandan-Hidatsa	36. Pawnee
12. White Mountain Apache	37. Oto
13. Havasupai	38. Jicarilla Apache
14. Walapai	39. Iowa
15. Arikara	40. Missouri
16. Menomini	41. Omaha
17. Wyandot	42. Pima
18. Iroquois	43. Papago
19. Delaware	44. Yavapai
20. Nanticoke	45. Cheyenne
21. Powhatan	46. Takhali
22. Tuscarora	47. Nez Percé
23. Yuchi	48. Pomo

INCIDENCE OF THE EMERGENCE TYPE IN NATIVE
NORTH AMERICAN TRADITION

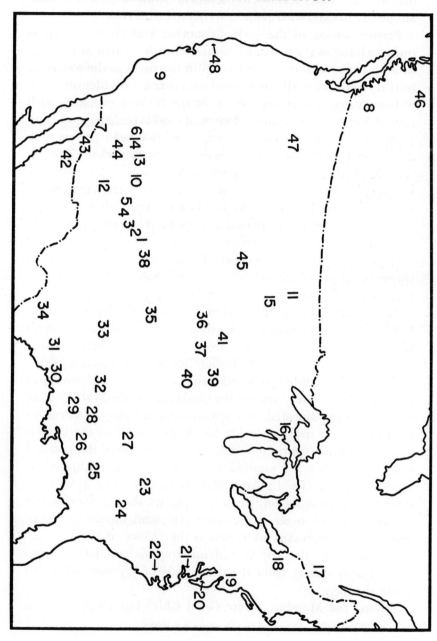

discover the ladder leading to the world below—a land of luxuri-
ant plenty stocked with game and covered with corn.[16]

Personification of the earth as mother and giver of food is
quite striking in the myth. Identified with the "earth Mother" is
Mother Corn, who is authenticated in the myth as the source of
fertility rites (primarily concerned with corn). This identification
of Corn Woman with the mother of the Indians and, also, with
the earth as mother of life and giver of food is perhaps most complete among the Pueblo. Her place has not been pre-empted,
and she is thought of as still residing in the underworld. She is
considered the source of corn and corn culture (what men live
by, in an extended sense) among the Pueblo[17] and charges her
people with the care of altars and bestows upon them the corn
fetish which they are to regard as herself. When they neglect to
pray to her and turn to another religion (because a Deceiver
comes and pretends to be a deputed supernatural), she withdraws
the food plants, which are returned only after a long period of
placation and sacrifice.

Among the Navaho, First Man and First Woman come into
being (through marriage of earth and sky) holding an ear of
white and yellow corn, respectively. During the first Blessing
Rite or ceremony (in Na 6*), Pollen Boy and Corn Beetle Girl—
ripener—take visible forms and return to their plant forms after
the ceremony. Thus, among the Arikara,[18] Corn Mother is an
ear of corn transformed into woman (taken from the Creator's
field of corn in the sky-world). She is the source of the bundle
songs and rituals connected with the purification of the people's
seeds before they are planted and is a means of ridding their
fields of evil spirits. In Ar 8 Mother Corn's voice guides the
people during migration; when she appears, she carries with her
the fragrance of sweet grass, cedar tree, and blooming plum;
further, the informant adds, hers is the "Voice of Vegetation."
It is noteworthy that the Woodland Iroquois say that corn and
other plants sprang from the dead body of Woman Who Fell
From the Sky.

Among the Mandan, where Good Chief Furred Robe (who

* See Bibliography of Versions in this paper, pp. 83–87.

was chief in the underworld) is now pre-empting Mother Corn, he originates "songs so there will be rain and good crops, sexual restrictions during growing time, the cleansing feast at the close of these restrictions, [and] tells the people to burn sage and rub themselves to remove the bad spirits in the fields."[19] (Compare with the section of the Navaho versions concerned with the separation of the sexes.) He has a robe which, if sprinkled with water, causes rain to come (in Man 1); it is he who gives success in raising crops (in Man 1, 2, 3). In Man 3 "before coming out, Corn was a man."

The symbol of Corn Mother has been extended to include the people who came from the underworld. Among the Arikara the people were grains of corn when underground; in Na 8 the first couple are created from two ears of white and yellow corn placed between buckskins and breathed upon by the wind, and the homes of the gods are decorated within and without with ears of corn. In other versions the clan originators are made out of ground cornmeal mixed with pollen, etc.

Sacred bundles are in some instances authenticated by the emergence myth. Two Mandan bundles, the Old Woman Who Never Dies Bundle[20] and the Skull and Robe Bundle belonging to Good Chief Furred Robe,[21] are thus authenticated.

In several instances there is an intimate connection between the emergence myth and ceremonies or rituals performed for the good of the people. In dramatized form the myth is presented as an integral part of the Hopi Powamu ("Bean") ceremony[22] and the Hopi (Walpi) Snake ceremony.[23] Among the White Mountain Apache the emergence myth serves as the basis for ant songs and the ant ceremony.[24] Among the Navaho the myth is primarily concerned with the evolution of the Hanelthnayhe ("Upward Reaching") Way. The pouch for this Way was first assembled by First Man in the eighth division and the ceremony first performed in the next world. Upward-Reaching-Way is accounted for by five sets of events in the basic myth itself.[25] The Tonkawa re-enacted the myth as a dance, showing how the wolf released their progenitors from the underworld and instructed them how to live. A live Tonkawa man was dug up during the ceremony.[26] The Arikara emergence myth is told as the origin myth for the bundle connected with the Buffalo ceremony, and gives the source for the Buffalo Dance. It also serves as origin myth for the Arikara Awaho bundle.[27]

Among the Yavapai the blind shaman who recited the story said that he had received it from the goddess Komwidapokuwia and that it marked the beginning of his shamanistic power.[28]

An interesting function which the emergency myth serves is to account for tribal or gens origins and names. Thus, the Tin-lineh (a tribe of the Yokuts group) derive their name from badger burrows, which their forefathers issued from.[29] The Yuma received their totemic names from the culture-hero of their emergence myth.[30] The Menomini emergence myth recounts how ten animals, invited to a feast by Sekatcokemau (Chief of Chiefs) immediately after his emergence from the earth in bear form, became the ancestors of dominant subgentes. Sekatcoke-mau himself sprang from the great underground bear.[31] So, too, among the Iroquois, the six families that issued from their underground (cave) refuge were the founders of the present Six Nations.[32] And, among the Oto and Missouri, members of the Bear gens relate the emergence myth as their origin story.[33] Members of the Omaha Honga gens say that their name ("eyes open in water") derives from the circumstance that they emerged from the water.[34]

As in nearly all origin myths, way of life and economic activities are accounted for in emergence myths, especially where a supernatural being assumes the role of culture-hero (or heroine —Mother Corn, Changing Woman, Mother of the Pueblo, Goddess Komwidapokuwia).

The migration accounts in the linked emergence-migration myths of the DE + DM and SE + DM types serve as pseudo-history for the various groups. Under a leader, either a supernatural or a human being, the people start traveling on earth, seeking a predestined location in which to settle ("navel of the earth," spot designated by the supernatural, etc.). The character of both content and atmosphere passes from one level of reality to another; hence the term "pseudo-history" is particularly applicable to the migration material.

II THE EMERGENCE TYPE

The emergence myth relates the ascent of the inhabitants of the lower world to the earth's surface and their subsequent settlement and/or migration.[35] Although the details vary, the component elements remain basically unaltered from the point of location in the underworld up to the start of migration.

Following ascent by natural or artificial means, the people and/or supernaturals (all living things)[36] issue from a hole in the ground after preparation of the earth for their habitation (or a scout's discovery of it as habitable).[37]

The hole is thought to be pre-existing or to be a cave or to have been bored by an animal, a series of animals, or by the culture hero(es).[38]

The means of ascent is either a vine, a stretching plant, a tree or mountain, a ladder, or a combination of two or more of these.[39]

The emergence is actuated either by the coming or subsidence of a flood (the termination of some other catastrophe)[40]—in which case the emerging peoples are refugees—or by the desire for a place lighter, larger, and better provided with subsistence forms than the underground habitation.[41]

While the portion of the story concerned with the emergence proper is sharply defined, the introductory action and post-emergence events have apparently developed by accretion, from the different centers of distribution, certain traits circulating in the body of tradition properly belonging to the flood story, the creation story, and the hero cycles—particularly those hero-cycles concerned with the Sun's children, "the old woman's grandsons" and Manabozho.

The "Earth-mother" concept of creation enters into the story as a motif; we have not gone into the study of it as a type, although certain of the versions do reflect the psychological attitude toward the emergence as childbirth in an extended sense, after a period of gestation (cf. Zu 4, 5 and Ar 7, 8).

The emergence type has a continental distribution along a belt hugging the eastern and southern limits of the United States, extending from the Iroquois and Delaware in the East to the Mohave and the Yokuts (Tinlineh) of California. Another belt of distribution extends north-south through the middle of the continent, from the Mandan and Hidatsa on the Upper Missouri River to the Atakapa and Tonkawa of the Gulf. Though the story type is retained, the collected versions show all stages of truncation and development from a bald statement of underground origin to a fully elaborated recounting of creation, genesis, emergence, migratory activities, population increase and decrease (because of encounters with monsters and warring groups), and evolution of economy.

In the Southwest the type borrowed heavily from the cycle of the Sons of the Sun ("Monster-slayers") among the Navaho, Pueblo, Apache, and Yavapai. On the western and northern peripheries it has been influenced by the earth mother and sky-father of genesis, the Plains-Plateau concept of origins. This genesis is one of supernatural progenitors of the race among the Navaho, the Pima-Papago, and Yuma; of all living things among the Thompson, Zuñi, Lipan Apache, and Arikara.

Throughout this area of distribution the concept of the underworld as the habitation of the gods (supernaturals) and as the setting for the creation of the peoples persists. As the story moved upward into the Plains and northeastward into the Woodlands, it accommodated itself to the belief in the sky world as the residence of the gods, and in the creation of the peoples in the sky or upon the earth.[42] The emergents are refugees in the Arikara and Woodland-Iroquois versions; among the Thompson, Mandan, Hidatsa, and Sioux, sky, earth, and underworld are points of origin for the people. It is no wonder one of the Mandan informants said—

I'm sure we once lived beside a lake because I've heard so many stories about it. Some people think this lake was under the ground and that we left it when we came up out of the ground. Others think it is on top of the ground. Our old people must have got some of their stories mixed because they tell of coming out of the ground as a tribe and also of the making of the world on top at the Heart River. Others say they came from the sky.[43]

In its new, Plains and Woodlands habitat the story gained the earth-diver element but lost the flood as motivating factor for emergence. Northeastward among the Woodland Iroquois it borrowed, for the activities of the hero, from the Manabozho cycle and that of the "old woman's grandsons."

In the Southeast the emergence story has become merely an incident in a pseudo-history more concerned with the migratory activities of the tribes and their encounters with warring groups.

Certain areal relationships emerge into focus when the versions are closely studied and analyzed.

The Navaho, Pima, Papago, and Yuman versions are bound together by the common traits of a contest among supernaturals actuating a flood, which terminates one world order and necessitates the building of another. The flood is the cause of the emergence, and the emergents are refugees. Among the Navaho the flood occurs in the underworld, and the people come to the upper(most) world as refugees. Among the Pima-Papago the flood occurs in the upper world, and the people who are taken underground by the culture hero or a supernatural are refugees who emerge after the subsidence of the flood, in order to repeople the earth. Among the Yuman Yavapai the flood terminates the first cycle of time and wipes out the first generation (who emerged from the underground).

Though among the Pima-Papago this flood is a direct result of the attempt by one supernatural to vanquish the other, among the Navaho it is caused by the water monster, which has been angered because of the theft of its babies by Coyote. Atavistic traces remain of this element in Yuman versions where the flood is connected with a "baby" found on the ground or left there, or is produced by waters welling from the hole to the underworld.

The shift in locale (for the flood) has not produced any significant changes in the elements comprising the story. Among the Pima-Papago a hole is bored by Elder Brother from the earth's surface through its core and to its other side, so his people may be safe. Among the Navaho the hole is likewise bored, but this time from the underworld up, opening into our world. First Man or the two heroes (like Elder Brother of the Pima-Papago) lead the underworld people out of the threatened place of habitation to one of refuge. The processes of re-creation of the earth to make it livable are present in versions collected from these areas we are considering, with this difference. In the Pima-Papago-Yuma versions the earth is dried and ordered after the flood has ravaged it; in the Navaho versions an earth covered with primeval waters is put in order.

If we seek to extend this complex to include all areas which have retained this trait or element, we find the Pueblo and Arikara-Pawnee to be within the orbit of influence of the particular trait we are discussing.

Te 2 takes after the Navaho versions of the creation story and Coch 1 after the other group of versions (Pima-Papago-Yuma). The flood is produced by one supernatural among the Pueblo in order to drown the "children" of a rival supernatural (Ker 1, Coch 2). The same situation noted above exists; leadership of the people is at stake (or settlement in a particular spot), and the flood takes on the aspect of a contest of power. The emergence already having taken place, however, the challenged supernatural revives her people to show her superiority. The defeated supernatural leads her people to another spot (other than the disputed one) to settle in. In Sia 1, Ker 1, and Zu 2 the trait has become, through progressive deterioration, a mere event in a pseudo-history and has ceased to be a motivating force in a story of origins.

The Atakapa version is on the farthest eastern periphery of this complex. The informant did not give a very connected story. He introduced the emergence with a flood story, but he then stated that the earth was still wet when the people came out. We are therefore in a quandary. Are the emerging peoples refugees and earth-people; or are they refugees who once inhabited the lower world and who are now fleeing from a flood therein? Is the earth wet because of primeval waters that have not completely disappeared, or because of a flood that has lately covered it?

When we come to the Arikara-Pawnee versions, we return to the concept of the emerging peoples as original inhabitants of the earth who had previously sought refuge underground. The deluge is sent by the creator to destroy a too-powerful first (or second) generation of human creations. Since these two traits (flood and destruction of imperfect human creations) are inseparably linked in this area,[44] assimilation of both was inevitable. So follows the traditional pattern of the leader, the boring of the hole, the migration and settlement, and the preparation for life on earth. But because the Arikara-Pawnee oppose no foil to the creator, a new supernatural, Mother Corn, is deputed to lead the people out to repeople the land.

Not Densmore alone[45] but all others who have noticed the phenomenon have commented on the lack of correlation between the two creation stories told by the Mandan (i.e., the story concerning the origin of first man and that concerning the appearance of the Mandan tribe on earth). The Mandan-Hidatsa versions reflect, though imperfectly, the form of the myth among the Pima-Papago and Yuma, where Earth Doctor, dissatisfied with his own human creations, evokes earth and sky out of nothing (cf. Th 1 also) to procreate a companion creator. Out of this union comes Elder Brother (the Lone Man of the Mandan-Hidatsa versions), who proves to be more powerful than Earth Doctor. (Logically this is corollary to the motif of successive human creations, as found among the Arikara; because they were too powerful—either being made of stone or being giants—and because they were patterned too much after the creator himself, the first and second creations are destroyed.)

Among the Mandan-Hidatsa (as among the Pima-Papago-Yuma) Lone Man is more than a worthy opponent to his creator. Thus the contest of power. However, since the contest occurs before the creation of the people and/or takes the tame form of sitting it out to prove which is older (immortal?) of the two, the involvement of the people in this struggle for power is lost. In the Yuma-Pima-Papago cycle, the people are divided among the warring camps. The struggle for power takes the form of a flood, and the first to issue from the waters—Elder Brother—liquidates or subordinates his defeated opponent(s) and leads out his people from their place of refuge under the earth. It is striking that the Mandan-Hidatsa versions have likewise failed to resolve the conflict *decisively*. This is so because the outcome no longer is significant in the context of the tale. Hence in almost all the versions Lone Man and Creator share in the preparation of the earth for the people. Furthermore, although an angered supernatural causes a flood in some of the versions, the emergence is not linked with it in any way. Lone Man takes his people to a corral refuge (or some other structure) high up on the bluffs. The same tendency that we found among the Pueblo to relegate the flood trait to an incident in a post-emergence pseudo-history is noted.

Other vestigial elements found among the Mandan-Hidatsa are the return of the supernatural, to do harm among the people (cf. Montezuma of the Yuma), and the Chief of the Underworld (Good Chief Furred Robe of the Mandan?). Montezuma, among the Yuma, has the chief of the underworld lead his people out to war on and pre-empt the earth people, who have angered him.

It is fair to state at this point that the Mandan share with the Pueblo, Arikara, and Navaho the "Mother Corn" trait. Bowers[46] is inclined to believe that fertility rites and dramatization of the people emerging as corn are comparatively recent accretions.

Woodland-Iroquois versions duplicate the following elements of the Southwest complex that we first discussed: (*a*) the sequence of events, (*b*) the nature of motivation for the underground location of the people, (*c*) the struggle for power, and (*d*) the concept of a specially prepared habitation below the ground for the refugees. The supernaturals involved in Woodland-Iroquois versions are the twin culture heroes, Good and Bad Minds. As with the geographically closer Mandan-Hidatsa, the Earth-Diver is a method of creation (note how the Pima-Papago versions tell of the creation of the world from a bit of clay), but primeval waters have replaced a flood.[47] The contest of power takes the form of a combat, and the flood trait is lost. The motif of cheating, or of deception, used in winning the contest, is found, too, among the Mandan-Hidatsa (the pile of whitened bones deceiving the supernatural into thinking that his opponent is mortal so that the supernatural gets up first) and the Pueblo.[48] Among the Pueblo the victor also kills the loser.[49]

The stylistic use of one of the heroes as foil (or alter-ego) is deteriorating among the Pueblo. A definite extension of psychological attitudes has been introduced in some versions, where the winner (and cheater) is identified with the Father of the Whites and the defeated, smaller sister as the Mother of the Indians. (Note that the pattern of the contest in some instances takes after that between Pueblo Gambler and his liquidator.)

In native North America, the Southwest seems to have been the area from which the emergence myth first diffused. This, however, is merely a suggested possibility. Study of the total distribution of the myth in the New World would be necessary before a valid historical conclusion could be arrived at with any certainty. However, if a Southwestern center of diffusion is posited, it is of interest to observe the differentiation of detail in the myth which has developed in North America as the myth has traveled in various directions. These details have been frozen into forms having independent distributional existence in one or several native groups. Examples of such details are: (a) vine as means of ascent—Mandan, Yuma; (b) pregnant or corpulent woman causes vine to break—Mandan, Kiowa (blocks log); (c) set pattern of obstacles during migration—Arikara; (d) emergence from cave/mound—Muskhogean, Powhatan and Nanticoke (mountain), Iroquois; (e) sun motivates emergence—Jicarilla Apache and Pueblo; (f) earth hardened or dried before emerging people can get out—Pueblo, virtually all Navaho versions, all Jicarilla Apache versions, one Lipan Apache version; (g) series of ascents through series of worlds—Navaho and Pueblo; (h) locust conquers water monsters—Navaho. Other examples are to be found in notes 35–41.

A particularly interesting, specialized form (emergence from water rather than from the underworld) developed among the Siouans; these versions are noticeably connected with the authentication of gens origins (Missouri Bear gens, Oto Bear gens, Omaha Honga gens). It is possible that this form retained the emergence type but with special emphasis on the element of point of origin as being either a lake or near a lake. (In some of the versions a shift has occurred, and the lake or water is identified, not with the point of origin in the underworld, but with the point of emergence in the upper world. The shift is not a difficult one to make since the Navaho-Pueblo-Jicarilla group tells of water covering the earth when it is first sighted.) It is also apparent that the Siouan redactor reflects the Plains-Plateau concept that the animals of the previous world order became the people of this one.[50]

The story developed certain structural explanatory elements with independent distributional existence also: (*a*) body or legs of first animal to emerge (generally, the badger) blackened permanently by the mud of the unripened earth; (*b*) animal first to emerge was blinded by light (sun's rays), now sees only at night and stays below ground during the day (said of the mole); (*c*) bird's (generally, the turkey's) tail feathers whitened permanently from contact with foam from rising flood waters; (*d*) underworld is world of the dead because the first to die returns there or portion of the people is left below either from choice, because the means of ascent breaks, or because an animal mischief-maker (supernatural) decides that it be so; (*e*) irregular placement of stars results from the actions of an animal mischief-maker; (*f*) the story is a legend told in connection with a topographic feature in the geographical environment.[51]

The link holding the Mandan-Hidatsa, Arikara-Pawnee, Pueblo-Navaho complex together can probably be found in the Corn-Mother trait. Among both Pueblo and Navaho it is Mother Corn who leads the people out of the underworld, creates them, and endows them with corn as a culture trait.

Among the Mandan, Good Chief Furred Robe has encroached upon her in her role as the bringer of corn culture. But note how in Man 3 the vine, by which the people are climbing up into the upper world, breaks when he is still below; note, too, that he gives to Waving Corn Stalk (his daughter, who reaches the top) the right to plant corn anywhere and deputizes her to carry on his "ways of doing things." Also, in Man 11 his sister is Yellow Corn Woman. Bowers[52] has found that ". . . new practices, particularly fertility or consecration of the seed rites . . . based on dramatization of corn as people coming from the ground"[53] have been added to older and more widely diffused ceremonies.

In Ar 1 ". . . they [the emergents] were not people; they were grains of corn . . ."; in Ar 2 during the long night vigil spent in singing songs that she teaches her people, Corn Woman sits behind them. At break of day they look where she sits; she has turned into an ear of corn. Thus, with the Arikara, the conceptualization is, if anything, more intense than with the Pueblo. The corn-ear fetish, actualized symbol of Corn Woman, exists both among the Arikara and Pueblo.

Sacred Ear of Corn Woman (Ac 1, Lag 1, Ker 1, Ker 2, Sn Fe 1, Sia 1, Sta A) also leads the people out of Shipap, is likewise a symbolization of corn as woman, is just as clearly thought of as a culture mother, and departs from the myth context for the underworld after impressing upon her children the sacred care of the altars and bestowing upon them the corn fetish.

Because the Arikara conceive of their creator as residing in the sky world, Corn Woman returns there; among the Pueblo the creator (Spider or Thought Woman) resides in the lowest world so Corn Woman returns thereto. Emergence is thus actuated from within the earth among the Pueblo rather than from without (as among the Arikara), and the obstacles that Mother Corn encounters, of (1) locating the people and (2) gaining access to the inner world in the Arikara versions, are not experienced by the Pueblo Sacred Ear of Corn Woman.

Her role is filled by Changing Woman among the Navaho. It is she who creates the progenitors of the Navaho nation from skin-rubbings of different parts of her body; she equips them for life on earth. She is both mother and giver of food. Before her children leave the creation "hogahn," she tells them it will be necessary to plant corn seeds at once. To her is entrusted future guardianship of the people; it is her duty to furnish he-rain and she-rain, fructify crops, and bring forth abundant grass and seeds.[54]

Binding the Southeastern, the Jicarilla Apache versions, and an isolated instance from the Delaware (Lenni Lenape), with the Navaho, Pueblo, Arikara, and Mandan is the trait of the supernatural actuating the emergence or releasing the people from the underworld. Since this is a primary role ascribed to the sons of the Sun, it is not surprising to discover that "the two boys" who provide the reeds by which the people ascend in the Navaho versions also "pierce the roofs" of the cave worlds in certain Pueblo versions. Among the Navaho they carry the sun and moon and issue from a spring. Since the monster-slayers are born from impregnation by the sun and the moon (or sun and falling water), the concept of Sun sending his emissaries (his sons in several versions) to actuate ascent to the upper world (found among the Pueblo and Jicarilla Apache) is not a surprising development. (Thus we have the pattern repeated of the sender and emissary where the myth posits no foil to the supernatural.)

Where this trait of release is lost, the story is reduced to simple emergence from the earth oftentimes because of an accidental discovery of a ready and more habitable world.[55]

Abbreviations

AA	American Anthropologist
AP-AMNH	Anthropological Papers, American Museum of Natural History
ARBAE	Annual Report, Bureau of American Ethnology
BAE	Bureau of American Ethnology
CU-CA	Columbia University, Contributions to Anthropology
FCM-P	Field Columbian Museum, Publications
FMNH	Field Museum of Natural History, Anthropological Papers
GSCan	Geological Survey of Canada, Anthropological Series
INMAI	Indian Notes, Museum of American Indian
JAFL	Journal of American Folklore
MAAA	Memoirs of the American Anthropological Association
MAFS	Memoirs of the American Folklore Society
MAMNH	Memoirs, American Museum of Natural History
PAES	Publications of the American Ethnological Society
P-CI	Publications, Carnegie Institute of Washington

PMASAL   Papers of the Michigan Academy of Science, Arts and Letters
PPMAAE   Papers of Peabody Museum of American Archaeology and Ethnology
UC-PL   University of California, Publications in Linguistics

III   BIBLIOGRAPHY OF VERSIONS

In the text the versions are referred to by the abbreviated caption in parentheses.

NORTHEASTERN: Algonkian

(Al 1) Algonkian 1 (Nanticoke, Powhatan): Brinton, D., *Myths of the New World* (New York: 1868), p. 224.

(Del 1) Delaware 1: Loskiel, G. H., *Geschichte der evangelischen Bruder unter den Indianen in Nordamerika* (Leipzig: 1789), p. 60.

WOODLAND CENTRAL: Algonkian

(Me 1) Menomini 1: Skinner, A., MAMNH, XIII, Pt. 1, 8–10.

WOODLAND: Iroquois

(Ir 1) Iroquois 1: Johnson, E., *Legends, Traditions and Laws of the Iroquois, or Six Nations* (New York: 1881), pp. 40–46.

(Ir 2) Iroquois 2: Loskiel, G. H., *History of the Missions of United Brethren Among the Indians in North America*, tr. La Trobe (London: 1794), p. 24.

(Ir 3) Iroquois 3 (Tuscarora): Cusick, David, *Sketches of Ancient History of the Six Nations* (Lockport, N. Y., 1848), pp. 14–21.

(Wy 1) Wyandot 1: Barbeau, C. M., GSCan, XI, 37–48.

(Wy 2) Wyandot 2: Schoolcraft, Henry R., *Oneota* (Philadelphia: 1875), pp. 207–210.

(Wy 3) Wyandot 3: Connelley, W. E., *Wyandot Folklore* (Topeka: 1899), pp. 67 ff.

PLAINS: Siouan

(Oto 1) Oto 1: Whitman, W., JAFL, LI, 173–177.

(Oto 2) Oto 2: Whitman, W., JAFL, LI, 177–183.

(Om 1) Omaha 1: Fletcher, A. C., and La Flesche, F., ARBAE, XXVII, 17 ff.

(Io 1) Iowa 1: Whitman, W., JAFL, LI, 201–204.

(Mo 1) Missouri 1: Whitman, W., JAFL, LI, 184–187.

(Man-Hid 1) Mandan-Hidatsa 1: Beckwith, M. W., MAFS, XXXII, 7–13.

(Hid 2) Hidatsa 2: Long, Stephen, *Expedition* (in R. Thwaites, *Early Western Travels*, XXIII), p. 316.

(Hid 3) Hidatsa 3: Wied-Neuwid, Maximilian, *Travels in the Interior of North America* (in R. Thwaites, *Early Western Travels,* XXIII), p. 316.

(Man 1) Mandan 1: Bowers, Alfred, *Mandan Social and Ceremonial Organization* (Chicago: 1950), pp. 156–162.

(Man 2) Mandan 2: Bowers, *ibid.,* 194–196.

(Man 3) Mandan 3: *ibid.,* 196–197.

(Man 4) Mandan 4: *ibid.,* p. 298 f.

(Man 5) Mandan 5: *ibid.,* p. 355.

(Man 6) Mandan 6: Catlin, G., *Letters and Notes on the Manners, Customs, and Condition of the North American Indians* (London: 1844), I, 178–179.

(Man 7) Mandan 7: Densmore, F., Bulletin LXXX, BAE, 6–7, 35.

(Man 8) Mandan 8: Dorsey, J. O., ARBAE, XI, 512.

(Man 9) Mandan 9: Lewis, M., and Clarke, W., *Expedition,* Hosmer ed. (Chicago: 1917), I, 148–149.

(Man 10) Mandan 10: Wied-Neuwid, Maximilian, *Travels,* pp. 306–316.

(Man 11) Mandan 11: Will, G. F., and Hyde, G. E., *Corn Among the Indians of the Upper Missouri* (St. Louis: 1917), pp. 218–220.

(Man 12) Mandan 12: Will, G. F., and Spinden, H. G., PPMAAE, III, No. 4, 138–141.

PLAINS: Caddoan

(Ar 1) Arikara 1: Dorsey, G. A., P-CI, No. 17, pp. 12–17.

(Ar 2) Arikara 2: Dorsey, *ibid.,* pp. 18–22.

(Ar 3) Arikara 3: *ibid.,* 23–25.

(Ar 4) Arikara 4: *ibid.,* 27–28.

(Ar 5) Arikara 5: *ibid.,* 31–32.

(Ar 6) Arikara 6: *ibid.,* 32–35.

(Ar 7) Arikara 7: Gilmore, M. R., INMAI, III, 188–193.

(Ar 8) Arikara 8: Gilmore, M. R., PMASAL, XII, 95–120.

(Ar 9) Arikara 9: Grinnell, G. B., JAFL, VI, 122–128.

(Pa 1) Pawnee 1: Grinnell, G. B., JAFL, VI, 114 ff.

(Chey 1) Cheyenne 1: Grinnell, G. B., JAFL, XX, 169–194.

(Kio 1) Kiowa 1: Mooney, J., ARBAE, XVII, 152–55.

(Wi 1) Wichita 1: Dorsey, G. A., JAFL, XV, 223.

(Wi 2) Wichita 2: Marcy, R. B., *Exploration of the Red River* (Washington: 1854), p. 69.

PLATEAU

(Th 1) Thompson 1: Teit, J. A., MAMNH, VIII, Pt. 2, 321–322.

(NP 1) Nez Percé 1: Spinden, H. G., JAFL, XXI, 13–14.

CALIFORNIA

(Tin 1) Tinlineh 1: Gatschet, A. S., *Creek Migration Legend* (Philadelphia: 1884), pp. 217–218.

(Po 1) Pomo 1: Powers, Stephen, *Tribes of California* (Washington: 1877), p. 147.

MACKENZIE–YUKON

(Tak 1) Takhali 1 (Carrier): Brinton, D., *Myths of the New World* (New York: 1868), p. 224.

SOUTHWEST

(Pi 1) Pima 1: Russell, F., ARBAE, XXVI, 206–221, 237.

(Pap 1) Papago 1: Lumholtz, C., *New Trails in Mexico* (New York: 1912), pp. 355–357.

(Pap 2) Papago 2: Mason, J. A., JAFL, XXXIV, 254–68.

(Pap 3) Papago 3: Neff, M. L., JAFL, XXV, 51–65.

SOUTHWEST: Yuma

(Moh 1) Mohave 1: Bourke, J. G., JAFL, II, 169–189.

(Moh 2) Mohave 2: Kroeber, A. L., AA, IV, 276–285.

(Moh 3) Mohave 3: Gould, M. K., JAFL, XXXIV, 319–320.

(Yum 1) Yuma 1: Harrington, J. P., JAFL, XXI, 324–348.

(Wal 1) Walapai 1: James, G. W., *The Indians of the Painted Desert Region* (Boston: 1903), pp. 188–195.

(Hav 1) Havasupai 1: James, *op. cit.*, pp. 209–213.

(Yav 1) Yavapai 1: Gifford, E. W., JAFL, XLVI, 347–351.

(Yav 2) Yavapai 2: Gifford, E. W., JAFL, XLVI, 347–351.

SOUTHWEST: Athabaskan (Navaho)

(Na 1) Navaho 1: Coolidge, M. R., and Coolidge, D., *The Navaho Indians* (Boston: 1930), pp. 121 ff.

(Na 2) Navaho 2: Curtis, E. S., *The North American Indian*, I, 83–98.

(Na 3) Navaho 3: Franciscan Fathers, *Ethnologic Dictionary of the Navaho Language* (St. Michaels, Ariz.: 1910), pp. 350 ff.

(Na 4) Navaho 4: Goddard, P., AP-AMNH, XXXIV, 1–170.

(Na 5) Navaho 5: Wheelwright, M., *Emergence Myth According to the Hanelthnayhe or Upward-Reaching Rite* (Santa Fe: 1949), pp. 100 ff.

(Na 6) Navaho 6: Wheelwright, M., *op. cit.*, pp. 3–85.

(Na 7) Navaho 7: Matthews, W., *Amer. Antiq.*, V, No. 3, 207–224.

(Na 8) Navaho 8: Matthews, W., MAFS, V, 63–159.

(Na 9) Navaho 9: Matthews, W., MAFS, V, 216–224.

(Na 10) Navaho 10: Sapir, E. and Hoijer, H., *Navaho Texts* (Iowa City: 1942), pp. 16–137.

(Na 11) Navaho 11: Schoolcraft, H. R., *Information Respecting the History, Condition and Prospects of the Indian Tribes of the United States* (Philadelphia: 1856), IV, 89–90.

(Na 12) Navaho 12: Schoolcraft, *op. cit.,* pp. 218–220.
(Na 13) Navaho 13: Stephen, A. M., AA, VI, 359–360.
(Na 14) Navaho 14: Stephen, A. M., JAFL, XLIII, 97–102.

SOUTHWEST: Pueblo

W. Keresan:
(Ac 1) Acoma 1: Stirling, BAE, Bulletin CXXXV, 1–98.
(Ac 2) Acoma 2: White, L. A., ARBAE, XLVII, 17–192.
(Lag 1) Laguna 1: Parons, E. C., AP-AMNH, XIX, 96, 114–117.
E. Keresan:
(Coch 1) Cochiti 1: Benedict, R., BAE, Bulletin XCVIII, 1–256.
(Coch 2) Cochiti 2: Dumarest, N., MAAA, VI, 137–237.
(Sn Fe 1) San Felipe 1: Bunzel, R. L., JAFL, XLI, 288–90.
(Sta A 1) Santa Ana 1: White, L. A., MAAA, LX, 1–357.
(Sia 1) Sia 1: Stevenson, M. C., ARBAE, XI, 26–58.
(Ker 1) Keresan 1: Boas, F., PAES, VIII, Pt. 1.
(N Ti 1) North Tiwa 1: Parsons, E. C., MAFS, XXXIV, 1–185.
(N Ti 2) North Tiwa 2: Parsons, E. C., AA, XLI, 222.
(Te 1) Tewa 1: Parsons, E. C., MAFS, XIX, 1–304.
(Te 2) Tewa 2: *Ibid.*
(Ho 1) Hopi 1: James, G. W., *The Indians of the Painted Desert Region*
(Boston: 1903), pp. 107–110.
(Ho 2) Hopi 2: Voth, H. R., FMNH, VIII, 1 ff.
(Zu 1) Zuñi 1: Benedict, R., CU-CA, XXI, Vol. 1.
(Zu 2) Zuñi 2: Parsons, E. C., JAFL, XXXVI, 135–162.
(Zu 3) Zuñi 3: Cushing, F., JAFL, XXXVI, 163–170.
(Zu 4) Zuñi 4: Bunzel, R. L., ARBAE, XLVII, 545–609.
(Zu 5) Zuñi 5: Cushing, F., ARBAE, XIII, 379 ff.
(Zu 6) Zuñi 6: Parsons, E. C., JAFL, XLIII, 2–4.

SOUTHWEST: Athabaskan (Apache)

(Coy 1) Coyotero 1: Gregg, J., *Commerce of the Prairies,* I (1844), 290.
(Jic 1) Jicarilla Apache 1: Curtis, E. S., *The North American Indian,* I
(Cambridge: 1907), 60–62.
(Jic 2) Jicarilla Apache 2: Goddard, P., AP-AMNH, VIII, 193–194.
(Jic 3) Jicarilla Apache 3: Mooney, J., AA, XI, 197–209.
(Jic 4) Jicarilla Apache 4: Opler, M. E., MAFS, XXXI, 1–406.
(Jic 5) Jicarilla Apache 5: Russell, F., JAFL, XI, 253–255.
(White Mt. A) White Mountain Apache 1: Goodwin, G., MAFS, XXXIII.
(Li A 1) Lipan Apache 1: Opler, M. E., MAFS, XXXVI, 13–26.
(Li A 2) Lipan Apache 2: Opler, M. E., *op. cit.,* pp. 26–37.

SOUTHEAST: Caddoan

(Ca 1) Caddo 1: Dorsey, G. A., FCM-P, XLI, No. 1.

(Ca 2) Caddo 2: Mooney, J., ARBAE, XIV, 1094–1096.

(Ca 3) Caddo 3: Parsons, E. C., MAAA, LVII, 67.

(Ca 4) Caddo 4: Schoolcraft, *op. cit.*, V, 682.

(Ca 5) Caddo 5: Swanton, J. R., BAE, Bulletin CXXXII, 25–26.

SOUTHEAST: Muskhogean

(Cr 1) Creek 1: Gatschet, A. S., *Creek Migration Legend* (Philadelphia: 1884), p. 244.

(Cr 2) Creek 2: Brinton, D. G., *National Legend at the Chakta-Muskokee Tribes* (Morrisania, N. Y., 1870).

(Avo 1) Avoyelle 1: Swanton, J. R., BAE, Bulletin XXX, Pt. 1, 118.

(Ali 1) Alibamu 1: Gatschet, *op. cit.*, p. 86.

(Choc 1) Choctaw 1: Bushnell, D. I., AA, XII, 526.

(Choc 2) Choctaw 2: *Ibid.*, p. 527.

(Choc 3) Choctaw 3: *Ibid.*, pp. 527–528.

(Choc 4) Choctaw 4: Bushnell, D. I., BAE, Bulletin XLVIII, 30.

(Choc 5) Choctaw 5: Claiborne, J. F. H., *Mississippi as a Province, Territory and State* (Jackson, Miss.: 1880), I, 519.

(Choc 6) Choctaw 6: Gatschet, *op. cit.*, pp. 105–107.

(Choc 7) Choctaw 7: Gregg, J., *Commerce of the Prairies* (in R. Thwaites, *Early Western Travels*, XX), 284.

(Chi 1) Chickasaw 1: Adair, J., *History of the American Indians,* ed. Samuel Cole Williams (Johnson City, Tenn., 1930), p. 203 fn.

(Tu 1) Tunica 1: Haas, UC-PL, VI, 19, 133–141.

(Ata 1) Atakapa 1: Swanton, J. R., BAE, Bulletin XLIII, 363.

(Yu 1) Yuchi 1: Gatschet, A. S., AA, VI, 279–282.

SOUTHEAST: Tonkawa

(Ton 1) Tonkawa 1: Schoolcraft, *op. cit.*, V, 683; Marcy, R. B., *Thirty Years of Army Life on the Border* (New York: 1866), pp. 174–178.

Notes

1. Al 1 vers.; Del, 1; Me, 1; Ir, 3; Wy, 3; Oto, 2; Om, 1; Mo, 1; Man, 11; Hid, 3; Ar, 9; Pa, 1; Chey, 1; Kio, 1; Wi, 2; Th, 1; NP, 1; Tin, 1; Po, 1; Tak, 1; Pi, 1; Pap, 3; Moh, 3; Yum, 1; Wal, 1; Hav, 1; Yav, 2; Na, 14; Ác, 2; Lag, 1; Coch, 2; Sn Fe, 1; Sta A, 1; Sia, 1; Ker, 2; N Ti, 2; Te, 2; Ho, 2; Zu, 6; Coy, 1; Jic, 5; White Mt A, 1; Li A, 2; Ca, 5; Cr, 2; Avo, 1; Ali, 1; Choc, 7; Chi, 1; Tu, 1; Ata, 1; Yu, 1; Ton, 1.

2. Middle and South American emergence myths, for example, have not been included in the present study, to say nothing of Old World forms.

3. Parsons thought that "Beliefs in Emergence and of an earth composed of several levels . . . probably throw back . . . to a very ancient source." (Elsie Clews Parsons, *Pueblo Religions* [2 vols., Chicago: 1939], I, 17 fn.)

4. Ar 1, 2, 3, 5, 6, 7, 8, 9; Man 3, 10, 12; Pa 1; Pa 2, 3; Ker, Te 1, Ho 2, Sia 1, Ac 1, Sta A 1, Sn Fe 1; Zu 2, 4, 5; Ca 1; Na 1, 5, 6, 12; Jic A 1, 3; Li A 1.

5. Ir 1, 3; Man 1; N Ti 1; Yum 1; Moh 1, 2; Choc 2; Cr 1; Tu 1; Chi 1.

6. Ar 4; Lag 1; Jic A 2, 5; Na 2, 5, 13.

7. Kio 1; Oto 1, 2; Om 2; Pi 1; Zu 6; White Mt A 1; Choc 2, 3, 4; Ali 1.

8. Wy 1, 3; Ir 2; Me 1; Hid 2, 3; Man 4, 5; Chey 1; NP 1; Th 1; Tak 1; Wi 1, 2; Tin 1; Pap 2; N Ti 1; Coch 1; Ata 5; Choc 5, 7; Ali 1; Coy 1; Ca 3, 4; Avo 1; Del 1.

9. Man 6, 7, 8, 9; Te 2; Mo 1; Ac 2; Ca 2; Na 11, 14; Cr. 2.

10. DE = Detailed Emergence.

11. DM = Detailed Migration.

12. SM = Simple Migration.

13. SE = Simple Emergence.

14. M = Migration tale.

15. Man 8, 9.

16. Senate Report on the Indian Tribes, p. 358 (Washington: 1867).

17. Sn Fe 1, Sia 1, Ker 1, Coch 1, Sta A 1.

18. Ar 1, 2, 4.

19. Man 1.

20. The Old Woman Who Never Dies is given the attributes of Corn Mother.

21. F. Densmore (BAE–B, Vol. 80, p. 35) observes: "It is interesting to note that the beneficent character of this traditional chief, or culture hero, has made him a living personality in the minds of those who, from contacts with the white man, have lost faith in the old legends." Thus a new myth out of an old one; all believe Good Chief Furred Robe to be a man and not a tradition.

22. Leo W. Simmons, *Sun Chief* (New Haven: 1942), p. 20. The Powamu ceremony is held in February, "to melt the snows, banish cold weather, and prepare the fields and gardens for planting" *(idem)*.

23. G. W. James, *Indians of the Painted Desert* (Boston: 1903), pp. 107–10.

24. White Mt A 1.

25. L. Wyman and I. Osanai, *Navajo Eschatology* (Anthro. Ser., Univ. of New Mexico Bull. IV, No. 1, 1942).

26. Ton 1.

27. Gilmore (Ar 8) says: "The story of origin has been formulated and orally transmitted from generation to generation in the recital of the rituals of their Sacred Bundles." He received one of the symbolic sheaves of sticks in the Sacred Bundle used in the religious festival and received orally the "volume of their teaching from Four-rings . . . a priest of the Hukawirat Sacred Bundle."

28. Yav 8.

29. Tin 1.

30. Yum 1.

31. Me 1.

32. Ir 1, 3.

33. Oto 1, 2; Mo 1.

34. Om 1.

35. Migration traits distributed as follows: (1) *Migration ordered*—Ar 1, 8;

Pap 3; Wal 1; Na 4; Ker; White Mt A 1; Jic 5. (2) *Leader in migration*—Ir 1, 3; Hid 2; Man 10, 12; Ar 1, 3, 4, 5, 6, 8, 9; Pa 1; Pap 2; Moh 2; Wal 1; Sia; Ker; Coch 1; Te 1 (several); Jic 2 (several); Jic 3; Ca 1; *restless pole*—Cr 1; Choc 6; Chi 1. (3) *Migration to seek navel (center of earth)*—Pi 1; N Ti 1; Sia; Zu 1, 2, 4; Jic 3. (4) *Dispersal and distribution*—Ir 1, 3; Wy 1; Oto 1; Man 3, 5; Ar 1, 2, 9; Pa 1; Pap 2; Moh 1, 2; Yum 1; Wal 1; Na 4, 7, 11, 13; Ac 1; Te 1; Ho 1; Ti 1; Sn Fe 1; Coch 1; Sta A 1; Zu 2, 4; Jic 1, 2, 3, 5; White Mt A 1; Li A 1, 2; Cr 1; Choc 4. (5) *Multiplicity of tribes (bands)*—Ir 1, 2; Wy 1; Man 7, 11, 12; Ar 8, 9; Pap 2; Moh 1, 2; Yum 1; Wal 1; Na 4, 6, 8, 9, 11, 13; Ac 1; Te 1; Ho 2; N Ti 1; Sn Fe 1; Coch 1; Li A 1, 2; Jic A 1, 2, 3, 5; White Mt A 1; Cr 1; Choc 3, 4. (6) *Multiplicity of languages*—Ir 1, 3; Man 10; Ar 1, 2, 9; Choc 3, 4; Li A 1, 2. (7) *Periodic stops on long journey*—Ir 1, 3; Man 1, 12; Ar 1; Pap 2; Na 3, 8, 9, 11, 12, 13; Sn Fe 1; Ker; Jic 3; Cr 1; Zu 4; Ali 1; Choc 6; Li A 1, 2. (7a) *White or Great House*—Pap 2, 3; Yav 2; Na 3, 6; Ac 1; Sn Fe 1; Sta A 1; Ker. (8) *Obstacles during migration*—Ir 1, 3; Oto 1, 2; all Ar versions; Pa 1; Pap 1, 2, 3; Pi 1; Na versions; Pueblo and Muskhogean.

36. Supernaturals alone emerge: All Na versions except 1, 2, 3, 11, 12; Ker 1; Wi 2 (progenitor alone); Ac 1 (2 progenitors only); Ca 3 (6 progenitors); Mo 1 (progenitor); Wal 1 (2 gods).

Supernaturals emerge together with the people: Wy 1, 2; Na 1, 2, 3, 11, 12; Jic A 2; Zu 1, 3, 4, 5, 6 (sons of Sun); Ho 1, 2; Te 1; Ac 1; Sn Fe 1; Coch 1, 2; Sia; Sta A 1; Ker 1, 2; Ar 2, 3, 5, 6; Choc 2.

Animals emerge with people: Del 1 (?); Man 2, 7, 10, 11, 12; Ar 1–9; Pa 1; all Na (dig in?); Zu 3, 4, 5; Sta A 1; Te 1, 2; Sia; Ac 1; White Mt A 1; Li A 2; Jic 1–5; Ton 1; Ca 2; Choc 2.

All living things: Sia; Ac 1; Sta A; Zu 3; Sn Fe 1; Ker; Coch 2; Zu 4, 5; Ar 7, 8; Th 1; Li A 1; Na 3(?).

37. Preparation for habitation immediately before emergence: Wy 3; Na (all versions); Sn Fe 1; Sta A 1; Sia; Ker; Zu 3; Jic 1, 2, 3, 4, 5; Li A 1, 2(?); Choc 6.

In all other versions, a ready, pre-existent earth receives the emergents; in almost all the fuller versions the creation story accounts for this order. Creation of worlds occurs in Pi 1; Pap 1; Ar 9; Pa 1; Th 1; Choc 6; Man 4, 5. Land alone is created either by the rolling away of primeval waters or the drying of earth: Na (all versions); Jic A (all versions); Te 1; Sia 1; Zu 3; Li A 1. By earth-diver: Ir 1, 3; Wy 1, 3; Man-Hid 1; Man 10 and 12.

Identity of scout: *Bird*—Man 11, Mo 3, Zu 4, Ho 2. *Man*—Wy 3; Man 3, 6, 9; Te 1; Ca 1; Chey 1; Ker 1; Sn Fe 1 (two boys); Ac 1 (sisters); Oto 1 (men). *Animal* (badger predominating—Na 3; Jic 1, 2, 3, 5)—Oto 1; Ar 4, 7; Na 2, 5, 8, 9, 14; Te 2. *Series of animal scouts*—Man 10; Sia 1; Jic 1, 2, 3; Li A 1. *Trees*—Sta A 1.

38. Hole a cave: Ir 1; Wy 1 (cavern); Man-Hid 1 (cavern); Ar 1, 3; Na 11; Li A 2 (?); Ca 2; Chi 1; Choc 1 (cavern in hill); Choc 2 (cavern); Choc 7 (cave in mountain).

Hole bored by animal: Del 1; Oto 2; Man 12; Ar 9; Pa 1; Na 1, 2, 3, 4, 6, 7, 13; Sia 1; Ton 1; Zu 4 (and reed); Ac 1 (and tree).

Hole bored by series of animals: Ar 1, 2, 3, 4, 5, 6, 7, 8; Na 9, 11, 12, 13, 14.

Badger as borer predominates: Ar 1, 2, 3, 4, 5, 8; Man 12; Na 9, 12, 13, 14.

Hole bored by plant or tree: Zu 4; Man 6; Ac 1. Hole enlarged: Man 1, 7, 10, 11, 12; Sta A 1; Sia.

Hole bored by hero: Wy 3; Pi 1; Pap 2; Zu 1, 2, 3, 5.

Earth opens and closes: Ac 1; Te 1; Coch 1; Na 13; Ca 5; Choc 5.

In all other versions the hole is pre-existing or thought to be so.

39. Means of ascent: *Vine*—Man 2, 3, 4, 5, 6, 7, 8, 9, 10, 11, 12; Moh 3 (ladder of vines); Yav 1, 2 (and tree).

Stretching reed(s)—Na 1, 2, 3, 4, 7; Te 2; N Ti 1; Sia; Jic 2; Zu 2 (plants).

Stick-like object—(1) *prayer-stick with notches:* Ker 1 and Zu 1; (2) *cane:* White Mt A 1; (3) *flute:* Na 11; (4) *bamboo:* Na 5; (5) *wand:* Na 6 (and stretching column),

Stretching tree(s)—Hid 3; Oto 2 (root); Yav 1, 2; Ac 1; Sta A 1; Zu 1 (on mountain); Zu 4.

Stretching mountain—Jic 1, 2, 3, 4, 5; Choc 3, 4 (mound).

Ladder(s)—Zu 3 (cane); Zu 4 (tree ladder); Zu 5 (grasses); Moh 3; Jic 1, 2, 4 (on mountain), 5.

40. Escape from impending flood actuates the emergence: Na (all versions); Ho 1; Yav 1 and 2 (as in Na versions, water issues out of hole into underworld; atavistic element of angered water-monster); Moh 3.

Emergence after flood subsides: Ar 1, 4, 6; Pi 1; Coch 1; Ata 1 (?). (In the following versions—Man-Hid 1; Man 1, 3, 10, 12; Moh 1; Sia 1; Ker 1; Zu 1—flood is considered an event in post-emergence history of the tribe. In all versions angered supernatural causes flood, and a hero saves portion of the people.)

41. Motivation for ascent is desire for place that is lighter, larger, or better provided with subsistence forms than underground habitation: Ir 2; Wy 2; Man-Hid 1; Man 3, 6, 9, 10, 11, 12; Ar 3, 7, 8, 9; Chey 1; Sn Fe 1; Sta A 1; Ker; Zu 1, 2, 3, 5; Jic 1, 3, 4, 5; White Mt A 1; Li A 1, 2; Ca 1; Choc 3, 4.

People are called forth by a supernatural: Ir 1, 3; Wy 1 (?), 2, 3; Ar 1, 6; Kio 1; Pi 1; Pap 1, 2, 3; Yav 2; *sun*— Zu 1, 2, 3, 4; *sun*—Jic 1, 2, 3; Ali 1.

42. Th 1; Man 4, 5; Ar 1, 2, 3, 4, 5, 6, 8, 9; Pa 1; Siouan and Woodland Iroquois versions.

43. Man 5.

44. Cf. Type No. 152 and its cognate, No. 233, in Remedios Wycoco, *The Types of North-American Indian Tales* (Doctoral dissertation, Indiana University, Bloomington: 1951), pp. 55, 64.

45. Man 7.

46. Alfred Bowers, *Mandan Social and Ceremonial Organization* (Chicago: 1950), pp. 156–62.

47. Woman Who Fell From the Sky—Woodland Iroquois—has her prototype in Komwidapokuwia of the Yuma (goddess floated in a log) and/or Changing Woman (impregnated by sun and water), who mothers the monster slayers of the Navaho. The "grandmother" trait is very convincingly explained in Moh 3 and Yav 1, 2. Traits that she combines: floating on water; magical impregnation by sun and falling water; birth of hero(es); grandmother; re-creation and peopling of earth through her progeny. Difference: primeval water replaces flood among the Woodland Iroquois.

48. Ker 1, Coch 1, Sia 1, Ker 2.

49. Coch 1 and Sia.

50. Wycoco, *op. cit.*, Type 201, p. 57.

51. (a) Ar 1, 2, 3; Na 2, 4, 5, 7, 8, 9, 11 (raccoon), 12, 14; Jic 1, 2, 3, 5.

(b) Ar 1, 2, 3, 7, 8, 9; Pa 1.

(c) Pi 1, Moh 1; Na 3, 4, 5, 7, 9.

(d) *Portion of tribe left below:* Ho 2; Ker 1; Coch 1; Sia; Jic 2, 4, 5; Tun 1.

First death seen through hole to underworld: Na 4, 6, 7, 8, 11; (return) Pa 1; Sn Fe 1; Sta A 1; Ker; Zu 2, 3.

Earth closes upon others: Ar 5, 7, 8.

Prohibition violated: Pap 3; Ca 1, 2; Avo 1; Tun 1.

Means of ascent breaks because of corpulent or pregnant woman: Man 2, 3, 6, 7, 8, 9, 10, 12; Hid 2; Kio 1.

(e) Na 2, 3, 4, 7, 10, 11; Coch 1; Sia; Ker 1; Zu 3.

(f) Al 1; Ir 1; Wy 2; Pa 1; Yav 1, 2; Na 5, 7, 8, 12, 13; Ho 1; Sia 1; Jic 2, 4; White Mt A 1; Avo 1; Chi 1; Cho 2, 3, 5, 6, 7; Cr 1, 2.

52. *Op. cit.,* pp. 156–62.

53. Distinctly Arikara; cf. Ar 1, 4, 6.

54. Na 2, 3, 6, 7.

55. Cf. Southeast versions enumerated in note 8.

Richard M. Dorson

INDIANA UNIVERSITY

BLOOMINGTON, INDIANA

Hugh Miller, Pioneer
Scottish Folklorist

On the death of Hugh Miller, by his own hand, the day before Christmas, 1856, the Scottish and English newspapers carried striking tributes to the stone mason who became a celebrated geologist, editor, and public figure.[1] These obituaries surveyed his various talents, in literature, science, journalism, and theology, but none described him as a folklorist—a term still young. The fame of Hugh Miller has gradually receded. His attempt to wed geological and Scriptural truth, while it won him the friendship of Agassiz in America, placed him on untenable scientific grounds; the Free Church movement he espoused is forgotten; and his heavily descriptive prose, contrived and prolix, though not without charm, cannot hold modern readers. Yet Hugh Miller deserves the close attention and firm respect of one audience today, for he contributed two very remarkable books to the first shelf of British folklore.

In *Scenes and Legends of the North of Scotland* (1835, new, expanded edition, 1850), published in his thirty-third year, Miller presented a wide range of traditional tales from his home town of Cromarty, an isolated peninsular seaport on the Highland border, windswept and gale-lashed from the North Sea. His autobiography, *My Schools and Schoolmasters* (1854), contains much incidental information on the varied sources of folklore to which he was exposed. These two books reveal what the whole literature of folklore rarely divulges, the place that folk tradition occupies in the life of a town, and in the life of a man.[2]

Miller never set out deliberately to record tales, in the manner of the modern field collector, but he possessed the folklore instinct, and eagerly drank in the "traditionary history" that surrounded him at every turn. To his Uncle James, a harness maker who absorbed all the antiquarian lore of castle and crag and sepulcher on his country journeys, he listened with unending delight. Visiting his cousin George in the Highlands, young Hugh sat in on evening storyfests about bitter and ancient Gaelic legends of giant Fions fighting great boars bearing poisonous bristles. Yarns of the sea had always washed over the Cromarty youth. As a boy he repeatedly heard mate Jack Grant relate the narrow escape of Hugh's father, a sea captain, in a storm that broke his ship on the Findhorn bar; a woman and child had drowned in an inside cabin, and Jack had earlier seen their wraiths walking on deck with the captain. Later, when Hugh voyaged along the Scottish coast, he spent evenings in the forecastle listening to sailors' narratives strongly tinctured with the supernatural. Coming across a band of gypsies, Miller was amazed at their power to lie, from the oldest to the youngest, who "lisped in fiction." He never forgot the old woman's marvelous lie of curing a young nobleman whose eye hung halfway down his cheek; she slit a hole at the back of his neck, seized the end of a sinew, and pulled the orb snugly into place—then tied a knot in the ligament to keep it there.[3]

The oral history which to this day folklorists have unfortunately slighted, Miller absorbed avidly. He never forgot the

older generation's recollections of stirring events now coated
with legend: of the battle of Culloden in the "Forty-Five," of
royalist horrors inflicted on the Highland rebels, of the buc-
caneer adventures of his own great-grandfather, John Feddes.

And I have felt a strange interest in these glimpses of a past so unlike
the present, when thus presented to the mind as personal reminiscences, or as well-attested traditions, removed from the original witnesses by but a single stage. All, for instance, which I have yet read of
witch-burnings has failed to impress me so strongly as the recollections of an old lady who in 1722 was carried in her nurse's arms . . . to
witness a witch-execution in the neighborhood of Dornoch—the last
which took place in Scotland. The lady well remembered the awestruck yet excited crowd, the lighting of the fire, and the miserable
appearance of the poor fatuous creature whom it was kindled to con-
sume, and who seemed to be so little aware of her situation, that she
held out her thin shrivelled hands to warm them at the blaze.[4]

Here the Cromarty stone mason described the word-of-mouth
history which in olden times and still today, on the lips of Indians or Europeans or Africans, invariably acquires folk elements. So he relates how the folk adjudged innocent a Highlander swinging on the gibbet when a white pigeon half en-
circled the corpse; and how an old woman's dog, separated from
the battlefield of Culloden by a lofty hill, howled eerily in its
direction, "looking as if he saw a spirit."[5]

Besides savoring folk history, Miller appreciated its kin, personal history, where an eloquent bard enlarged on his own
strange and wonderful experiences. In a garrulous stone mason
named Jock Mo-ghoal, he found a most masterful saga man.

As recorded in his narratives, his life was one long epic poem, filled
with strange and startling adventures, and furnished with an extraordinary machinery of the wild and supernatural; and though all
knew that Jock made imagination supply, in his histories, the place of
memory, not even Ulysses or Aeneas . . . could have attracted more
notice at the courts of Alcinous or Dido, than Jock in the barrack.

The workmen used, on the mornings after his greater narratives, to look one another full in the face, and ask, with a smile rather incipient than fully manifest, whether "Jock wasna perfectly wonderfu' last nicht?"[6]

In one of his sagas, Jock told how he spied a girl friend in Edinburgh across the street—his future wife—and in walking over to greet her was struck by a chariot. His sweetheart took him, in great pain, to an old hag who offered to defer the agony; Jock acquiesced, made his way home safely in spite of robbers, mists, and snowstorms, and four weeks later, as the hag had stated, he heard the rattle of a chariot, felt a smashing blow on his breastbone, and staggered to bed for six weeks. Perceptively Miller commented that such fabulous autobiographers can always be found in the "less artificial" states of society.

With so wide a range of oral sources at his command, and the impulse to absorb them, the Cromarty author was in a position to write an unusual volume of folklore. On the other hand, no disciplined approach to the field as yet existed to guide him, and he knew only the doubtful techniques of Sir Walter Scott, who embroidered legends to harmonize with wild and romantic settings. Though he knew Allan Cunningham and Robert Chambers, fellow Scots delving into lore, they were equally gropers, guided, too, by Scott. Nevertheless, the *Scenes and Legends of the North of Scotland* exceeds all expectation for a pioneer collection of local narratives and merits a recognition it has never received, as a superb record of folk traditions seen in their full context of village society and history. Miller knew the bleak Scottish town, not yet robbed by the great industrial cities of its cultural individuality, with an intimacy no visiting collector could ever attain.[7] Unspoiled by preconceptions of modern folklore science, he set down whatever he heard and saw in the way of traditions.

Detailed contemporary letters from the early 1830's afford us considerable insight into the purposes and circumstances governing the publication of the *Scenes and Legends*. This work was intended by Miller to launch a promising literary and intellectual

career; previously he had printed only a volume of poems at his
own expense, whose faults he soon perceived, and a pamphlet
on the herring fisheries. Young Miller had high aspirations, and
enjoyed local celebrity in Cromarty for his learning, but he
sought a larger audience. Knowing his birth town best of all
subjects, through his long-established family roots and antiquarian interests, he conceived the idea of writing a "traditional history" such as Gilbert White's *Natural History of Selborne* (London: 1789). What White had done to illuminate the atmosphere of every English town, Miller would do for Scottish parishes, through the representative model of Cromarty.[8] This larger
ambition explains the inconsistencies in the book, which records
grim folk belief and rude dialect alongside artificial literary
passages describing emotions and landscape. Miller wished to
take his place in English literature, by virtue of a book on
folklore.

He found the usual difficulties in securing a publisher. For
three years, from 1833 to 1835, his letters reveal his efforts and
frustration. In one priggish statement he declares his unwilling-
ness to publish by subscription, but in the end, after Edinburgh
publishers had rejected his manuscript with some praise and
criticism of its too lengthy moralizing, he concluded a subscription arrangement with Adam Black, future Lord Provost of
Edinburgh.[9] Miller had continued to polish his *Scenes* all the
while, writing that "If ever my Traditions get abroad they will
be all the better for having stayed so long at home."[10] The book
made its way slowly, even with favoring reviews and Miller's im-
ploring letters to literary friends and patrons.[11] Curiously, when
Miller's reputation ultimately justified a reissue, by 1850 (and
thereafter the work went through successive editions), it appeared in enlarged form, despite the criticisms of the first publishers' readers. The author added sketches he had contributed
to *Chambers Journal*, after the publication of the *Scenes*, and
others he had written before 1835 but not included in the first
printing.[12]

Neither Miller nor his public understood very precisely what
he had written. The line between oral tradition and creative fic-

tion had not yet been clearly drawn; Miller admits to merging memory and imagination, and discloses his bias in one especially revealing aside. "This part of the country contains a rich and as yet unexplored mine of tradition; but some of the stories are of too wild and fantastic a character for furnishing a suitable basis for a prose tale; and the great bulk of them, though they might prove interesting when wrought up together, are too simple and too naked of both detail and description to stand alone."[13] He is always thinking of tradition in terms of literary possibilities and goes on to say that he has imaginatively endowed legends with landscape and dialogue and movement. Some fictional efforts did come from his pen, but shortly after the publication of the *Scenes* he turned to journalistic and scientific writings.

The Cromarty mason must have been something of a character himself. "He was tall and athletic," recalls one traveler to Cromarty, "and had a large head, made to look huge by a rusty profusion of not very carefully remembered hair." The visitor described the red sandstone whiskers, the keen gray eyes, freckled face, and slouching walk, borne down as it were by his own massive intelligence and brooding ambitions.[14] Hugh Miller achieved the fame he so earnestly wished in his own lifetime, but posterity may remember him best for this literary excursion of his youth.

In regarding folklore as the raw stuff of literature, Miller drew inspiration and technique from his illustrious countryman, Sir Walter Scott, whose name runs through the *Schools and Schoolmasters* like a household god. When he moved to Edinburgh to edit *The Witness,* awestruck Hugh lingered in Castle Street for a glimpse of the great man, without success. He refers familiarly to Scott's *Letters on Demonology and Witchcraft* and quotes Scott's folklore tales and notes to illuminate Cromarty legends. The water kelpie whom Sir Walter described in *Guy Mannering* —the stream's spirit cries, "The hour's come but not the man," whereon a rider rushes up to the bank and perishes in attempting to cross—reminded Miller of a striking variant in his own Ross-shire. When the courier rode up to the stream, following the kelpie's cry, a group of Highlanders cutting corn seized him

and thrust him into a nearby chapel, to save him from his fate.
When the hour of death had passed, they unlocked the door and
found the man lying dead, his face buried in a small stone font
whose few pints of water had suffocated him when he fell down
in a fit.[15] Again Scott sharpens Miller's insight, in connection
with the grey-bearded goblin that haunted Craighouse Castle.
A herdboy told Hugh, "Oh, they're saying it's the spirit of the
man that was killed on the foundation-stone, just after it was
laid, and then built intil the wa' by the masons, that he might
keep the castle by coming back again; and *they're saying* that a'
the verra auld houses in the kintra had murderit men built intil
them in that way, and that they have a' o' them their bogle."
Miller immediately recognized the antique tradition of building
sacrifice, and quoted Scott on its modern transference to pirates,
who customarily buried a Negro or a Spaniard with their loot to
keep it guarded.[16]

Thus inspired by Sir Walter and driven by his own urge for
recognition, the humbly born writer explored every aspect of
Cromarty life for its sheaves of lore and gathered them into his
Scenes and Legends. Some sketches Miller elaborated from the
bare motifs, as he admitted, with imaginary dialogue and scenic
backdrop, but others he set down plainly, in their grim, tart, or
comic oral style. Historical and humorous tradition he treated
more scrupulously than supernatural incidents, which tended to
stimulate his fancy.

The coastal sea, and the bay of Cromarty, figure prominently
in the mass of tales. Fishermen, sailors, and smugglers crowd the
pages, for the men of Cromarty divided their time between farm
and fishery. We hear a wealth of marine belief: of whistling for
winds and soothing the waves; of the Witch of Tarbat, who
transported a ship inland, and drowned her own husband and
son in a hurricane; and of the conviction that relatives of the
drowned always persecute the wreck's survivor.[17] When the herrings suddenly deserted Cromarty, folk explanations arose to
explain the disaster; fighting men had spilled angry blood in the
sea, or a minister had cursed taunting fishermen packing their
catch on a Sunday. Tradition claimed that in one lucky season

surplus fish were used to fertilize the fields—a reason given in Cornwall for the disappearance of the hake.[18] A quarantine fleet that lay off Cromarty to isolate the cholera in the eighteenth century gave rise to rumors that mysteriously surfaced again in 1831, when another fleet dropped anchor. The fish were said to be poisoned, from eating victims thrown overboard; a grave robber found not the money he sought but the dread fever; one ingenious soul saved his townsmen by trapping the plague, formed into a yellow cloud, in a linen bag and burying the bag under a churchyard stone.[19] Fragmentary reports clustered around the mermaid, who Cromarty folk were wont to spy along the shore, braiding her long yellow tresses and defying a hardy man to best her. To one who could, she granted three wishes, and John Reid thus compelled her to guarantee him his beloved. Only under compulsion would the mermaid use her power for good, and the sight of her might presage evil; shortly after she was seen washing bloody clothes in a loch, the church roof collapsed and killed many inside.[20]

Throughout the dour chapters of Cromarty life, the kirk stands sharply athwart the town, an edifice of Calvinistic granite hewn by staunch Presbyterian Covenanters. To folklore it contributed the religious stories about Donald Roy, the Presbyterian elder, and Miller's own great-great-grandfather, stories passed down through the family line as wondrous truth. Donald became converted when, returning from the playing fields instead of the church on successive Sundays, he found his cattle dead. He developed the power of second sight and could foretell catastrophe and good fortune. Praying once in a Catholic lady's home, he caused twelve images to topple in the chapel and brought about his hostess' conversion.[21]

With clever perception, Miller bracketed the visionary Presbyterian with a Highland seer, whose uncanny prophecies still agitated the talk of later generations. The so-called heathenism of the one and the Christian faith of the other incorporated the same class of "neutral superstitions," which carry over from the false to the true religion. Unlike temperamentally as were the Highland clansman and the Covenanting elder, they shared an

ancient and universal belief in dream, vision, and miracle. So
Miller boldly introduced Kenneth Ore, the seventeenth-century
seer from Ross-shire. Kenneth first learned of his divinatory gift
when gazing at a smooth stone that warned him of a plot against
his life. Ever after he foresaw troubled events and foretold that a
raven would drink blood three days running on a hill in Suther-
landshire, that a cow would calve on top of Fairburn Tower, and
that dramshops would arise at the end of every furrow.[22] Miller
is sceptic enough to declare that only the fulfilled prophecies
are remembered.

Moving now into the murky area of popular credulity in unnatural beings, the folk historian of Cromarty speaks on evil
spirits, ghostly apparitions, and green fairies. Wherever he
scratched the surfaces of Scottish border life, wells of supernatural belief opened up. Pondering in the burying grounds of St.
Regulus and Kirk-Michael or recalling the ghost tales of an
"elderly relative" with whom he journeyed through neighboring
parishes, Miller evoked a score of spectral narratives. The very
apartment in which he wrote had seen and heard wraiths and
distress cries that presaged death.[23] The Devil appeared in divers
guises in the north of Scotland, as a black dog emitting flame
when Donald Roy thought evil, or an ugly beast who vanished
in a lightning flash, or a lively stranger who paused at the edge
of a clergyman's light. In two instances the Evil One claimed a
human soul for services rendered, and a servant who used the
Devil's name caught sight of his lost mistress chained in a cavern
and guarded by two large dogs.[24] A variety of revenants pester
the living. One returns to fulfill a death compact, another to re-
buke a farmer courting near the grave of his late wife (he died
within a fortnight), a third to redeem her sin in stealing the pack
of a murdered pedlar. The ghost of a second murdered pedlar
walks until his natural life span is up—which leads Miller to
wonder if this is not an Arminian rather than Calvinist tradition!
A protective mother returns from the grave to unlock her chest
and cover her freezing babes. Not all ghosts are purposeful,
Miller recognizes, and in one elaborate episode involving the
mysterious death of a miller, he stresses the lack of motivation in

the specter that afterward haunted the miller's companion.[25]

Where ghostly revenants are known around the world, other beings display a purely Celtic background. Green goblins and sylphs commit evil in vague traditions. The genius of smallpox takes the form of a wandering green lady; another green lady bathes a goblin child in the blood of a household's youngest inmate; yet a third implores a deaf farmer reading a Bible to tell him if there is any hope for such as she.[26] Unlike such goblins, the fairies are diminutive, three feet in height, wearing gray suits with red caps, and seem better known in popular memory. Only shortly before Miller's lifetime, specified individuals had beheld the fairies at the Burn of Eathie, and many had reported activity in the meal mill of Eathie at night, when the miller had gone home. One ne'er-do-well who attempted to stay the night at the mill was seen no more (some say he came back after seven years), but a bold young farmer accomplished the feat, and saved himself in the manner of Ulysses in the cave of Polyphemus. He told an inquisitive old fairy that his name was "Mysel' an' Mysel' " and then hit him in the face with a roasted duck. The blinded creature screamed to his companions that "Mysel' an' Mysel' " had done the injury.[27]

Some of these witch, goblin, ghost, and fairy legends clung to definite landmarks in and about Cromarty, and geographical sites offered Miller the chief thread of his desultory and rambling volume. He wanders along the shore or across the bluffs and woods and meadows, and pauses at the spot where a celebrated event allegedly occurred. This technique possessed the advantage that many Cromarty traditions were local legends, and besides the writer's taste led him to associate scenery and tales. "There is a natural connexion," he wrote, "between wild scenes and wild legends," and he missed no opportunity to support the contention. His opening pages discuss etymological legends about the Sutor Mountains, said to be named either for giant shoemakers (soutar—shoemaker) who used the promontories as work stools, or by an ardent maiden who pointed out to her reproachful lover the embracing peaks that resembled "tongueless suitors."[28] Sludach Spring gushes irregularly ever since a tacks-

man flung mud in it, even though he later atoned by wiping the
spring with a clean linen towel.[29] A high precipice known as the
Caithness-man's Leap memorializes a tremendous and fortuitous
descent by a thief in a pea field, shot by the enraged farmer.[30]
Behind the magical properties of Fiddler's Well lies a strange
account. A consumptive young man whose best friend has just
died of consumption is told by a field bee to dig at the spot where
the well now flows, and drink its water in the morning, to be
cured. Others also have benefited from the water.[31] A widely honored European tradition, the Sleeping Host, who will arise when
a visitor blows the bugle or smites the mace within his mountain
fastness, becomes attached to the Dropping Cave. There daunt-
less Willie Millar blew the bugle, but the charm failed to work,
and he found himself tumbling on the sod before the cave.[32]

Such *Natursagen* early attracted the attention of Continental
folklorists, but the historical legends which Miller gathered with
equal zest still remain virgin territory. He set down stark and
vivid memories of the "Forty-Five," the fateful year (1745) when
the Stuart Pretender (Charles Edward) and his Highland allies
marched on the throne, pillaging the border and lowland towns
on their way, until they met their Armageddon on the battlefield
of Culloden (1746). Often these remembrances dwelt on humorous incidents tied to the Highland marauders. One lone follower
of the Pretender rushed out to greet them, crying "You're welcome." "Welcome or not, give me your shoes," replied an in-
vader. Amazon Nannie Miller, when the Cromarty men had fled,
dealt summarily with two Highland warriors who sought to
"spulzie" (rob) her, but instead fled precipitately before her
wrath, after she had ducked one in the meal barrel. Anyway, it
was said that the ill-gotten gains of looters in the "Forty-Five"
would never benefit their possessors. One poor fisherman, seeing
his boat broken by the King's men in their pursuit of the Pretender, sighed out, "Gain King, gain Pretender, waes me, I'm the
loser gain wha like." Hugh's grandfather had seen one disap-
pointed Jacobite who swore he would never cut or comb his hair
until Charles Edward was crowned, and walked around like a
huge mobile cabbage, "for his hair stuck out nearly a foot on each

side of his head, and was matted into a kind of felt."[33] The
American and French Revolutions too generated traditions. A
ballad grew around the tragic killing by Donald Munro of his
two sons, who had enlisted in the English army for the purpose
of seeing their father in America. Omens and prodigies were seen
on the outbreak of war with France, armies fighting in the air
and the sky deluged with blood. The horrors of epidemic and
starvation as well as of wars lingered in folk memory.[34]

Probably the richest vein of lore that Miller tapped lay in the
local characters, whose idiosyncrasies he described with sympathetic fidelity. These are pertinacious, obdurate, and fanatic per-
sonalities, whose eccentric behavior had passed into the unwritten history of Cromarty. Chiefly they possess an unswerving
single-mindedness. Donald Miller steadfastly rebuilt the bul-
warks separating his farm from the stormy sea and finally conquered it by constructing a fourth bulwark. Threatened with the
loss of his farm if he voted against his laird's choice for minister,
and locked in his room by his goodwife to make sure he didn't,
Roderick Ross crawled out the narrow window and sped to
church to give his self-dooming vote. Sandy Wood carried his
determination beyond the grave. His garden mysteriously shrunk
each year, till he discovered his neighbor stealthily shifting the
boundary stones that separated their lands; then the rogue ac-
cused Sandy of the deed, before the townspeople. To insure
getting the ear of the Lord first on Judgment Day, Sandy had
himself buried hard by the moor of Nativity, where God was expected to interview the risen. A visiting Englishman, hearing the
tale, heaped dirt on Sandy's grave, to keep him from securing this
unfair headstart; happily, the villagers, who had come to appre-
ciate Sandy's side, shoveled off the dirt. Other portraits deal with
the genteel, impoverished painter Morrison, who once painted
two sisters without realizing one had taken the other's place;
with the fierce Dominie, such a terror to his pupils that a lady,
seeing him in church years after she had sat in his class, fainted
dead away; with the shiftless lad who failed as a ploughman and
cabinetmaker but who achieved national fame as an inventor of
nautical instruments. Some odd sticks Miller strokes in with a

single telling anecdote, like the simple curate, father of twenty, who admired the bonny lass on his knee and wished she were his daughter—which indeed she was. Little Jenny grew up to be Hugh Miller's great-great-grandmother.[35]

Still other kinds of folk matter are scattered throughout the *Scenes and Legends*. Of the local sayings that acquired a prover-bial currency, three became attached to the lone pro-American Whig in town, John Holm. "All in vain, like John Holm's plan of the fort," referred to a cat's knocking over with its tail the replica of Fort George carefully traced by John in the hearth-stone ashes. Local customs are represented in the incongruous practice of cockfighting under the supervision of the parish schoolmaster, and in Scottish versions of Halloween rites. Haunted homes and castles, prophetic dreams, and curious tra-ditions that defy neat classifying—the presence of a cock averts a meteor's fall; a web of linen made from stolen lint soars into the air and drops in a lake—these intersperse the meaty volume.[36]

One sets it down marveling at the density and breadth of oral narration within the borders of a single community. Yet the major fictional forms of storytelling, complex *Märchen*, humor-ous exaggeration, romantic novelle, are all lacking. This is a country of legend, of the believed tale, and fictions that wander into town are sharply localized. The most meaningful distinction among the multiple narratives, and one hinted at by Miller, lies in layers of belief. Tales nearest in time, like those about the "Forty-Five" or Donald Roy the elder, are most implicitly re-ceived, while the ones dating from remote, perhaps pre-Christian days, when giants and evil goblins formed part of a comprehen-sive mythology, seem shadowy and are only half credited.[37] In this conception he anticipates Gomme, who believed that folk-lore could be used to reconstruct past historical periods. But he also foreshadows Lang, who held that mankind everywhere thinks alike in the savage state that precedes civilization. Miller notes the resemblance between old Scottish and New Zealand native battle-axes and of the giant legends whereby Tonga Island-ers and the early inhabitants of Cromarty explain the appearance of mountains.

Though making little attempt to segregate his materials into rigid categories, the future geologist did speculate on their natural divisions. Lacking any terminology for labeling stories, he divided them into "three great classes," those founded on real local events, those which are pure invention, and those which blend fact and imagination.[38] Clearly he placed many tales into the first rather than the third group, because of his own credulity in both supernatural and unusual natural events. Like Andrew Lang, he possessed his own modicum of belief, and saw a spectral arm the night his father drowned.[39] Again, he accepted as true many extraordinary occurrences simply because they departed from precedent.

Invention generally loves a beaten track—it has its rules and its formulas, beyond which it rarely ventures to expatiate; but the course of real events is narrowed by no such contracting barrier; the range of possibility is by far too extensive to be fully occupied by the anticipative powers of imagination; and hence it is that true stories are often stranger than fictions, and that their very strangeness, and their dissimilarity from all the models of literary plot and fable, guarantee in some measure their character as authentic.[40]

The recurrence of folktales around the world has borne out Miller's shrewd insight that plots and motifs are easier to borrow than to create. But with greater access to collections of legends, he might have recognized a "beaten track" in some Cromarty happenings. The very episode that prompted the above induction, a fugitive's mighty leap over a cliff, finds its close counterpart across the Atlantic (see n. 30). Still, the stone mason realized the peregrinations behind certain traditions and observed that the same rumors attached to a quarantine fleet stationed in the bay in the seventeenth century had become attached to another such fleet nearly a hundred years later.

His mind plays briefly with classes of tellers as well as tales, and he recognized "that the different sorts of stories were not lodged indiscriminately in every sort of mind"—the people who cherished the narratives of one particular class frequently rejecting those of another. But he ends up lamely, saying that women, being more poetical, are attracted to the more imaginative legends. One factor in impressing him with the truth of stories lay in the minute detail provided by rural narrators, whom he likens to the Dutch painters.[41] These hints at inspection of oral style he unfortunately fails to pursue.

For the most part Miller recorded and presented his folklore unanalytically, aware that he was dealing with "traditionary history," but never consciously attempting to found or further a new study. Perhaps this lack of technical training gives his work its greatest value, for he never separated lore from life, as does the modern collector, but set his narratives amidst the bleak and unrelieved rigors of Scottish border existence.

Notes

1. See the "Memorials of the Death and Character of Hugh Miller," in Hugh Miller, *The Testimony of the Rocks* (Boston: 1857), pp. 7–30.

2. *The Jonny-Cake Letters* of Shepherd Tom Hazard (Providence: 1880) is another rare example of local traditions seen through the eyes of a country resident [see my article, "The Jonny-Cake Papers," *Journal of American Folklore*, LVIII (1945), 207–15].

3. *My Schools and Schoolmasters* (Edinburgh: 1907), pp. 34–35, 104–5, 357–58, 386–87.

4. *Ibid.,* p. 125.

5. *Ibid.,* 125–26, 128; for reminiscences of Culloden see also Miller's *Essays, Historical and Biographical, Political, Social, Literary, and Scientific,* ed. Peter Bayne (Boston: 1865), "The Centenary of the 'Forty-Five,'" pp. 101–2.

6. *My Schools,* pp. 208–9.

7. According to W. M. Mackenzie, *Hugh Miller, A Critical Study* (London: 1905), p. 2, Cromarty at this time numbered about 1,500 population.

8. See his letter to Sir Thomas Dick Lauder (to whom he inscribed the *Scenes*) of March, 1833, in Peter Bayne, *The Life and Letters of Hugh Miller,* 2 vols. (Boston: 1871), II, 43–45.

9. *Life and Letters,* I, 300–2; II, 50.

10. *Ibid.,* I, 374.

11. See his letters to Allan Cunningham and Sir George Mackenzie, *Life and Letters,* II, 45-49. The reception of the book is described in *My Schools,* pp. 512–13.

12. Lydia Miller (Mrs. Hugh Miller), in the Preface to her husband's *Tales and Sketches* (6th ed.; Edinburgh: 1872), p. xiii, and Miller's note to the second edition of *Scenes and Legends.*

13. *Life and Letters,* I, 420.

14. J. R. Robertson, in *Life and Letters*, I, 383.

15. *My Schools*, pp. 202–3. See Motif M341.2.3, "Prophecy: death by drowning." Accounts of the water kelpie are given in John G. Dalyell, *The Darker Superstitions of Scotland* (Glasgow: 1835), pp. 543–44; Walter Gregor, *Notes on the Folk-Lore of the North-east of Scotland* (London: 1881), pp. 66–67; John G. Campbell, *Superstitions of the Highlands and Islands of Scotland* (Glasgow: 1900), p. 215; Alasdair A. MacGregor, *The Peat-Fire Flame: Folk-Tales and Traditions of the Highlands and Islands* (Edinburgh and London: 1947), pp. 68–71, 116–19.

16. *My Schools*, pp. 222, 233. See Motifs S261, "Foundation sacrifice," and N571, "Devil (demon) as guardian of treasure."

17. *Scenes and Legends of the North of Scotland; or, The Traditional History of Cromarty* (8th ed.; Edinburgh: 1869), pp. 58–59, 282–89, 62. For sea lore, see Motifs G283, "Witches have control over weather," D2142.0.1, "Magician (witch) controls winds," and D2151.3, "Magic control of waves"; Eve B. Simpson, *Folk Lore in Lowland Scotland* (London: 1908), "Fishermen's Superstitions," pp. 118–44. G. L. Kittredge, *Witchcraft in Old and New England* (Cambridge, Mass.: 1928), chap. 8, "Wind and Weather," pp. 159–60, gives examples of witches who traffic in winds; R. M. Dorson, *Jonathan Draws the Long Bow* (Cambridge, Mass.: 1946), pp. 245–47, abstracts Maine sea superstitions from the writings of George S. Wasson.

18. *Scenes and Legends*, pp. 256–57. Simpson gives folk reasons for the desertion of the herrings, pp. 141–42. For the disappearance of hake from the Cornish fishing towns, see Robert Hunt, *Popular Romances of the West of England* (London, 2nd series: 1865), pp. 152–53; R. M. Dorson, *Bloodstoppers and Bearwalkers* (Cambridge, Mass.: 1952), pp. 110–11.

19. *Scenes and Legends*, p. 244. An Englishman frightened an Indian in colonial New England by declaring that a hole in the ground, used for storing powder, contained the plague; an Indian chief later asked the Englishman to release it against his enemies (*America Begins*, ed. R. M. Dorson [New York: 1950], p. 302, quoting Thomas Morton's *New English Canaan*, 1632).

20. *Scenes and Legends*, chap. 20, pp. 290–304. Motif B81 is "Mermaid." Legends of Cornish mermaids are given by Robert Hunt, *Popular Romances of the West of England* (London, 1st series: 1865), Nos. 56–62. In "The Old Man of Cury" (pp. 159–63), a captive mermaid gives her captor three wishes in payment for her release. See also Campbell, "The Mermaid," in *Superstitions*, pp. 201–2; MacGregor, "Mermaid Traditions," in *The Peat-Fire Flame*, pp. 105–6.

21. *Scenes and Legends*, pp. 145–50. Accomplishments of Protestant ministers in popular fancy often closely parallel Catholic saints' legends; see C. Grant Loomis, *White Magic* (Cambridge, Mass.: 1948), chap. 5, "Divine Foresight and Knowledge," and chap. 6, "Power Over Matter."

22. *Scenes and Legends*, pp. 163–65. Kenneth Ore is presented at full length in Alexander Mackenzie, *The Prophecies of the Brahan Seer*, with introductory chapter by Andrew Lang (Stirling, Scotland: 1924). Lang points out that the Brahan seer, unlike his fellow Highlanders, used a divining stone. Mackenzie quotes Hugh Miller on Ore, pp. 7–8. I also have a copy of a tenth edition, dated 1942.

23. *Scenes and Legends*, p. 358. Scottish death omens and wraiths are discussed by James Napier, *Folk Lore: or, Superstitious Beliefs in the West of Scotland within this Century* (Paisley: 1879), pp. 56–59; also by Gregor, 203–5; and see the section,

"Apparitions, Wraiths, the Second Sight," in *Scottish Fairy and Folk Tales,* ed. Sir George Douglas (London: n.d.), pp. 193–215.

24. *Scenes and Legends,* pp. 146, 166, 168, 169–176. See Motifs G303.3, "Forms in which the devil appears," and G303.9.5, "The devil as an abductor." Dalyell, *(Darker Superstitions),* has material on evoking Satan, Satan's forms, and Satanic pacts, pp. 528, 547, 553–55, 577–80; Gregor *(Notes),* speaks of "Devil compacts," pp. 74–75, and Campbell *(Superstitions),* of "The Devil," pp. 292–312.

25. *Scenes and Legends,* pp. 359–70, 376. See such motifs as E411, "Dead cannot rest because of sin"; E413, "Murdered person cannot rest in grave"; E415, "Dead cannot rest until work is finished"; E323.2, "Dead mother returns to aid persecuted children." Scottish ghostlore can be found in Gregor, chap. 13, "Ghosts," pp. 68–70; MacGregor, "Ghost Tales and Haunted Places," pp. 282–311. Louis C. Jones stresses the neutrality of many modern ghosts in "The Ghosts of New York: an Analytical Study," *Journal of American Folklore,* LVII (1944), 246.

26. *Scenes and Legends,* pp. 70–73. The classification of these evil demons is not easily made, the more so since green is the characteristic fairy color (Campbell, p. 155), and since the diminutive fairies and Satanic metamorphoses are often popularly confused (Dalyell, p. 534). Motif V361 is suggested here: "Christian child killed to furnish blood for Jewish rite."

27. *Scenes and Legends,* pp. 466–70. This is Motif K602, "Noman." W. A. Clouston gives variants from Northumberland and Finland in *The Book of Noodles* (London: 1888), 194n. Campbell gives abundant material on "The Fairies" and "Tales Illustrative of Fairy Superstition," in the first two chapters of *Superstitions of the Highlands and Islands of Scotland,* pp. 1–155; see also MacGregor's first chapter (in *The Peat-Fire Flame*), "Faeries: Their Propensities and Activities," pp. 1–28; Simpson *(Folk Lore in Lowland Scotland),* "Fairies," pp. 82–117; Douglas *(Scottish Fairy and Folk Tales),* "Fairy Tales," pp. 103–39.

28. *Scenes and Legends,* pp. 13–15. Place-name legends are, of course, common in folklore; the juxtaposition here between an old myth and a modern pun has special interest. Some New England examples are given in R. M. Dorson, *Jonathan Draws the Long Bow* (Cambridge, Mass.: 1946), pp. 188–98.

29. *Scenes and Legends,* pp. 5–7. See Motifs H1193, "Causing dry spring to flow again task," and H1292.1, "Why has spring gone dry." MacGregor tells of an abused well that moved its locale, p. 145.

30. *Scenes and Legends,* pp. 264–66. Peabody's Leap, on the Vermont side of Lake Champlain, similarly commemorates a tremendous jump, by pioneer Timothy Peabody in escaping from Indians (Charles M. Skinner, *American Myths and Legends* [Phila. and London: 1903], I, 52–54).

31. *Scenes and Legends,* pp. 339–41. Well legends of Celtic Scotland, often involving curative properties, appear in MacGregor, chap. 12, "Well Lore," p. 144–56.

32. *Scenes and Legends,* pp. 332–36. This is Motif E502, "The Sleeping Army." E. S. Hartland has a full discussion of this migratory legend in *The Science of Fairy Tales* (London: 1891), pp. 207 ff.

33. *Scenes and Legends,* pp. 320–25. MacGregor testifies that this cycle of traditions survives to the present; see his chap. 23, "Folk-Tales of the '15 and the '45," pp. 312–28.

34. *Scenes and Legends,* pp. 475–76, 485, 246–49, 308–17. The ballad story suggests Motif N731.2, "Father-son combat" (Sohrab and Rustum). Seventeenth-cen-

tury omens of war are reprinted in *America Begins*, ed. R. M. Dorson, pp. 399–400, 150, 151.

35. *Scenes and Legends,* pp. 30–36, 349–54, 215–20, 415–16, 424–31, 144. Local characters have not as yet been studied or much collected by folklorists. Many New England town histories contain accounts of such characters.

36. *Scenes and Legends,* pp. 476–77, 420–23, 63–66, 73–74, 61. In *My Schools and Schoolmasters* Miller gives a delicious example of proverbial coinage, relegated to a footnote (p. 298). Some lads gave an eagle, shot by Hugh's Uncle James, to a half-witted old woman called "Dribble Drone," saying it was a great goose. She cooked and ate it, and was heard to remark, "Unco sweet, but oh! teuch, teuch!" The saying was later applied to any tough fish or meat.

37. References to the different time layers behind folklore can be found in *Scenes and Legends,* pp. 58, 70, 161; to the uniformity of human invention, pp. 15–16. Mackenzie *(Hugh Miller)* has a perceptive chapter on "History and Folklore," where he points out Lang's polygenetic theory as stated by Miller (pp. 69–70).

38. *Scenes and Legends,* pp. 3–4. Miller stoutly affirms the inimitability of the common people's style in telling true narratives, as distinct from fictitious ones.

39. *My Schools,* p. 24. See also the omen of the sandstone slab, pp. 236–37, which Hugh dropped over a wall for an augury in a mood of depression. Instead of smashing, it lit on its edge in soft greensward, whereupon Hugh believed he was meant to recover.

40. *Scenes and Legends,* p. 40.

41. *Scenes and Legends,* pp. 7, 4.

William Hugh Jansen

UNIVERSITY OF KENTUCKY

LEXINGTON, KENTUCKY

Classifying Performance in the Study of Verbal Folklore[1]

During the past quarter century, there has been a growing concern among folklorists about a rather imponderable quantity called performance—particularly performance of the folktale and folksong. Although the desirability of biographical notes about informants (in some instances, read *performers* for *informants*) has been stressed, it is still an unusual collector who gives even the sketchiest data about the human sources whence came the songs or tales he presents. The folklorist reviewing a published collection of folklore most commonly regrets the inadequacy or the total absence of notes about the informants. Even more urgent than the need for such biographical information is the need for notes about the conditions of the actual performance, notes that reveal the informant's attitudes toward his particular material and its relation to him and to his audience, notes that reveal the audience's attitudes toward the performer and toward his handling of the particular material. Elsewhere it has been already pointed out that performance notes—rather than performer notes—and performance notes alone will enable the scholar to utilize a folklore collection as a fully reliable commentary upon aspects of the particular folk group whence the collection was taken.

Here I intend to outline a rather tentative proposal for measuring or classifying the performance of verbal folklore and to advance a few suggestions, even more tentative, for various applications of such a classification. The proposal can be only tentative until it has been mulled over by collectors with varied field experience and by specialists in the many genera of verbal folklore.

Social anthropologists, as many folklorists should know, can classify the elements in the culture of a given society according to the fraction of that society which participates in those elements.[2] This classification ranges from the 100 per cent of complete participation in *Universals* down through *Specialties* and *Alternatives* to the zero of nonparticipation in *Individual Peculiarities*. These last elements are, of course, since they are completely unshared, not strictly parts of culture although they may have once been, or may at some future time become, integrated into a culture. Strikingly for the folklorist, Dr. Ralph Linton in passing points out a relationship between this classification and the understanding of cultural transmission and gives, among others, the example of learning to play marbles. A child is not likely to acquire the skill from an adult, even if that adult remembers the game clearly. Equally significant for the folklorist is Dr. Linton's insistence that what is a Universal in one society may fall into any one of the other categories in a different society.

Despite some palpable parallels, what I am proposing is not, I feel, the same as this anthropological classification, which—in so far as it applies to folklore—basically concerns the content of folklore. Certainly the folklorist is, and must be, primarily concerned with the content, the material of folklore. It is his first and most important consideration. Naturally, therefore, classification systems have been—and, we hope, are being—developed. Aarne, Thompson, Taylor, Child, Grundtvig are among the synonyms for catalogs and classifications of the materials of verbal folklore. New names will be added to the list as other types of folklore are classified, and some old names will be magnified or obscured by the new classifications. But in addition to activity in studying the content of folklore, and perhaps as both a supplement and a complement to the knowledge gained from that studying, there should be more consideration of the manner of folklore, of that dual but inseparable process of performance and reception.

Fully conscious of the qualitative connotations in percentages, I presented the classification of the anthropologists as ranging from the 100 per cent of universal participation to the 0 per cent of nonparticipation. Still bearing in mind the qualitative connotations in percentages, one must now invert the scale to connote the desired qualitative values in the classification to be proposed here: i.e., from the 100 per cent of unique individual performance (or complete nonparticipation) to the 0 per cent of fully general performance (or universal participation). The latter quality should probably not be labeled performance at all, in the sense intended here.

Here arise two questions which must be answered before any discussion of the proposed distinctions can begin: What is meant by performance? And, what are the degrees of performance? To begin with, and as an answer in part to both questions, when one speaks of oral verbal folklore, one must employ the term *performance* in something like its theatrical or dramatic definition. The very existence of a piece of verbal folklore, however insignificant, implies an auditor, frequently a group of auditors, and, of course, some person or occasionally persons to "do" that piece of folklore for that audience. This truism applies to language itself, for, in its existence also, a speaker and a hearer are implicit. But in folklore, the element that I can find no term for except *performance* does not exist until the "doer," the speaker, or the reciter of the bit of folklore steps outside himself as an individual and assumes a pose toward his audience, however small, that differs from his everyday, every-hour-in-the-day relationship to that same audience. Integral in this posing is a purpose. The poser is *as poser* a teacher, a monitor, or an entertainer; he may be any one or any combination of the three. In order that a verbal folk item may be (in the sense I intend) *performed,* there must be some amount of this posing on the part of the individual who makes that item oral, and I think this posing will have as its purpose—implicit or explicit or conventional—one of three aims or something very akin to them: didacticism, admonition, or entertainment. (All of these alternates are necessitated by the disparate nature of verbal folklore, including as it does ballads, proverbs, *märchen,* riddles, legends, and so on.)

Let us regard quickly a few illustrations, always remembering that both the practice and function of folklore differ from group to group. I have tried to select mundane examples that most Americans are likely to have encountered.

1. A family group, arising early, finds that a rain that started during the night is still going on. Anyone in the group, from the oldest to the youngest, that has begun to absorb the group's traditions may recite, and with complete approval from the other members of the group, "Rain before seven, clear before eleven." The purpose is obviously a kind of didacticism mixed perhaps with creating assurance and conserving knowledge. Still the degree of performance is small and insignificant—the demands upon the sayer's artistic capacities are few.

2. A whistling bobby-soxer enters her family's presence and is greeted with:

> A whistling woman and a cackling hen,
> Neither comes to any good end.

We know without being told that in all probability the reciter is an older member of the group. If the reciter is too young, we have a sense that the situation is wrong—the verse is not serving its function of admonition. It has become ridiculous, funny, or cute. Occasionally, if the reciter is of the offender's immediate generation, the verse may serve the perverted and unusual ironic purpose of mockery. But its normal purpose is, of course, didactic, and, while it is small, the amount of posing required is not insignificant.

3. Tradition, semi-literary, makes much of the pompous portly gentleman dangling his pocket watch before the eyes of an infant. But there is a very real folk tradition that in some societal groups impels the adult male to greet every newly met child with this or some similar formula:

> Round as a turnip, busy as a bee,
> Prettiest thing that you ever did see.

In communities such as those of modern rural America, the purpose of such a formula is primarily, though perhaps not exclusively, entertainment. The suggestions of pose are obvious.

4. A curious visitor, let us say an inquisitive folklorist, is entertained by a rural householder who launches out with, "Well, once there was a fellow who lived right here in Beeville that used to say he'd been out hunting" and continues with a summary of the miraculous hunt story (Aarne-Thompson Mt. 1890 ff.). Here the purpose is likely to be, in varying fractions, didacticism and entertainment, and the amount of performance skill involved may, or may not, be very high.

5. Then there is the mill hand sitting in a barber shop with some fellows from his shift. He starts, "You know four years ago when we had that lay-off? I got tired of loafing around; so I went up to see my uncle that lives in the Catskills," and he's off into a first-person narration of the same miraculous hunt story with himself as the hero. Clearly the purpose here is entertainment, and the performance quotient is high, or should be.

Although many other illustrations offer themselves, these must suffice. They have been, of course, selected and arranged to prove a point or several points. In each of the five items, the very form or content suggests, in varying degree, performance. Each of the situations described, along with the function of the particular material in that situation, suggests varying demands for skill in performance, even for the presence or absence of such skill. Finally, various kinds of performers induce various expectations about the nature of the performances. These then are three ways to weigh the degree of performance or the anticipation of performance: the implications in the form and/or the content of an item; the function of the item in a particular situation; and the actual as opposed to the ideal performer for the item.

The first three bits of folklore used in the examples all happen to incorporate in their form both rhyme and rhythm. The presence of either implies, naturally, some degree of performance; yet both, obviously, may be absent and a high degree of performance still be involved, as in the miraculous hunt tale cited. The weather rhyme is so common in content that it sets up almost no expectation of performance qualities, despite its rhythmic rhyming. The content of the admonition anent whistling, however, and of the riddle, too, suggests more than a minimum of performance and, in addition, sets limits upon the ranks from which the performers may come. I wish there were time to amplify upon the suggestions about performance and performers inherent in both the first-person versions of folktales and the "conventional" first-person tags in the so-called impersonal folksongs: e.g., "Never have I seen" or "heard," "I will sing you," "Come all ye," and so on. In short, in the content or form of verbal-folklore items many indications may be made about the degree of performance skill and about the kind of performer demanded for those items. The demand, of course, may not be met. At the same time, even when little or no demand is present in either form or content, an item may still receive very skillful performance. Thus a valid folk belief may be recited in a most offhand way without any reflection upon its validity or upon its performer, but it may also be stated in an atypically impressive way by a skillful performer motivated by aesthetic reasons or purposes that are related to my next point.

The function served by a particular bit of folklore in one situation may differ distinctly from the function of that same bit in another situation. Thus, conceivably, a riddle recited in a social situation by an adult desiring to establish friendship with a child calls for a greater degree of performance than does the same riddle later recited in private by the same child to another child.

And a catch intended to embarrass one hearer for the amusement of other hearers—particularly if these latter already know the catch—probably exacts a much higher degree of performance than the riddle does in either situation. I dare say that in most modern, post-literate societal situations it is the function of entertainment that most frequently implies a high degree of performance. This supposition, however, does not always hold, for there are many simple anecdotes, having the obvious function of entertainment, that may be, and are, told by anyone. In a group which is bent upon anecdote narration, there is likely to be chaos if everyone wants to tell the story he has been "reminded of"; but if the group includes one or more who are recognized as superior storytellers, the tendency is certainly to let them tell the anecdotes.

Thus, the third and last quantity that affects the degree of performance and its anticipation is the performer himself. Wherever there is an individual who is considered a performer, whether by others or by himself, there is a source of folklore items with a high degree of performance—whether the content, form, situation, or function of the items leads to an anticipation of performance or not. Perhaps it is a matter of *noblesse oblige*. Such an individual may be recognized as an adult who tells stories well to children, as the best performer in an immediate or an extended family, as the person whom a whole community regards as its singer or teller, or finally and very rarely as the performer whose reputation extends beyond his community or generation. One of the most exacting implied demands for performance rests in the belief that a particular item of folklore "belongs to" a particular, recognized storyteller, and the greatest possibility for fulfilling that demand lies with another recognized performer who does such an item in the manner of its "owner," who may be far away in time or space.

It should be possible to determine from these three yardsticks at least whether a high or a low degree of performance is to be expected of a specific folkloristic item at the moment of its recording. If it is the high degree, then one must determine whether that expectation has been fulfilled. Discovering the degree of success in such performances would be the subject of a different paper, but we can suggest here that the measures would include the folk's judgment, the performer's attitudes, the presence of virtuosity or originality in manner and treatment (not in content), and the collector's or student's own common sense.

To return to imaginary percentages for a moment, one may suppose that a 100-per-cent expectation of performance, or anything near it, would mean, for example, that a group would absolutely restrict the telling of a particular tale to one of its members. Such cases must be rare, practically nonexistent. The zero percentage, in which a group thinks of a particular item as being available for retelling by any of its members, must be quite common with some sorts of folk materials. Naturally exact percentages in such nebulous matters are ridiculous and should never be established, but trends, groupings, comparables, differences should become clear upon a little study. Certainly in much verbal folklore, a sharp division becomes quickly evident between that in which a high expectation of performance qualification is implied and that in which no such implication exists.

If we accept the proposal that the relative expectation of *performance* (another term for this quantity is badly needed) can and should be determined for a given item of folklore, then what? A number of influences of varying significance upon the study of folklore are possible. First of all, this proposal would naturally complicate the collector's life, since he would have more responsibilities to the scholar and more things to look for. Certainly, however, it would give the scholar new means of evaluating collections already made and collections to be made: a standard of validity, as it were. Where the expectation of performance is low, any accurately recorded version of an item is as "good" as any other. Bare content rather than style or form is what is important to the folk and the scholar. But where the expectation is high, no matter how accurately recorded, only those versions of an item that fulfill the expectation can be termed "good." For one item in such an instance, there may be poor, good, and excellent versions. Here, to the folk, style and form obviously mean more than content, although for the scholar all three probably must be given equal weight. Recognizing the proposed division should help the student, too, to distinguish between versions simply reported by unqualified informants and those performed in more suitable manner. It should make him very wary of such ridiculous categories as "mere jokes," a term which might describe the form but never the content or the potential function of any story. It might help him, also, to arrive at a division of folksong more meaningful than "ballads, lyrics, and miscellaneous."

In describing his collection activities, a friend asserts that he can sometimes recognize a *cantefable* before the first recitative passage occurs. I am sure that this is so and that it shows a relationship felt in the auditor between actual performance and the ideal norms of performance. That is, if the listener has a pattern of performance associated with a certain type of folklore, signs of the pattern will lead him to expect the type of folklore or the type of performance, either one. (Remember that *cantefable* really describes a manner of performing and the form itself of the item rather than the content of the thing performed.) Thus, observing this difference may provide the student with a more sturdy ladder to the study of the aesthetics of folk-narrative performance, the relation of audience and performer, and, perhaps more revolutionary, a reappraisal of originality and conformity in folklore. It would certainly lead to different emphases upon the function and situation of a given item and their influence upon the performance of that item. And it should lead to closer descriptions of the folk performer and a recognition of the fact that what he does may be, at various times and for various reasons, an art, a craft, a common skill, or a universal and general capability.

Notes

1. With gratitude I acknowledge that specific ideas herein are the result of discussions with my colleague at the University of Kentucky, Professor Irwin T. Sanders, and with Professors Herbert Halpert and Leonard W. Roberts of Murray State Teachers College (Murray, Ky.) and Union College (Barbourville, Ky.), respectively.

2. See chap. XVI in Ralph Linton, *The Study of Man* (New York: 1936). The use of percentages is my own device.

Warren E. Roberts

INDIANA UNIVERSITY

BLOOMINGTON, INDIANA

Folklore in the Novels of

Thomas Deloney

This paper is an attempt to demonstrate that much can be learned about the folklore of a past era by a close study of the works of an author of that era, especially if that author be one who wrote for a popular audience and one who was in close contact with the common people. Such an author is Thomas Deloney, "the Balletting Silke Weaver of Norwich,"[1] who wrote three novels between 1596 and 1600. Although not too much is known of his life history, there is no doubt that Deloney was acquainted with the common people as few other English authors have been. This acquaintance is shown by a number of facts. He composed innumerable broadside ballads for the delight and inspiration of the Elizabethan common man. Not only were his prose works frankly directed at an audience of commoners, but also they deal to a large extent with characters of this class. The praise of homely virtues and the glorification of shoemakers and clothiers are the predominant themes in *Jack of Newberie, The Gentle Craft,* and *Thomas of Reading.* Moreover, Deloney shows a knowledge of everyday tasks and a close acquaintance with the open country, the small towns, and the main cities in England. It is, therefore, not surprising that Deloney knew a great deal of folklore and that he used a large amount of it in his novels.

In discussing the folklore that appears in Deloney's novels, I will proceed by taking up in its turn each of the categories that he used. Before commencing this discussion, however, I would like to point out that in some cases I can only suggest that Deloney was drawing upon traditional lore, for it is not always possible to cite an exact folklore analogue for his material. It is sometimes necessary to show that Deloney's material is similar to known items of folklore and then suggest that folklore may have been his source. In this way it may be possible to point out some items of Elizabethan folklore that otherwise would remain unrecognized and unknown.

LEGEND AND FOLKTALE

In general, it may be said that Deloney frequently used legendary material in his novels, for much of the narrative that he gives about such historical figures as Simon Eyre, Richard Casteler, and Sir John Rainsford probably came from oral sources. It is true that Deloney could have found out something about Simon Eyre and others from chronicles, but from these written sources Deloney could have gotten only the barest bones of his story. The innumerable incidents that he relates were either composed from whole cloth by Deloney or were gathered from oral sources. Since Eyre, for instance, had been a famous and well-loved figure, and since he had been dead less than a century and a half, it is possible that stories about him were still current in Deloney's time. A few samples of this kind of legendary material, however, will suffce. From Stowe's *Survey,* Deloney could have found that Sir Simon Eyre was a draper, the mayor of London, and a public benefactor.[2] Yet Deloney recounts a lengthy biography of Eyre, telling how he started his career as a shoemaker, how he introduced to England the low-cut shoe, how he became wealthy by a lucky accident, and how he established the custom of the apprentices' feast on Shrove Tuesday and the custom of the Pancake Bell.[3] Although it is possible that Deloney invented these incidents, they sound very much as if they were legendary accounts that he encountered in oral circulation. They may well have been, therefore, part of the immense stock of the folklore of Elizabethan England.

Another type of legend that Deloney used is the folk etymology. An especially good example occurs in *Thomas of Reading* when Deloney tells of a cripple who stole a silver weathercock from the top of St. Paul's Church and who later built a gate on the north side of the city which to this day is called "Cripple-Gate."[4] F. O. Mann, Deloney's most recent editor, feels that Deloney has invented this story to explain the name.[5] It seems more likely, however, that Deloney is repeating a folk etymology, for stories like the one he gives are often found connected with an unusual name. Other examples of what may well be folk etymologies explain the origin of the term "Tom Drum's entertainment," the naming of Colebrook, the River Cole, Exeter, and Gloucester, and the practice of referring to cobblers' tools as "Saint Hugh's bones."[6]

Deloney seems not to have used any complete *Märchen* in his novels. From time to time, however, he makes references which seem to indicate an acquaintance with certain *Märchen,* and he uses certain motifs which are found in *Märchen.* The most interesting reference occurs in *Thomas of Reading,* where Deloney speaks briefly of a servant named Crab who makes a rhymed prophecy. Deloney introduces the prediction in this way: "With that Crab, according to his old manner of prophesying, said thus: . . ."[7] Crab, as far as I have been able to discover, is not a common Elizabethan Christian name. It may be, therefore, that Deloney had in mind "Doctor Know-All" (Type 1641), whose

hero, a sham soothsayer, is often named Crab. This tale seems
never to have been recorded in England. It is, however, known
in Ireland,[8] and it has often been recorded in America from
Negro storytellers.[9] It would seem possible, therefore, that the
story was known in Elizabethan England but that it has since
died out in England.

In the seventh chapter of *Jack of Newberie* an honest weaver,
fearing that his wife had made him a cuckold, threatens her, saying, "I will send thee to salute thy friends without a Nose."[10]
Mutilation of this sort is certainly not a common Elizabethan
punishment for adultery. This punishment is, however, part of
a folktale, "The Cut-Off Nose" (Type 1417), which is known in
some parts of Europe. In England the story is found in an Elizabethan jestbook,[11] and in the third act of Massinger's play of 1633,
The Guardian. Deloney may also have known the story and may
have referred to it.

Motifs from *Märchen* are also used by Deloney. In *The Gentle
Craft,* a king whose daughter has been spirited away announces
that the man who finds her "should be honoured with the marriage of his fair daughter."[12] I need not elaborate on the prevalence of this motif, T 68.1, in *Märchen.* When Sir John Rainsford finds the body of a pauper refused burial because the widow
is penniless,[13] we meet another motif (E 341.1) from the "Grateful Dead" cycle of stories (Types 506, 507, 508). Motifs L 111.2.1.,
"Future king found floating in water," and H 171.3., "Horse indicates election of king," also appear in *Jack of Newberie.*[14]

Deloney may have used elements from yet another kind of
folktale, the *Schwank,* or humorous anecdote, or jest. In a comic
subplot in *Jack of Newberie* an Italian merchant is led to believe
that he is to pass the night with a virtuous English servant girl
whom he has been trying to seduce. When he climbs into bed in
her darkened room, however, he discovers that a sow has been
substituted for the young lady.[15] In "The Foolish Bridegroom,"
Type 1685, a bride, angered by the foolish actions of her bridegroom, puts a goat into the bridal bed and returns to her parents.[16] A well-known jest, "Old Hildebrand" (Type 1360C), tells
a story very much like one which Deloney has included in

Thomas of Reading. In both stories, the husband, suspecting an intrigue, pretends to leave his house and then, from his hiding place, is able to overhear his wife and her lover singing a song about their amorous intentions. In both stories, of course, the lover is discomfited.[17] It is possible that Deloney knew the folktale in some form and consciously modeled his narrative after it. The story has been collected in England and in America from English sources.[18] Moreover, there is an English chapbook version of this tale extant from the year 1655, but certainly older than that date.[19] In *Jack of Newberie* a woman comes home late at night and begs her husband to let her in the house. At first he refuses, chiding her for her lateness, but eventually he complies. She, angered at his refusal, later succeeds in locking him out.[20] Exactly the same story is told in Type 1377, "The Husband Locked Out." The tale had been previously used by Boccaccio, but, as Mann points out, there were probably no translations of the *Decameron* in English in Deloney's time.[21] It is possible, therefore, that Deloney had heard the story orally.

BALLADS

In addition to his prose novels, Deloney composed many broadside ballads. We would therefore expect him to be acquainted with the popular song and the folksong of his day. First of all, two traditional ballads, "The Fair Flower of Northumberland" (Child No. 9) and "Flodden Field" (Child No. 168), are included in their entirety in *Jack of Newberie*.[22] Some incidents which Deloney describes make it seem possible that he knew other traditional ballads. He mentions "a notable Theefe named Wallis, whom in the north they call Mighty Wallis,"[23] the hero of the ballad "Gude Wallace" (Child No. 157). It must, of course, be admitted that the ballad is but one of many sources of information that Deloney could have known. Deloney's Wallis has the shoes of his horse and those of his men's horses reversed to confuse pursuers, just as ballad characters do in "Jock o the Side" (Child No. 187) and "Archie o Cawfield" (Child No. 188).[24] Twice Deloney uses the time-honored humorous device of having a commoner exchange sharp words with a member of the nobility whom he does not recognize.[25] This device, though found in prose narrative, is used in "King Edward and the Tanner of Tamworth" (Child No. 273) and "A Gest of Robin Hood" (Child No. 117). Twice also Deloney tells how an apprentice boy or servingman wins the heart of the young widow who is his mistress and marries her despite the richer men who are courting her.[26] This is a common motif (T 121.) in all kinds of stories, of course, but it is found in three traditional ballads, Child numbers 109, 232, and 252. Finally, a bit of rough comedy is found in *Jack of Newberie,* where the servants revenge themselves on a bothersome old woman by getting her drunk and having her carried about the town in a basket.[27] This harsh treatment of the old lady may be compared to a similar episode in a humorous ballad, "The Keach i' the Creel" (Child No. 281), where an inquisitive old woman falls into a basket and is thoroughly jolted.

In one case a folksong may have suggested an episode to Deloney. A heartsick maiden in *The Gentle Craft* says that she would not rise from her bed if her father, mother, brother, etc., sent for her. When she hears that a messenger from her lover is downstairs, however, she leaps from her bed.[28] In a folksong, "Whistle, Daughter, Whistle," a girl persists in refusing to whistle although she is offered many fine things. When she is offered a man, though, she whistles at once.[29]

PROVERBS

The student of Elizabethan proverb lore will find in Deloney's novels a veritable treasure-trove of material. Deloney's acquaintance with the commoners of his time, his portrayal of characters drawn from the lower classes, especially workingmen and craftsmen, his obvious intention of writing for a popular audience, and his gift for reproducing racy, realistic dialogue all help to explain his frequent use of proverbial material. Some indication of the amount of proverbial lore in the novels can be shown by pointing out that the indefatigable student of Elizabethan proverbs, Morris Palmer Tilley, included in his great collection, *A Dictionary of the Proverbs in England in the Six-teenth and Seventeenth Centuries,* only about half of the mate-rial that Deloney used. In order to avoid duplicating Tilley's collection, I list here only the material that is not included in the *Dictionary.*[30] Moreover, in the list below is included only that material that Deloney may have known from oral tradition. Occasionally Deloney adopts the fine phraseology of Euphuism, especially when treating a romantic subject. Proverbs are one of the standard Euphuistic ornaments, but many of the ornamental proverbs are translated from foreign sources and were never current in England. Deloney undoubtedly borrowed these prov-erbs from Lyly or one of his followers just as he borrowed the style.

It is not always easy to recognize a proverb in the works of an author of an earlier period. Many times, of course, we can recognize a proverb because it has been used by other authors or because it is still current at the present day. Occasionally, too, an author is explicit, using, as Deloney does, a phrase such as "an old saying" to refer to a proverb.[31] Many of the examples which are listed below do not meet these requirements, however. These examples have been included either because they are similar to known proverbs or because they have something of the true proverbial ring.

TRUE PROVERBS

(Page numbers in the following lists of true proverbs and pro-verbial comparisons refer to *The Works of Thomas Deloney.*)

Abundance groweth from riches, and disdain out of abundance [p. 121].[32]

Many have runne neer the goale, and yet have lost the game [p. 14].

Howsoever things do frame,
Please well thy Master, but chiefly thy Dame [p. 93].[33]

Men gather no grapes in January [p. 162].

The longer she lives, the worse she is [p. 19].[34]

Faint Souldiers never finde favour [p. 5].[35]

They are worthy to know nothing, that cannot keepe something [p. 6].

Three things are to small purpose, if the fourth be away [p. 12].[36]

Proffered ware is worse by ten in the hundred than that which is sought [p. 5].[37]

Hee is most poore that hath least wit [p. 144].

Women are not Angels, though they have Angels faces [p. 148].

Such as are in their youth masters, doe prove in their age starke beggars [p. 238].[38]

PROVERBIAL COMPARISONS

As errant a Cuckold as Jack Coomes [p. 161].

Thou art not worth so much as goodman Luters lame nagge [p. 177].

You are like to Penelopes puppy, that doth both bite and whine [p. 128].

To stand, like Saint Martins begger, upon two stilts [p. 207].

SAYINGS

Poore people, whom God lightly blesseth with most children [p. 213].[39]

SUPERSTITIONS

In dealing with the superstitions or the folk beliefs of the Elizabethan era, one must always be aware that there were two traditions. One is the usual oral tradition. The other, however, is a learned tradition, consisting largely of "unnatural natural history" and based often upon Pliny. Since "unnatural natural history" is one of the usual embellishments of the Euphuistic style, and since Deloney sometimes imitates Euphuism, there are several examples of this learned tradition in Deloney's novels. When one encounters statements such as "The fierce Lion is kind to those who doe him good . . . and the very Dragons are dutefull to their nourishers,"[40] one may rest assured that Deloney is drawing upon a learned, not an oral, tradition. These two traditions were not always separate, of course, and it is probable that many items passed from the learned to the oral tradition and vice versa. The list below, however, includes examples of superstitions which Deloney probably knew from oral sources.

If the tongue of a frog is placed on the breast of a sleeping person, the sleeper will answer any question put to him, "for by that means Dick Piper knew he was a cuckold."[41]

If a traveller puts six leaves of mugwort in his shoe, he will never be weary.[42]

Mugwort keeps ale from souring.[43]

Houseleek protects a place from "thunder."[44]

Pimpernel protects against witchcraft.[45]

It is unlucky to meet a hare on a journey.[46]

It is unlucky to meet a sergeant on a Sunday morning.[47]

The right leg of a turtledove or the head of a crow will function as love charms if carried about the person.[48]

The stumbling of a horse bodes danger.[49]

Bleeding of the nose bodes danger.[50]

Screech owl and raven cries forebode death.[51]

From an analysis of Deloney's novels, therefore, some additions to our knowledge about specific items of folklore can be made. This analysis has also demonstrated that Deloney used a considerable amount of folklore, most of which he knew as part of the immense stock of Elizabethan oral tradition. The folklore that Deloney used is, of course, only a small sampling from that immense stock, but it can give us some indication of what the whole was like.

Notes

1. Francis O. Mann, ed., *The Works of Thomas Deloney* (Oxford: 1912), p. vii. The epithet was coined by Thomas Nashe.

2. See *Works*, p. 523.

3. *Works*, pp. 109–33.

4. *Works*, pp. 234–35.

5. *Works*, p. 554.

6. *Works*, pp. 190, 260, 242, 89.

7. *Works*, p. 236.

8. Seán Ó Súilleabháin, *A Handbook of Irish Folklore* (Dublin: 1942), p. 584.

9. See Ernest W. Baughman, *A Comparative Study of the Folktales of England and North America* (Doctoral dissertation, Indiana University, Bloomington: 1953; University Microfilms, Ann Arbor, Michigan, publication No. 5855), Type 1641.

10. *Works*, p. 51.

11. William C. Hazlitt, ed., *Shakespeare Jest Books* (London: 1864), III, 14–15.

12. *Works*, p. 106.

13. *Works*, pp. 181 ff.

14. *Works*, p. 42. Hyder Rollins, "Thomas Deloney's Euphuistic Learning and *The Forest*," PMLA, L (1935), 679–86, shows that the entire section in which these two motifs appear was borrowed from Fortescue's *The Forest*.

15. *Works*, pp. 47 ff.

16. Motif K1223.1.

17. *Works*, pp. 229 ff.

18. Baughman, Type 1360C.

19. Walter Anderson, *Der Schwank vom Alten Hildebrand* (Dorpat: 1931), pp. 311–16.

20. *Works*, pp. 17–19.

21. *Works*, p. 507. The first complete translation of the *Decameron* into English was in 1620.

22. *Works*, pp. 25–26, 33–36.

23. *Works*, p. 243.

24. Motif K534.

25. See Motif P15.1.1.

26. *Works*, pp. 4–19, 191–201.

27. *Works*, pp. 63 ff. Motif K1663.

28. *Works*, pp. 163–64.

29. N. I. White, ed., *The Frank C. Brown Collection of North Carolina Folklore* (Durham: 1952), II, 457–58.

30. Following are the numbers of proverbs in Tilley's *Dictionary* (Ann Arbor: 1950) which also appear in Deloney's novels: A 172, B 363, B 587, B 591, C 529, C 940, D 99, D 513, D 567, F 280, G 222, L 495, M 39, M 163, P 646, S 44, S 240, S 709, S 903, S 919, S 1025, T 199, T 257, W 686, W 794.

31. *Works*, p. 12.

32. Cf. Tilley, A 12, "The abundance of things engenders disdainfulness." The proverbs in the above list are arranged alphabetically according to the first important noun or pronoun.

33. Deloney calls this "the admonition of an old Journey-man."

34. Cf. Tilley, O 38, "The older the worse."

35. The earliest extant edition of Deloney's *Jack of Newberie*, that of 1619, reads as above. The Mann edition of Deloney's *Works* reads "Some Souldiers never

finde favour." I am indebted to Merritt E. Lawlis for information concerning the 1619 edition. Cf. Tilley, H 302, "Faint heart ne'er won fair lady."

36. Deloney calls this "an old saying." Listed in G. L. Apperson, *English Proverbs and Proverbial Phrases* (London: 1929), p. 629.

37. Cf. Tilley, S 252, "Proffered ware stinks."

38. Cf. White, *The Frank C. Brown Collection*, I, 443, "An early master makes a long servant."

39. Cf. Tilley, C 331, "Children are poor men's riches."

40. *Works*, p. 268.

41. *Works*, p. 88. For references to this belief see F. Hoffman-Krayer and Hanns Bächtold-Stäubli, *Handwörterbuch des Deutschen Aberglaubens* (Berlin: 1927–42), III, 131. This belief may be from learned tradition, for it is found in Pliny. The fact that Deloney puts it in the mouth of a shoemaker and the fact that he connects it with "Dick Piper" may indicate that Deloney knew of the belief from oral sources.

42. *Works*, p. 88. *Handwörterbuch*, I, 1007. This belief is also in Pliny, but it is known all over northern Europe at the present time in oral tradition and may also have been known in Deloney's day.

43. *Works*, p. 88.

44. *Works*, p. 88. *Handwörterbuch*, I, 1412.

45. *Works*, p. 88. *Handwörterbuch*, I, 1224.

46. *Works*, p. 174. *Handwörterbuch*, III, 1514–1515.

47. *Works*, p. 174. "Sergeant" probably refers to a constable.

48. *Works*, p. 187. *Handwörterbuch*, V, 368, and VIII, 701–2.

49. *Works*, p. 256. *Handwörterbuch*, VI, 1620–1621.

50. *Works*, p. 256. *Handwörterbuch*, VI, 972–73.

51. *Works*, p. 258. *Handwörterbuch*, II, 1073, and VII, 445–46.

Thomas A. Sebeok

INDIANA UNIVERSITY

BLOOMINGTON, INDIANA

Toward a Statistical Contingency Method in Folklore Research

1. *Purpose, and general procedure.* From the methodological point of view, the purpose implicit in several preceding studies[1] was to explore the possibilities of applying to a wider range of problems than had theretofore been the case, first, the formality of structural linguistics, together with, second, the quantitative approach of content analysis, to the end that the construction and stylistic characteristics of sets of texts—in the instances cited, folkloristic texts of magico-religious function from a single culture—be clarified.[2] The procedure is, roughly, as follows. Collections of texts which perform like functions in a given culture are selected for study. This corpus is examined to determine the least common denominator shared by all the texts within it, and this is stated in the most economical form that seems possible. This operation yields what we have called the "structure" of the texts. Each text is then re-examined in order that its unique qualities may be isolated, an operation which yields what we have called elements of "content"; these elements are coded, and the relations of the resulting units expressed, insofar as possible, in quantitative terms.

2. *Content, especially in contrast to structure.* We discuss, briefly, first, the relation of structural analysis to content analysis, and, second, the latter technique itself more fully. We assume[3] that structural unity characterizes all folklore texts, whether these be such simpler forms as proverbs, riddles, weather predictions, dream portents, and the like; or texts that are more complex and frequently intricate, such as some prayers and most folktales;[4] or yet forms like the folksong where the structure of the verse interacts with the musical pattern.

From this it follows that any quantitative approaches which overlook that unity are likely to be self-stultifying. The variables which are worth quantitative investigation will be those related to a view of the whole system. As a necessary preliminary to identifying these variables a great deal of nonquantitative work must be done. We believe that we must identify and clarify our Gestalten before we can intelligently measure their frequencies or even consider quantitative relations between their parts. Quantitation we regard as a postscript, a verification and testing of essentially nonquantitative hypotheses.[5]

We begin the description of a text with an exhaustive identification of its relevant elements, and with a statement of the relationship prevailing among these elements: it was found possible (1) to state the parts of the whole and the relationship of the parts within the whole, without (2) making statements about the nature of these component parts themselves. (Again, the first procedure is what we have called structural analysis; content analysis focuses on the component parts themselves.) The distinction between the two techniques lies mainly in the presence or absence of strict criteria of relevance. Content analysis, which involves relatively loose criteria of relevance, is on a much lower level of abstraction than is structural analysis, thus appearing vaguer, more fluid, more arbitrary, more subjective. In structural analysis, including especially linguistic analysis, it is possible to tell what does and what does not belong to the structure, i.e., what is and what is not relevant. On the other hand, the categories of content analysis—like the elements of cultural anthropology and like the motifs of the folktale—are obtainable by what has been felicitously called (with reference to culture traits) "a sophisticated awareness of their comparative implications."[6] To bring out the distinction still more clearly, but without pressing this analogy too far, perhaps one could tentatively apply the model of language study, and say that, in folklore research, structural analysis is to content analysis as, in linguistics, grammatical analysis is to lexical study.

It is generally agreed that "content analysis stands or falls by its categories."[7] The validity of the categories selected will ultimately depend on the investigator's professional skill, and may always remain arbitrary to a greater or lesser extent. The ideal content analyst of a given corpus of folklore texts will search out his categories on the basis of his knowledge of the entire cultural, and in particular the folkloristic, matrix in which the texts lie embedded and also of parallel corpora of texts from neighboring peoples.[8]

3. *The analysis of explicit content.* Content analysis is, of course, a technique well known in a variety of social sciences, having been applied both to a large and diverse group of materials as well as to a large and diverse set of problems; the technique is less well known in the humanities and relatively new to folklore research. Variously defined by different workers, it is defined in this way by Berelson: "Content analysis is a research technique for the objective, systematic, and quantitative description of the manifest content of communication."[9] Any sort of communication, private or "mass," can be so analyzed. Though specific applications have been made in many areas, we call attention here only to the various attempts which have been made in applying content analysis to stylistic features; Berelson's bibliography of such studies includes some 35 references.[10]

In published studies of folklore texts only Bernard Wolfe, to our knowledge, has essayed something approaching quantitative content analysis of any sort, along lines indicated in this quotation:

All told, there are twenty-eight victories of the Weak over the Strong; ultimately all the Strong die violent deaths at the hands of the Weak; and there are, at most, two very insignificant victories of the Strong over the Weak. . . . Admittedly, folk symbols are seldom systematic, clean-cut, or specific. . . . But still, on the basis of the tally-sheet alone, is it too far-fetched to take Brer Rabbit as a symbol—about as sharp as Southern sanctions would allow—of the Negro slave's festering hatred of the white man?[11]

This method of content analysis has also been applied to such other folklore media as the movies. Also, of course, qualitative content analysis of folklore materials is not uncommon, and has been preferred by many analysts, perhaps because, in a sampling sense, the content under analysis tends to be too small or inexact to justify formal and precise counting; or again perhaps because its themes have appeared as *Gestalten* rather than as bundles of measurable features into which such texts can be decomposed. Quantification is useful, however, when precision and objectivity are necessary or desirable, when the materials to be analyzed are many, or when a high degree of specification in comparing sets of data is required.[12]

With the exception, however, of the method described under the following heading, existing methods of content analysis deal only with explicit content; that is, in one way or another—and this is true even of the "coefficient of imbalance"[13] technique—they come down to counting the frequency of occurrence of certain items: so, for instance, the relative frequencies of favorable *vs.* unfavorable evaluations of particular referents are counted. Participants in the interdisciplinary seminar of psychologists and linguists at Cornell University pointed in their report[14] to three major weaknesses of these current methods of content analysis: "(a) The units of sampling have generally been based upon expediency . . . (b) The categories employed in deciding when a certain type of content is present or absent in a given unit have been largely arbitrary ... (*c*) Existing methods of content analysis are limited to simple comparisons of frequencies rather than measuring the internal contingencies between categories." It was the feeling of this group that the transitional relations among semantic events are also important for content analysis. What is more, we may add here, these transitional relations are likely to be especially relevant and illuminating in the content analysis of folklore texts; and, since our preliminary attempts to apply this new research tool to a sizeable body of Cheremis folktale motifs have proved exceptionally promising,[15] it seems appropriate to outline our conclusions in this volume, dedicated to Stith Thompson, who has stressed the importance of investigating folktales so as "to give the findings some statistical validity."[16]

4. *The analysis of implicit content.*[17] The fundamental logic of this statistical contingency method is quite simple: in fact, it is nothing more than an application of the law of association by contiguity, upon which all theories of learning—including Frazer's theory as to the psychological basis of the principles of magic—are, in one way or another, founded. If one idea or concept appears in consciousness, for whatever reason, other ideas or concepts related to it in meaning will also tend to appear; i.e., semantic determinants operate upon the sequential patterning of communicative acts. With respect to communicative products —for example, a folktale—it should be possible to find out, by appropriate analysis of the greater-than-chance contingency of units in the products he emits, what ideas (in this case motifs or component parts of motifs) tend to go together in the thinking of the informant. By way of illustration, a much higher than chance association was revealed between the notion of writing and the devil in Cheremis folktales—an insight which is as revealing as it was unexpected.

There are five principal steps in contingency analysis of content. The first of these has to do with the SELECTION OF CATEGORIES, which, in our case, involves a host of empirical considerations— including the comparative reliabilities of different categories, the situation of mutual exclusion between like categories, and so forth—which cannot be discussed here even in general. As in all content analysis, so also here one starts with the frequencies of certain categorized entities. Usually the particular categories selected are determined by the analyst's purpose—by the kind of information he wants. It is desirable to strike a neat balance between categories broad enough to include all references to the same thing but not so broad that incompatible things are included. Among types of categories we have experimented with were themes in a corpus of prayer texts and motifs of the folktale. One result of our research with the folktale was the observation that the motifs employed in Stith Thompson's index of folk-literature already have internal contingencies in different ratios built into them, so that we found it necessary, for our purpose, to break motifs down to more elementary categories of syntactic classes. Thus, for instance, Q261, "Treachery punished," which occurs eight times in the corpus, if counted as a single unit, can reveal nothing about whether the co-occurrence of the deed and its punishment is due to chance or whether it is "significant." It was therefore necessary to calculate separately the relationship of all sorts of actors ("churlish person" or "courteous person" [cf. Q2] to various goals and various actions and various modifiers and the like: "deeds rewarded" [Q10-99], "deeds punished" [Q200-399], "kinds of punishment" [Q400-599], and so on).

The second step in contingency analysis of content involves the SELECTION OF UNITS: contingency is defined by the co-occurrence of two items but, one must add, "within a certain unit." In our case, the obvious unit (but not necessarily the ideally appropriate unit) was the text which, we had already assumed, possessed structural unity—say, a prayer or a tale. This, of course, was based on a prior psychological assumption, by no means demonstrated, that such a text falls within the temporal span through which the effects of one event persist. Yet even in prayers of extreme length and elaborate design, as are those of the Eastern Cheremis in the corpus we have examined, this assumption seemed to be borne out. It appears to be additionally sup-

ported by such statements in the ethnographic literature as this:
"Die Hauptbedingung eines Priesterkandidaten ist neben tadel-
losem Lebenswandel ein gutes Gedächtnis, damit er das lange
Gebet, welches fast eine halbe Stunde in Anspruch nimmt, ohne
sich zu irren hersagen kann."[18]

The CODING OF MATERIAL comes next. A trained analyst (or,
preferably, several trained analysts working independently)
reads through the original text (not a translation), noting by
symbols the occurrence within the text of the items searched for.
This coder's sole task is to judge the presence or absence of
reference to a particular item in each unit. For example, in a
hypothetical corpus of 10 folktales, motif A ("Mythological")
occurred in certain texts, B ("Animal") in others, C ("Tabu") in
others, and so on, as summarized in this table:

TEXT NO.	1	2	3	4	5	6	7	8	9	10	% of units
Motif A	X			X	X		X			X	.50
Motif B	X	X		X	X		X		X	X	.70
Motif C	X		X				X	X		X	.50

The determination of SIGNIFICANT CONTINGENCIES is the fourth
step. Given (carrying on from the above illustration) that each
motif occurs in a certain percentage of units (A, .50; B, .70; C,
.50), the *chance* contingency is simply the product of the two percentages: AB ("Mythological" times "Animal"), .35; AC ("Mythological" times "Tabu"), .25; BC ("Animal" times "Tabu"), .35.
The *obtained* contingencies (AB, .50; AC, .20; BC, .30) can be
evaluated against the chance contingencies in terms of the significance of differences in percentage. In the example above it
would appear that "Mythological" with "Animal" motifs occur
significantly more often than they would be expected to occur
by chance, but that this is not true for either "Mythological"
with "Tabu" or "Animal" with "Tabu" motifs. It is interesting to note that two motifs might also appear together less frequently than they would be expected to by chance, that is, as
if the occurrence of one would tend to inhibit the occurrence
of the other.

Though the above information would seem to be useful in

itself, we also want to know something about the interrelationship of the entire set of items measured. Thus the fifth and last step has reference to these CONTINGENCY RATIOS, which may be expected to reveal the interrelationship. To obtain a matrix of relations which can then be treated so as to yield a cluster analysis, the contingencies must be expressed as ratios which have certain of the properties of correlation coefficients. Osgood and his group have checked and evaluated several possible indices, one of which is the ratio $(A_B + B_A)/(A + B)$, where A_B is the number of units on which A's are contingent upon B's, B_A is the number of units on which B's are contingent upon A's, A is the total number of units for this A item, and B is the total number of units for that B item. It will be seen that if, in a given tale in which there are "Animal" motifs, *no* instances occur of "Mythological" motifs, the ratio must be .00; and that if *all* occurrences of "Mythological" motifs are contingent upon "Animal" motifs and vice versa, then the ratio must be 1.00. In the illustration above, the "Mythological" with "Animal" contingency ratio is $(5 + 5)/(5 + 7)$ or .83.

The final matrix analysis may well provide us with something beyond a mere description of the web of interrelationships that obtains among the set of items being measured. It should, at the very least, afford some information as to the manner in which those items are interrelated in the particular informant's thinking and, further, should allow us to measure the degree of difference between individual informants, say, tellers of tales. Such a difference measure, D, has indeed also been developed, actual computations of which generate a D-matrix which, when tabulated, gives the "distances" of every item (e.g., motif) from every other item in equivalent units (e.g., versions) and thus makes it possible for us to compare two different items for the same individual and the same item between two persons or between two time points of measurement.

It seems useful in this connection to recall the classic experiments of F. C. Bartlett with the repeated and serial reproduction of folktales[19] and, a decade later, those of Werner Wolff, who, among others, has shown individual determinants that act upon memory. Wolff performed some experiments in the course of which he read his subjects a fairy-tale love story, far from their usual experience yet evoking their personal participation. The experimenter checked, after a series of reproductions, to see whether certain "omissions, variations, perseverations, suppressions, and displacements were made by chance" and found that, to the contrary, these were due to deeper motives corresponding to the subject's personality acting in conjunction with certain additional objective processes that Wolff referred to collectively as "structuration."[20]

But, more than this, the analysis may well provide certain insights as to the attitudes of preference of the society in which the informant is a member, and these insights are likely to prove centrally characteristic of the culture. That there is a correspondence between the specific organization of a culture "and the traits and dispositions which characterize the psychological make-up or 'type' of the group" has been demonstrated, for instance, in a very interesting experiment conducted by S. F. Nadel[21] with two tribes of Northern Nigeria, the Yoruba and the Nupe, who are markedly different in culture. In one part of the experiment—the repeated reproduction of a quasi-folktale—"the responses which the contents and structure of the story evoke in the experimental subjects" were analyzed, and the two groups were shown to have responded rather differently in certain specified respects. Though the general trend of this correspondence, in particular, its reflection in folklore, has been well known— Boas, for example, alluded to it[22]—it may now become possible, with the aid of some such tool as a statistical contingency method, to construct a bridge more solid than has heretofore been available between systems of verbal behavior and the other systems of learned behavior shared by the members of a society.

Notes

1. Cf. Thomas A. Sebeok and Francis J. Ingemann, *Studies in Cheremis,* Vol. II, *The Supernatural* (Viking Fund Publications in Anthropology, No. 22; New York:

1956), Part Two. The present paper was submitted in the spring of 1954; the author's point of view has since been modified as a result of his participation, in February, 1955, in an interdisciplinary work conference on the subject of content analysis, under the sponsorship of the Social Science Research Council; see now "Linguistics and Content Analysis" (with S. Saporta), to appear as a chapter in *Content Analysis Today*, Ithiel de Sola Pool, ed.

2. Thus these studies differ in both aims and procedures from those of discourse analysis, which rather seeks to determine the structure of a single connected text at a time by setting up, so to speak, partial synonymity classes for it. Its procedures are akin to the formal procedures of descriptive linguistics but yield relatively little information that goes beyond. Cf. Z. S. Harris, "Discourse Analysis," *Language*, XXVIII (1952), 1–30; "Discourse Analysis: A Sample Text," *Language*, XXVIII (1952), 474–94.

3. But cannot document here for lack of space; see the various applications in the volume cited in note 1.

4. Cf. the extreme position of the Soviet folklorist V. Propp: "All fairy tales are uniform in their structure" (quoted by Roman Jakobson, "On Russian Fairy Tales," *Russian Fairy Tales* [New York: 1945], p. 641). Propp develops this statement in *Morfologiya skazki* (Leningrad: 1928), and "Transformacii volshebnikh skazok," *Poetika*, IV (1928).

5. Jurgen Ruesch and Gregory Bateson, "Structure and Process in Social Relations," *Psychiatry*, XII (1949), 123.

6. C. F. Voegelin and Z. S. Harris, "The Scope of Linguistics," *American Anthropologist*, XLIX, (1947), 592.

7. Bernard Berelson, *Content Analysis in Communication Research* (Glencoe, Ill.: 1952), p. 147.

8. "Since content analysis is only a technique applicable to communication materials and since communication materials can contain almost everything people say or do, the production of relevant categories is limited only by the analyst's imagination in stating a problem for investigation and designing categories to fit the problem" (*ibid.*, 148).

9. *Ibid.*, 18.

10. *Ibid.*, pp. 66–72, 208–10. Josephine Miles's *Eras & Modes in English Poetry* (Berkeley and Los Angeles: 1957) is a major new contribution in this area.

11. "Uncle Remus and the Malevolent Rabbit," *Commentary*, VIII (1949), 32.

12. See Harold E. Driver, "Statistics in Anthropology," *American Anthropologist*, LV (1953), 42–59, for a historical survey of quantification in the various branches of anthropology.

13. This is a general formula which may be applied to classified content data in order to present an over-all estimate of the extent to which favorable, neutral, or unfavorable treatment is accorded to the topic or symbol being analyzed. See Irving L. Janis and Raymond Fadner, "The Coefficient of Imbalance," *Psychometrica*, VIII (1943), 105–19.

14. John B. Carroll, Frederick B. Agard, Stanley S. Newman, Charles E. Osgood, and Thomas A. Sebeok, *Report and Recommendations of the Interdisciplinary Summer Seminar in Psychology and Linguistics* (Mimeographed; Ithaca, N. Y.: 1951), pp. 26–27.

15. The statistical samples were prepared by J. R. Mickey, based on the motif analysis of some 285 tales published in *Studies in Cheremis Folklore*, I (Indiana University Publications, Folklore Series, No. 6, Bloomington, Ind.: 1952).

16. Stith Thompson, "The Star Husband Tale," *Studia Septentrionalia*, IV (1953), 95.

17. Cf. also Charles E. Osgood and Thomas A. Sebeok, eds., *Psycholinguistics: A Survey of Theory and Research Problems* (Indiana University Publications in Anthropology and Linguistics, Memoir 10, 1954). The author is indebted to Professor Osgood for many hours of stimulating discussion of problems in this area.

18. H. Paasonen, *Tscheremissische Texte* (ed. Paavo Siro), *Mémoires de la Société Finno-Ougrienne* (Helsinki: 1939), p. 184.

19. *Remembering* (Cambridge: 1932). On Bartlett and folklore see, however, the strictures of William Hugh Jansen, in the *Journal of American Folklore*, LXIX (1956), 396. Bartlett's experiments were twice repeated under conditions more sophisticated from the point of view of folklore theory; the results, however, were analogous—indeed, in part, even more drastic; see Walter Anderson, *Ein volkskundliches Experiment*, FCC, No. 141 (Helsinki: 1951). See also Anderson's *Eine neue Arbeit zur experimentellen Volkskunde*, FFC, No. 168 (Helsinki: 1956).

20. *The Expression of Personality* (New York: 1943), pp. 203 ff.

21. "A Field Experiment in Racial Psychology," *The British Journal of Psychology*, Vol. 28, pp. 195–211 (1937–38).

22. So, for instance, in *Kwakiutl Culture As Reflected in Mythology* (New York: 1935): "Tsimshian and Kwakiutl mythologies present such a contrast well, for the social structure of the tribes is based on different concepts. . . ." (pp. 171–72).

C. F. Voegelin and

John Yegerlehner

INDIANA UNIVERSITY

BLOOMINGTON, INDIANA

UNIVERSITY OF ARIZONA

TUCSON, ARIZONA

Toward a Definition of Formal Style, with Examples from Shawnee

It was not until Stith Thompson asked one of us how we would treat the question of value in style—good style *vs.* bad style, successful style *vs.* style that fails artistically—that the collaborators realized how fortunate they had been to have discussed two difficult questions of style without becoming enmeshed in this one.[1] The question of value in style is a question apart. It can be put to one side and conveniently isolated for good—or at least until the other questions are answered. The other questions concern formal style; and when analysis reaches a definition of that for any given genre, then the constituents of formal style can be given a value rating —by the analyst following a rating scale or else by persons-in-the-culture expressing preferences. (Cf. Yurok basketmakers

comparing their own baskets with those of their colleagues before arriving at statements of artistic preference.[2])

Though isolable from valuation, the two major questions
which we do discuss appear to be not separable from each other.
One concerns the advantage to be gained by eschewing content in the identification of style—to find style in formal features only; the other involves the relation of style to the products
of linguistic analysis. These two questions are now discussed in
reference to the statements made in the few really successful
papers on style in American Indian folklore (Gayton and Newman's,[3] Opler's,[4] Goodwin's,[5] Reichard's,[6] Shimkin's,[7] and Erminie Wheeler-Voegelin's[8]), and also in reference to examples
from two genres in the unwritten literature of an Algonquian
culture. The two items in our sample are "Shawnee Laws" and
"Boneless Brother," the latter a folktale with animal and human
actors about evenly distributed.[9]

STYLE VS. CONTENT
AND STYLE VS. STRUCTURE

The identification of our two Shawnee genres can, of course,
be made by content—"Shawnee Laws" concerns injunctions or
advice to do so and so; "Boneless Brother" tells a tale of aban-
donment, adventure, and heroic climax. The former might be
classified as a sermon or speech, partly in reference to the situation in which it was told and partly in reference to its content;
the latter is, of course, a folktale.

Subclassification of the folktale genre is also sometimes made
on the basis of content. Thus for heroic myths alone, Shimkin
distinguishes a simple subclass (which contains a single cycle of
adventure) from a more complex subclass, the latter including:
introductory phrase, cause for starting travel, preparing equip-
ment for trip, the trip itself, adventures en route, crises or climax of the adventures; then a second cycle including final
victory, explanatory element, anticlimax, and final ending.

In Coeur d'Alene that part of a tale content which is plot or action is distinguished from that part which is not, as a period of desertion in an inter-action part of the tale—desertion when the plot action stalls and before a new plot action begins; or as an explanatory motif unrelated to the motivations of the tale plots.

Similarly, the "initial element" in the 14 published Tubatulabal tales—an utterance stretch of from 2 to 19 words—is distinguished by content from the following content of the tales, and that following content from the "final element"—an utterance stretch of from 4 to 8 words.

Most Yokuts tales collected by Gayton and Newman are myths in the Boasian sense, action occurring in an era before men and other life forms existed in the world as it is known today. Content identifies this genre as a whole and is relevant to the problem of smaller units. Thus in one distribution an episode (animal transformation) occurs which, though it may have been fully elaborated as a myth in its own right, serves the special function of a closing incident. In other variants the ending is lacking or is a simple, direct variety of the usual closing phrases which have received so much comment from collectors all over native America (in translation from Yokuts: *That is the end;* in texts recorded in English: *And that's all*).

Opler is most explicit about the crisscrossing and overlapping nature of folklore classification based on content. For Jicarilla Apache stories, his own classification is two-part: (1) those concerned with what is sacred and with ceremonies; (2) those concerned with the secular or profane. But he immediately notes that he has placed one tale (misbehavior of women of the emergence) under his (2)—part of the coyote cycle—though recognizing the occurrence of the same tale under (1)—part of the origin story. Opler is also explicit in distinguishing between native theory and observed fact—between the theory that there is one correct way to tell the origin story and the fact that every individual who tells it tells it differently from anyone else (differences lying in the content—"events"—included and in the order of their arrangement). Some items of content ("clusters of episodes") appear without raconteur variation; the included episodes always follow the same order. If any raconteur tells of the killing of the prairie dogs by

Coyote, he can be counted on to tell next the theft of the killed prairie dogs by Wildcat; next, Coyote's attempt to retrieve a prairie dog which he has thrown away; next, Coyote's revenge on Wildcat.

Having identified—on the basis of content—genre, subclass of genre, and segments (initial, introductory, plot, inter-plot motif, explanatory motif, final) within a given text of whatever genre, folklorists are faced with an alternative choice: (1) to find formal stylistic features which are always or generally or often or, perhaps, only sometimes associated with the genre, subclass, or segment in question; (2) to equate directly such content-identified units and their distribution as style itself.

Choice (2) usurps for the label *style* what in most fields is called *structure*. If a motif list is more or less like something out of a dictionary or an atlas, then a full statement of folktale types is like something out of a grammar; comparative folklore comes close to comparative linguistics, even to the point of achieving reconstructions of a parent type based on the structure of daughter types. Style is an enormously difficult thing to grapple with when it is perceived as having the dimensions of structure, as having, for instance, the length of content-identified units.

Choice (1) is that made by most scholars—to isolate content units, small and large, as a first step, and only then to come to grips with style.

Thus Shimkin can distinguish statistically between his simple and complex heroic myths by the stylistic device of intentional repetitiveness for artistic effect, a device found in both but more commonly in the latter, which are also longer—up to 10,000 words.

Stylistic devices may serve to characterize actors rather than genre, subclass, or segment within tales. Thus Reichard gives an impressive list of sound effects which distinguish a dozen different actors. For snoring Coyote goes *xwu xwu* (instead of normal *xuxu*), and in general he clowns the Coeur d'Alene language.

Though both the "initial element," as pointed out above, and the "final element" in Tubatulabal tales are identified by content, these same utterance stretches are associated with a stylistic device—the first word of each stretch always ends in the quotative (*it is said*); in other parts of the tales the quotative is randomly distributed. It is found not at all in personal narratives, except when the narrator is too young to remember a part of his life which he has by hearsay (e.g., *I was born, it is said*).

In contrast to the Tubatulabal, the neighboring Yokuts have such a striking uniformity in their style that personal narratives, myths, and tales are all said to show the same stylistic qualities.

The extra-folkloristic differences among Jicarilla Apache genres loom large, as in the association of clear skies with the telling of Hactcin stories and cloudy bad weather with the telling of Coyote stories. Associated stylistic features are not emphasized. When the exact meaning of names is in doubt, as "Hactcinyoyi," this may imply that the name is exclusively associated with the Hactcin story—a defining property of it, stylistically speaking. Goodwin notes for the closely related White Mountain Apache the stylistic devices of voice qualifier (voice raised to high pitch and then lowered) and the use of the quotative at the end of every sentence or group of related sentences.

The above sample illustrates the tendency of scholars to begin work on style after they have identified longer and shorter units in folklore on the basis of content—whole genres, as well as subclasses thereof, as well as segments having to do with plot and non-plot. Instead of beginning with content and going on to associated style, would it be possible to begin with style? To identify longer and shorter units in folklore on the basis of formal style? To do so would be theoretically interesting and experimentally possible. We do not experiment with this in the following section, where we give the formal style of two Shawnee genre; we cannot experiment because we did not stumble upon the texts as undifferentiated *qua* genre—we knew them to be distinguished by the usual criteria of content. Nevertheless, for its theoretical interest, we treat the two texts below as though we were attempting to find out whether they belonged to the same genre or different genres—without resorting to explanation via content.

To facilitate comparisons between two Shawnee genres, we label the folktales *A* and *B,* corresponding, respectively, to "Myth of the Boneless Brother" and "Shawnee Laws." Our presentation of stylistic features is in terms of their distributional occurrences: within *A* but not *B;* within both *A* and *B;* within *B* but not *A.*

Features peculiar to *A* (that is, not occurring in *B*) are as follows; the list is not exhaustive.

(1) An ab(c)a pattern, one stretch being repeated with a stretch or stretches intervening: thus, yaayalawiiki . . . hapaʔ-kweekiwiyawʔθi . . . tθeneeyewaapaki . . . yaayalawiiki   *they always hunt* (= a) . . . *they have a roof of meat* (= b) . . . *everyday* (= c) . . . *they always hunt* (= a). Another example is: hoteʔ-kwaapha . . . hoteʔkwiheemʔkwa . . . hoteʔkwaapha *he dipped it up* (= a) . . . *with his wooden spoon* (= b) . . . *he dipped it up* (= a).

(2) A pattern including inverse forms (verbs containing the suffix -ekw- and translated in English as a passive) and non-inverse forms (translated in English as active). It happens in this text that inverse forms invariably refer to actions which are directed toward the main character (hereinafter labelled *X;* all other characters are labelled *Y*); non-inverse forms refer to actions which the main character performs and, alternatively, to actions which the main character is commanded to perform. Thus, tayeečiwinitaʔmame . . . waʔsiwiʔθeniya . . . hotelaali . . . neeloʔčihini . . . hotekooli . . . nili . . . kčikaapeeθali   *I (X) can't get it . . . what I (X) eat . . . he (X) told him (Y) . . . no sense in that . . . he (X) was told by him (Y) . . . that . . . Snowbird (Y).*

(3) Repetition of a sequence of words with substitution of word (*Q*) for word (*R*). Thus, howenoʔki . . . tooto . . . keʔwiʔko-ma . . . piyaate . . . keʔwiitamawa . . . waašašimʔθeelemači *now*

*also . . . a frog (R) . . . you must call him . . . when he comes . . .
you will tell it to him . . . what use you will derive from him.*
Compare with this a sequence which differs only in the substitution of ši?šiikweeθa *speckled snail (Q)* for tooto *frog (R)*:
*now also . . . a speckled snail (Q) . . . you must call him . . . when
he comes . . . you will tell it to him . . . what use you will derive
from him.* This concludes the list of features peculiar to the
folktale *A*.

Next we treat features shared by *A* and *B* whose respective
frequencies in the two texts differ to such an extent that it is
possible to differentiate the texts on the basis of this difference
in frequency. This is, in effect, statistical. Certain of the affixes
which combine with verb stems are grouped into four sets of
paradigms. The paradigms relevant here are those called the
independent mode and those called the subordinate mode.[10]
The former occur with greater frequency in *A* than in *B*; the
latter occur with greater frequency in *B* than in *A*. Thus while
in text *A* the particle hiini *that, this is,* frequently precedes a
verb with independent mode affixes, such a sequence does not
occur in *B*. When this particle precedes a verb in text *B*, the
verb appears with subordinate mode affixes. An example from
A is: hiini . . . kehikwa *that . . . you will be told by him.* An
example from *B* is: hiini . . . weečiθaaθayaakeθiči *that is . . .
the reason he is always pure.*

Next we treat features peculiar to *B*; the two listed below are
not exhaustive.

(1) One subclass of particle is here termed subordinating *P*,
referring to weeči in the examples below. This subordinating *P*
may be preceded by hiini. Although sequences of hiini plus
subordinating *P* plus verb do occur in *A*, such sequences are
much more frequent in *B*; some morpheme sequences including
subordinating *P* occur after hiini only in *B*. Most common of
these instances with unique *P* is weeči *the reason.* hiini . . .
weeči- is a sequence that occurs repeatedly in text *B*.

(2) Sometimes hiini . . . weeči appears in combination with
another feature peculiar to *B*. This second feature may be characterized as a type of repetition in which a few stems are held

constant before different suffixes. A series of such repetitions is sometimes first preceded and then interrupted by occurrences of hiini . . . weeči-. Thus, hiini . . . weečiwaakotaki . . . hina . . . yeešipakθenaki . . . meeme?teeletaka . . . hiini . . . weečipakθ-enaači . . . wa?šikiteminaakweelemaawaači . . . ni?ki . . . mane-tooki . . . peepakθenooθočki *that is . . . the reason he knows it . . . that one . . . the way she turned it loose . . . the one who creates it . . . that is the reason she turned him loose . . . so that they may take pity on him . . . those . . . manitos . . . the ones who are turned loose.* (In smoother translation: *That is the reason he knows the way the one who creates it turned it loose. That is the reason she turned him loose, so that those manitos, the ones who are turned loose, may take pity on him.*) Com-pare- pakθen- preceded by yeeši-, weeči-, and the changed initial with reduplication before various suffixes: yeešipakθenaki *the way she turned it loose,* weečipakθenaači *the reason she turned him loose,* peepakθenooθočki *the ones who are turned loose.*

The beginning of text *B* (as well as passages scattered through-out the text) is characterized by a series of repetitions of this sort. In the part of the texts which contains the first thirty noun and verb words—that is, excluding particles, which are unin-flected—there are eleven verb stems and three noun stems. In this passage verb stems are repeated more often than noun stems. The point at which all this repetition (which we have charac-terized formally) abruptly ceases is identical with the point at which a content analysis would say the introduction ends. In other words, we have here shown how a text introduction may be defined formally.

Methods in modern linguistic analysis conversely parallel those in folklore which begin with content and sometimes later list associated features of style. In linguistics it is content or meaning which is secondary; either of these may be later associ-ated with morphemes and their order of occurrence. When the goal is to discover the structure of a language, no one kind of content is better than any other. Any genre will do as a point of departure. Analysis is undertaken on a corpus of homogeneous or heterogeneous texts, a corpus whose individual parts are not relevantly characterized as to genre because the distributional statements resulting from the analysis are not generally restricted in application to one genre or to a group of related genres. (It sometimes happens that a few exceptions or residual features turn up whose description calls for more than their distribution within the system; such extra-systemic features are found in exclamations, and the like.)

The products of linguistic analysis may be brought to bear on making statements about genres which will turn out to be of more than trivial interest. Initially, linguistic analysis makes no reference to genres. Rather, it considers itself successful when considerations of genres are excluded from all points in the procedures of analysis, but this very fact makes significant such implications about genres as may be found resulting from linguistic analysis. Hence, when the products of linguistic analysis do relate to statements about literary genres, the statements are non-circular.

Notes

1. We acknowledge with thanks the stimulation and helpful criticism obtained from professional folklorists attending the Folklore Institutes at Indiana University and, in addition, the bibliographic guidance given us by Professors Erminie Wheeler-Voegelin and Stith Thompson.

2. L. M. O'Neale, *Yurok-Karok Basket Weavers* (University of California: Publications in American Archaeology and Ethnology [1932], 32.1–184).

3. A. H. Gayton and Stanley S. Newman, "Yokuts and Western Mono Myths," *Anthropological Records*, V:1 (1940).

4. Morris Edward Opler, "Myths and Tales of the Jicarilla Apache Indians," *Memoirs of the American Folk-Lore Society*, XXXI (1938).

5. Grenville Goodwin, "Myths and Tales of the White Mountain Apache," *Memoirs of the American Folk-Lore Society*, XXXIII (1939).

6. Gladys A. Reichard, "An Analysis of Coeur D'Alene Indian Myths," *Memoirs of the American Folk-Lore Society*, XLI (1947).

7. D. B. Shimkin, "Wind River Shoshone Literary Forms: An Introduction," *Journal of the Washington Academy of Sciences*, XXXVII (1947), 329–52.

8. Erminie W. Voegelin, "Initial and Final Elements in Tubatulabal Myths," *Southwestern Journal of Anthropology*, IV (1948), 71–75.

9. These two texts are among the Shawnee materials collected by Voegelin. They were transcribed from the lips of the informant. A second version of the Shawnee Laws text was obtained on magnetic tape. A translation of a portion of the first version (coincident in length with the first five minutes of the second version) is being prepared for publication: John Yegerlehner, "The First Five Minutes of Shawnee Laws in Multiple Stage Translation," IJAL (1954). This five-minute portion constitutes one of the texts in our sample. It is roughly comparable in length to the "Myth of the Boneless Brother," the other text in our sample.

10. For the meaning of these terms, see Leonard Bloomfield, "Algonquian," in *Linguistic Structures of Native America,* by Harry Hoijer and others (Viking Fund Publications in Anthropology, No. 6 [New York: 1946]; pp. 85–129); and C. F. Voegelin, "Productive Paradigms in Shawnee," in *Essays in Anthropology in Honor of Alfred Louis Kroeber* (Berkeley, Calif.: 1936), pp. 391–403.

Samuel P. Bayard

PENNSYLVANIA STATE UNIVERSITY

STATE COLLEGE, PENNSYLVANIA

A Miscellany of Tune
Notes

*I*t is unlikely, in the nature of things, that students of folk music will ever be able to assemble a workable melodic-thematic index of national or international tunes comparable in scope and organization to the *Motif-Index of Folk Literature,* by the eminent scholar in whose honor these notes are set down. To me it is doubtful whether attempts in this direction would be helpful to scholars, as Aarne-Thompson or the *Motif-Index* has been; for the tune items we collect seem themselves to be our basic units, which have to be examined as wholes or in sections of such length that the relation of parts is not obscured.

In the analysis of these items we can apply section-by-section (or bar-by-bar) comparisons to identify individual melodic entities, and thus become aware of certain continuities in our folk

music besides those of style, formula, and performance. That is
the method generally employed in the present notes, which try
to exemplify the survival in tradition of certain old British
tunes, or their effects on national folk-music repertories. My
points of departure are naturally the *English Dancing Master*
of 1650,[1] the Skene MS of the early 17th century,[2] and William
Chappell's *Popular Music of the Olden Time*.[3] It is hardly accurate to say, as Baring-Gould did, that the latter work is "a
monument erected over the corpses of dead melodies, which,
indeed, it enshrines and preserves."[4] As implied in the ensuing
notes, Chappell is of enormous value to the tune comparativist.
These old popular airs were genuine *timbres,* used freely by folk
and art musicians both, and probably staying vigorously alive
long after they were officially supposed to be "dead." Some, if not
already folk tunes when first published during the 16–18th
centuries, speedily became so—taking their places beside the
immemorial airs and types known internationally since medieval
times and contributing to traditional style and formula. I wish
briefly to annotate a few tunes in these and other early sources.
In the headings of the following music tables the number in
parentheses refers to the corresponding note in the text [e.g.,
"Table II (3)" illustrates item 3—*Wooddicock*—in text].

   1. *Parsons Farewell,* DM 1650(6). An earlier version is
"Ostend" in the Skene MS, Dauney No. 14 (Table I). The air
can be traced still farther back in the Low Countries—a fact that
gives point to the Skene MS title. It appears in Adriaen Valerius,
Nederlandtsche Gedenck-Clanck, 1626, ed. P. J. Meertens and
others (Amsterdam: Wereldbibliotheek, 1943), p. 146; and the
editors refer to Starter's *Friesche Lust-Hof,* 1621, and the Thysius
Lute book, *ca.* 1600, for versions. In both Valerius and Starter
the tune is called a *bourrée* (Valerius, "Laboree"; Starter, "de
nieuwe laboré").
   2. *What High Offences Hes My Fair Love Taken,* Skene MS,
Dauney No. 72. This is apparently not a Scottish tune, being a
set of "Est-ce Mars, le grand dieu des alarmes," discussed by
Florimond van Duyse, *Het Oude Nederlandsche Lied,* II (Am-

TABLE I (I)

I Skene MS, Dauney 14

II DM 1650 (6)

I

II

I

II

I

II

sterdam: 1905), 1136–46, with many examples. About the set in
Valerius' *Gedenck-Clanck,* 1626, the 1943 musical editor says
(Introd., p. xlix) that although Valerius seems to owe the tune
to the French, it is the air of a yet older English seaman's song,
"The new Sa-hoo."

3. *Wooddicock,* DM, 1650(15), Fitzwilliam Virginal Book. A
Welsh harp (and dance?) tune, "The delight of the men of
Dovey,"[5] is said by Chappell (p. 64, note *a*) to be "an inferior
copy of 'Greensleeves.'" Actually it is a fuller copy of *Wooddi-
cock* (see Table II, p. 154)[6], which appears in van Duyse, *Oude
Nederl. Lied,* II (1905), 1104–07, with five 17th-century sets.

TABLE II (3)

Valerius' set in the *Gedenck-Clanck* is named "Engels Wodde-cot," and since the tune was set by Giles Farnaby in the Fitzwil-liam Book, it must have been known in 16th-century England. Of the Netherlandish sets, all have a high tonic ending but one, which shares the downward octave jump of Farnaby's variant; and no older set shows the length and *ABBA* organization of the Welsh variants. Hence, the evidence indicates that the Welsh forms are examples of secondary lengthening (a phenomenon hard to pin down in folk music), and are borrowings from the English or Dutch tradition.

4. *Flying Fame,* or *Chevy Chace,* Chappell, 198–9; *Pills* 1719, IV, 1, etc.[7] A reader who compares the sets in Chappell, *Pills,* or the early 18th-century ballad operas, with Alton C. Morris, *Folk-songs of Florida* (Gainesville, Fla., 1950), p. 302 (air to *Sir Hugh,* Child 155); with George Korson, *Pennsylvania Songs and Leg-ends* (Philadelphia: 1949), p. 37 (air to *Sir Hugh*); and with C. J. Sharp and M. Karpeles, *English Folk Songs from the Southern*

Appalachians (London: 1932), I, 124, vers. *M* (to *Lord Thomas and Fair Annet,* Child 73), will see how an old *timbre* lives on in oral tradition and gets re-created by folk singers.

5. *Lord of Carnavons Jegg,* DM, 1650, (44). A close set, showing continuity of country-dance-book traditional practices, is John Walsh's *Compleat Country Dancing-Master, 1731,* No. 148 (henceforth called "Walsh DM 1731"). An earlier version is Skene MS, Dauney No. 6, "Blew Ribbenn at the Bound Rod" (see Table III).[8] A much later version is Gow's *Complete Repository,* II, 1802, 4, 5, reprinted by Dauney, p. 351, "Blue Ribbon, Scotish Measure." To me the style of the air seems Scottish; I have not detected any Welsh sets.[9]

TABLE III (5)

6. *Watton Town End,* DM, 13th ed., 1707 (51)—having appeared in DM from 1665 on; Walsh DM, 1731, No. 170; *Pills,* 1719, II, 150, IV, 40, and elsewhere; Chappell, 220, etc. See Table IV[10] for a traditional American version of this air, and compare another, "Loving Hannah," Josephine McGill, *Folk Songs of the Kentuckey Mountains* (N.Y.: 1917), pp. 88–90.

7. *Callino Casturame,* Chappell, 793, Fitzwilliam Virginal Book. For a short account of this, the earliest recorded Irish tune known, see Donal O' Sullivan, *Irish Folk Music and Songs* (Cul-

TABLE IV (6)

I DM 13th ed., 1707 (51)

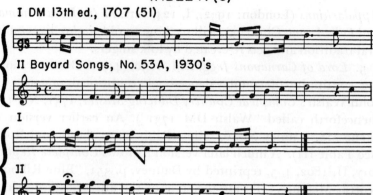

II Bayard Songs, No. 53A, 1930's

I

II

TABLE V (7)

I Chappell, 793

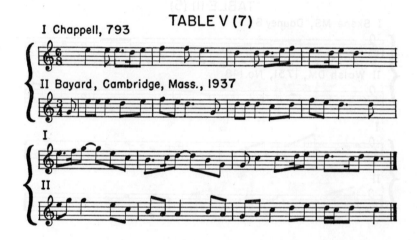

II Bayard, Cambridge, Mass., 1937

I

II

TABLE VI (8)

Skene MS, Dauney 2

tural Relations Committee of Ireland, Dublin: Three Candles, 1952), pp. 8, 9. Table V[11] shows a modern Irish folk version, set to Carroll Malone's ballad "The Croppy Boy" ("Good men and true in this house who dwell, / To a stranger bouchal I pray you tell," etc.). Malone's ballad, in its life as a folksong, seems to be set regularly to this air, evidently its "proper" tune.[12] Whether the tune has been in oral tradition since Elizabethan days, or has been recently revived and re-learned, can hardly be determined. But the extant modern sets definitely indicate a period of time in oral currency.

8. *Peggie Is Over Ye Sie Wi' Ye Souldier*, Skene MS, Dauney No. 2. For the tune, see Table VI. In John A. and Alan Lomax, *Our Singing Country* (N.Y.: 1941), pp. 164–65, is a song, "The Lame Soldier," recorded in 1938 in Indiana, in which Peggy leaves her husband to go overseas with a soldier who afterward mistreats her. The second line of the Lomax tune is nearly identical with the 1st–2d lines of the Skene MS air; and it is likely that we have here a modern version of both ballad and melody.

9. *The Breast Knot*, Jas. Johnson, *The Scots Musical Museum*, III (1790), No. 214, "The Breast knots." John Glen, in *Early Scottish Melodies* (Edinburgh: 1900), p. 131, traces the tune to 1758, as a reel named "The Lady's Breast Knot." A very popular fiddlers' and fifers' tune in North America, known by several names but perhaps oftenest called "The Jay Bird," is a modern representative of this melody.[13] Its second strain, in both Scottish and American versions, is also the tune of the exceedingly widespread game– and play–party song "Skip to my Lou." The English Morris called "The Breast Knot," Chappell, 681, corresponds with the Scottish air only in its first half. See Table VII,[14] on following page.

10. *John Come Kiss Me Now*. See Chappell, 147–48 for the history of this 16th-century air, and Glen, *Early Scottish Melodies*, p. 27, for an array of early versions. The tune was part of the Welsh harpers' tradition under the name "Pen Rhaw" (the spade head.)[15] Second strains differ in nearly all sets—whence it appears that they were joined independently to the first strain, which must be the nucleus. See Table VIII,[16] on following page.

TABLE VII (9)

I Museum, No. 214

II Bayard Instr. No. 56, Penna., 1929

I

II

I

II

I

II

TABLE VIII (10)

I Chappell, 148

II Jones Relicks, 1794, 165

I

II

11. *The Glory of the West,* DM, 1650(94): Chappell, 444. This tune was also known to the Welsh harpers as "Blodeu'r Gorllewin" (flowers of the west). See Table IX.[17]

TABLE IX (II)

12. *The Banks of Banna.* See Alfred E. Moffat, *The Min-strelsy of Ireland,* 4th ed. (London: 1897), pp. 312–13. This, the

air of Thomas Moore's "When thro' life unblest we rove," seems Irish as far back as it can be traced. Moffat cites its 18th-century popularity (which was due to George Ogle's song "Shepherds, I have lost my love"), noting that it "is merely an adaptation of the old air *Sin sios agus* [suas] *liom*, or 'Down beside me,'[18] published in Daniel Wright's *Aria di Camera, ca.* 1730, and many later works, and to which Moore wrote his song 'Oh, where is the slave'" (i.e., "Oh where's the slave so lowly").

The earliest set I have found of *Sin sios agus suas liom* is in *The Merry Musician, or a Cure for the Spleen*, pt. 1 (London: 1716), pp. 327–28, as "An Irish Song. Sung by Mr. Abel at his Consort at Stationers-Hall."[19] (See Table X.) The words given with the tune are:

Shein sheis shuus lum	Tamagra sa souga
Drudenal as fask me;	Ta she Loof her Layder;
Core la boe funareen,	Hey ho, rirko,
A Homon crin a Party;	Serenish on bash me.

Of this I cannot make out enough even to tell whether it is nonsense. Perhaps the final line is for "Saor anois ón mbás mé" (Save me now from death), but this guess may be quite wrong. Only an Irish scholar could pronounce upon the sense of the words.

TABLE X (12)

Merry Musician, 1716, 327

13. *Chestnut (or Doves Figary)*, DM, 1650, (85). This tune seems to have no early song words—with the striking exception

of a carol, for the tune of which see the accompanying table—
and may not have lasted long in DM. From what information I

TABLE XI (13)

I DM 1650 (85)

II Brit. Harmony, 1781, No.17

III D. Gilbert, 1823, No. 7, p.20

I

II

III

I

II

III

have available, it was eliminated before the 10th edition, 1698.
However, it became part of Welsh harpers' stocks, with the
names "Hyd y Ffrwynen" (length of the rushes), "Y Vrwynen
Las" (the green rush), and "Llanciau y Dyffryn" (the lads of the
valley). Sets are in John Parry (of Ruabon, *British Harmony*,

1781, 22, No. 17; W. Bingley, *Sixty of the Most Admired Welsh Airs, ca.* 1810 (1803?),[20] p. 23; John Parry (Bardd Alaw), *The Welsh Harper,* II, 1848, 47; Nicholas Bennett, *Alawon fy Ngwlad* (lays of my land), I, 1896, 61. Evidently the air has been traditional in Wales for some time; but whether it was originally Welsh or borrowed from outside is hard to guess.[21] Perhaps its West-English use as carol tune helped to give it currency in Wales. See Table XI,[22] on preceding page.

14. *Red House,* or *Where Wad Bonie Annie Ly. Museum,* No. 164. In *Early Scottish Melodies,* p. 164, Glen traces this melody to DM 1695 as "Red House," and under this title it continued to be included in dance-tune books. Also known as "Where shall [will] our goodman laye [ly]," it is the original of the well-known "John Peel": see Miss A. G. Gilchrist's article "The Evolution of a Tune: 'Red House' and 'John Peel,' " *Journal of the English Folk Dance and Song Society,* IV, 80–84. The earlier sets seem to have been minor-mode, the later ones major. The object of this note is to show how the tune survives in simplified form in modern American instrumental folk-music tradition. See Table XII.[23]

15. *The Health,* DM, 1650, (55); Chappell, 288. The tune must also have been current in the Netherlands when it was first printed in DM; van Duyse (*Oude Nederl. Lied,* II, 1182) gives a close set from *Den singende swaan,* Antwerp, 1665, with a tune title indicating a folk round-dance song.

16. *The Happy Clown,* or *One Evening Having Lost My Way,* Chappell, 675; Johnson's *Museum,* No. 251; *Beggar's Opera,* air XLVII, etc. Chappell traces the tune to 1718; Stenhouse, in his commentary on the *Museum* tunes,[24] claims to have it in a MS of 1709 (see Glen, *Early Scottish Melodies,* p. 144). How the tune came down to later tradition in Ireland may be seen by comparing Chappell (or any source cited by him or above) with Stanford-Petrie[25] Nos. 1397, 1398, "Is truagh mar' chonairc me aen bhean a-riamh" ('Tis pity I e'er saw a woman). One bar in the older sets corresponds to two in the Petrie versions, which may have been harpers' renderings.

17. *The Mask,* or *Hey to the Camp,* DM, 13th ed., 1707 (148);

TABLE XII (14)

I Walsh DM 1731, No III

II Oswald Companion, VII, 1755, p.22

III Bayard Instr., Penna, 1944

Walsh DM 1731, No. 221. This tune lives on in Irish and American tradition under a variety of names, such as "What would
you do if you married a soldier," "[when the praties are dug
and] the frost is all over," etc.[26] Table XIII sets it beside a modern version.[27]

TABLE XIII (17)

18. *Rock and Wee Pickle Tow,* Johnson's *Museum,* No. 439.
Glen, *Early Scottish Melodies,* p. 197, traces the tune to the 1663
edition of Playford's *Musicks Hand-Maid* as "A Scotish March,"
and as "Montrose's March,"[28] to Playford's *Musick's Recreation,*
1669. According to Glen, the title "A Rock and a Wi Pickle
Tow" dates from Oswald's *Curious Collection of Scots Tunes,*

1740. The tune has been extraordinarily popular in fiddlers' and fifers' traditions of southwestern Pennsylvania, and some of their versions have an irregularity, or extension-bar, as the earliest recorded sets have. See Table XIV for examples.[29] The tune also persists in Irish tradition, being sometimes associated with the

TABLE XIV (18)

I Scotish March, Musica Antiqua II, 1812, 175 (from Playford—1678)

II Pocket Companion VII, 1755, p.32

III Bayard Instr. No. 284, Penna., 1930's

IV Bayard Instr. No. 341, Penna., 1930's

V Bayard Instr. No 312, Penna., 1930's

I

II

III

IV

V

TABLE XIV (18) cont.

rhyme "There was an old woman tost up in a basket (blanket),"[30] etc. (like "Lilliburlero," cf. Chappell, 571).

19. *Oh Dear Mother What Shall I Do,* or *Blue Bonnets Over*

the Border. Johnson's *Museum,* No. 236. Glen *(Early Scottish Melodies,* pp. 137–38) possessed a MS of 1710 containing a vocal version of this tune, and refers to its use in Allan Ramsay's *The Gentle Shepherd,* 1725. Stenhouse also had a copy "from an ancient manuscript" (given in table); and it is plain that the earlier versions were vocal, not fast-paced, and were called "Oh dear mother [minnie], what shall I do?" It is also plain that this *moderato* tune was supplanted in tradition by a jig– or quick–marching version universally called "[All the] blue bonnets [are] over the Border," or some variant or derivative of that title.

Evidently the expression "all the blue bonnets are [come, came] over the Border" was a common one in the 18th century: James Hogg, in his *Jacobite Relics of Scotland,* I (1819), 5, 6, prints a song containing the expression in the first stanza. This song was imitated in Sir Walter Scott's "March, march, Ettrick and Teviotdale," which first appeared in 1820, and which used and further emphasized the line. (See G. Farquhar Graham & J. M. Wood, *The Popular Songs and Melodies of Scotland* [Balmoral Ed.; Glasgow: 1908], pp. 54, 55.) Furthermore, a tune in James Oswald's *The Caledonian Pocket Companion,* II (1740's?), 34, is called "Blow Bonnetts," and a reel (marked "old") in the 5th book of Niel Gow & Son's *Collection of Strathspeys, Reels,* etc. (1809), p. 23, is called "Blue Bonnets over the Border." (Hogg's Jacobite song had been set to a piece entitled "Leslie's March.") All these tunes are different from the one under discussion here.

In Vol. III of the *Pocket Companion* (also 1740's?), Oswald had printed "Oh dear mother what shall I do" with variations, of which the last (pp. 10, 11), called "Giga," is essentially the jig-time "Blue Bonnets" tune as it appears later (see table). It is very likely that Oswald thus recomposed the old air and launched it as a quick 6/8 piece. By 1818, in Niel Gow & Sons' *Part the First of the Beauties of Niel Gow,* p. 12, a variant of this jig-time "Oswald" version was printed with the title "Blue Bonnets over the Border." Whereas Oswald's "Giga" had been marked "Brisk," Gow's set was marked "Slow with exprn."[31] Finally, R. A. Smith, in *The Scotish Minstrel* (1820-24), V, 10, printed Scott's "March,

march" (as "Blue Bonnets" to another close variant of the "Oswald" version, marked "With spirit," and again called "Blue
bonnets over the border." This is the set that Graham reprints
(*loc. cit.*) and terms "the modern tune."

What evidently happened was something familiar to students
of instrumental folk music. Oswald's (?) quick-time recomposi-
tion of the older vocal air became traditional. Its older name was
then lost, and a familiar, "floating" instrumental tune title, already associated with at least two other melodies, became attached to the Oswald re-make, and supplanted the earlier title,
as the jig-version itself had supplanted the old vocal set. Table
XV[32] shows the two versions and illustrates the survival of the
Oswald set in modern American currency.

Still another remodeling of the old "Oh dear mother" melody
is in Niel Gow and Sons' *Complete Repository of Original Scots
Slow Strathspeys and Dances,* I (1799), 20—this time in the form
of a reel, with title "The Braes of Auchtertyre." The editors'
note is "This Tune is the Original of O Dear mother what shall
I do." But see commentaries of Stenhouse and Glen on Johnson's
Museum, No. 236. This form of the tune has likewise had a com-
plicated history in subsequent tradition; but its developments,
British and American, would require treatment in a separate
article.

I have space for only a few more notes, and I wish them to
illustrate further the participation of Welsh traditional music
in the British tradition—supplementing (as some of the foregoing notes have tried to do) Chappell's remarks about the presence of English airs in Welsh music (Chappell, p. 64, note *a*). It
is evident already that the Welsh harpers were influenced—
naturally, no doubt, and probably more than Welsh peasant
singers—by English popular music of the 17th and 18th centuries. Possibly even more airs than we now detect in Welsh folk
music were borrowed from outside sources and disguised by native development. The proposition is made likely, I think, by
the way in which the Welsh harpers liked to overlay their tunes
with arpeggios, broken chords, and sequential and diatonic-scale
passages.

TABLE XV (19)

I Stenhouse re Museum No. 236

II Pocket Companion III, p. 10

III Bayard Instr. No. 332, Penn., 1930's

The early currency of some British folk melodies is shown by their presence in the music of diverse nationalities. The common Anglo-American tune to (20) *The Golden Glove* (see Sharp-Karpeles, *English Folk Songs from the Southern Appalachians,* I, 377–78, 424 f.) is a fair example. One early version is Welsh: the tune "As I came home," in John Thomas, *Cambrian Minstrel,* 1845, p. 173. But versions recorded still earlier are "Isbel Falsey," C. St. George's *Mona Melodies,* 1820 (A. E. Moffat, *Minstrelsy of Ireland,* 4th ed., 1897, p. 351, No. xxiii); "Wilzham Wallas' March," in Alexander Campbell, *Albyn's Anthology* (Edinburgh), II, 1818, 72; and a Dutch song tune from a MS of the end of the 18th century, in Van Duyse, *Oude Nederlandsche Lied,* I, 1903, 185, No. 32C. Van Duyse also reprints *(ibid.,* p. 187, No. 32D) a modern Flemish version, first published 1879.

Instances may be multiplied from single collections, even without becoming involved in the complex matter of Welsh and Irish folk-musical relations. For example, in Nicholas Bennett's *Alawon fy Ngwlad,*[33] I, 38, "The Red Fox's Delight" is a quite individual version of the harp tune "The Blossom of the Raspberry" in the 4th vol. of Oswald's *Caledonian Pocket Companion,* p. 17, appearing as (21) *Miss Hamilton's Delight* in Johnson's *Museum,* No. 176. On p. 45 of the same Bennett volume, the tune "White Lime" is a version of the old dance tune (22) *The White Joak,* appearing in Walsh DM, 1731, No. 6, and in ballad operas. Again, the 3d air on p. 56 is (23) *The Irish Jigge* or *The Irish Trot,* see *Pills,* V, 108;[34] and "Captain Gwynn's Attack," p. 80, is the familiar (24) *Stingo, or The Oyle of Barley,* DM, 1650, (10). The same tune crops up in a curious set in Bennett's 2d vol., p. 97, "Judge a Point." The first air on p. 105 of Bennett, Vol. II, is (25) *The Cobbler's Jigg,* Walsh, DM, 1731, No. 22; Chappell, 277 f.

In Parry's *Welsh Harper,* II, we note that *The Irish Trot* appears again (p. 6, from Miss Williams' earlier collection)[35] and also that "William Owen's Delight," p. 31, strongly resembles (26) *Kemps Jegg,* DM, 1650, (25); and the tunes "Cwynvan y Bardd" (p. 36) and "Lament of Britain" (p. 99) are both seen to be close forms of (27) *Godesses,* DM, 1650, p. (52), that is, of the very old *Bailiff's Daughter* tune. In John Parry's *British Harmony,* 1781, the air "Gruffydd ap Cynan," p. 21, is (28) *Hark the Thund'ring Cannons Roar,* once a much-used broadside ballad tune; see *Pills,* I, 300, Walsh DM, 1731, No. 84. In Richard Roberts (of Carnarvon), *Cambrian Harmony* (Dublin: 1840), p. 5, "The King's Joy" is (29) *When the King Enjoys His Own Again,* Chappell, 434 ff. And in Edward Jones, *Cambro-British Melodies* (1820, the third volume of his *Relicks*), we see (30) *The Chester Waits,* p. 5, with this title simply rendered in Welsh, and in a set almost identical with Chappell, 551; and "The Heiress of Montgomery," p. 15, a set of (31) *Lochaber No More,* or *Limerick's Lamentation,* in a version very close to the old form "King James's March to Ireland," of 1692 (see Glen, *Early Scottish Melodies,* p. 89, for settings in parallel arrangement). In Edward Jones's *The Bardic Museum* (London: 1802; the second volume of his *Relicks*), p. 104, and in W. Bingley's *Sixty of the Most Admired,* etc., p. 41, a tune "The First of August" is nothing but the once popular English (32) *Come Jolly Bacchus,* or *Glorious First of August,* Chappell, 658.[36] The second edition of Jones' *Musical and Poetical Relicks of the Welsh Bards* (London: 1794), p. 163, has a tune, "The Beckoning Fair One," which is a good and distinctive, but unmistakable, set of (33) *Mall Sims* (see Chappell, p. 178).

Sometimes the marked stylistic resemblance between Welsh harp tunes and popular English airs of the 17th–18th centuries reminds a reader of something for which he sets out on a hunt through English collections—with occasionally surprising results. For instance, a favored Welsh harpers' air, appearing in Edward Jones' *Relicks,* 1794, and other collections,[37] "The Allurements of Love" (Serch Hudol), turns out to be the air of (34) *A Song. Set by Mr. Motley,* in *Pills,* V, 305–6. The commoner set has some manipulation and mingling of the first and second parts (as in *Relicks,* 1794, p. 135); but in his *Cambro-British Melodies,* 1820, Jones actually prints not only a version exceedingly close to that in *Pills* but likewise sets it to the very words of the *Pills* song: "Draw Cupid draw and make fair Sylvia know / The mighty Pain her suffering Swain does for her undergo"!

On the other hand, some discoveries are quite unexpected because of the "Cymrization" of an originally non-Welsh melody. Thus, the tune "Long Life to Mary" (Hir oes i Vair) in John Parry's *Welsh Harper*, II (1848), 15, which sounds very characteristically Welsh, reveals itself as a slightly contracted version of the air of (35) *The Loyal Subject's Wish. By Mrs. Anne Morcott* (*Pills* 1719, VI, 83–4). The song in *Pills* begins, "Let Mary live long."

Notes

1. For tunes quoted in this article, I use the uncopyrighted reprint "John Playford, THE ENGLISH DANCING MASTER, Now Reprinted for the first time from the first edition of 1650, with the tunes in modern notation. Edited by Leslie Bridgewater and Hugh Mellor, 1933. Published by Hugh Mellor, 10, Bolt Court, Fleet Street, London, E. C. 4." Hereinafter called "DM 1650."

2. The third edition of *Grove's Dictionary of Music and Musicians* (New York: 1947), dates the Skene MS as "between 1614 and 1620" (II, 16) and "between the years 1615 and 1635" (IV, 696); the Rev. Alexander Keith, in his edition of Greig, *Last Leaves of Traditional Ballads and Ballad Airs* (Aberdeen: 1925), p. 128, dates it not later than 1630. Tunes are taken from the edition of William Dauney, *Ancient Scotish Melodies* (Edinburgh: 1838), and are quoted with the number Dauney gives them.

3. William Chappell, *Popular Music of the Olden Time* (London: 1855–59). Called "Chappell" in references; since the pagination is continuous, no citations of the separate volumes will be given.

4. Quoted by C. J. Sharp in *English Folk-Song: Some Conclusions* (London: 1907). I use the reprint of 1936, in which the quotation appears on p. 118, at the end of chapter IX. It is, moreover, hardly in good taste to take this point of view toward Chappell today, because, unhappily, the time is at hand when the same words will apply to practically any regional collection of English folk music.

5. Welsh title, "Difyrrwch Gwyr Dufi (Dyfi)." Variants occur in John Parry, *British Harmony* (London: 1781), p. 25, No. 21; Edward Jones, *Musical and Poetical Relicks of the Welsh Bards*, 2d ed. (London: 1794), p. 129; John Thomas, *The Cambrian Minstrel* (Merthyr Tydvil: 1845), p. 90; W. Bingley, *Sixty of the Most Admired Welsh Airs* (London: 1803 or 1810), p. 26.

6. Table II: The Chappell set given here is that used by Giles Farnaby, whose lovely variations on "Woody cock" are now available in the album "Early English

Keyboard Music," on the London long-playing record LL 713, recorded under the auspices of the British Council. See note 5 for the other set.

7. By *Pills* I mean Thomas D'Urfey, *Wit and Mirth, or Pills to Purge Melancholy*, 6 vols. (London: 1719), where the tune "Chevy Chace" is printed to several songs.

8. Table III: The Skene MS set was noted an octave higher by Dauney, and the set in Walsh DM 1731 was in G. Throughout these tune-table examples, I have not hesitated to transpose melodies into other keys or registers, in order to facilitate comparison; I shall pass silently over the remaining instances of this practice in the tables. The tunes are not otherwise altered, of course.

When I give as examples items from my own collections, the words "Bayard Songs" refer to my folksong material, and "Bayard Instr." refers to my collection of folk instrumental tunes.

9. W. S. Gwynn Williams, in *Welsh National Music and Dance* (London: 1932), p. 121, lists this air, but remarks on the general uncertainty as to whether it is Welsh or not.

10. Table IV: No. II is "Lovely Molly," sung by Mrs. Emma Jane Phillips, Greene Co., Pa. The song is the same as "Loving Hannah," cited in the tune note; this tune, which I have heard often in southwestern Pennsylvania, seems to be persistently associated with the song.

11. Table V: No. II is "The Croppy Boy," sung by Mrs. Anastasia F. Corkery (née Warren), born near Macroom, Co. Cork, where she learned the song. I heard her sing it at various times in 1936–37, in Cambridge, Mass. I did not record the words, for Malone's ballad may be found in M. J. Brown's *Historical Ballad Poetry of Ireland* (Dublin & Belfast: 1912), pp. 212–13, and in Charles Welsh, *The Golden Treasury of Irish Songs and Lyrics* (New York: 1907), pp. 32, 33, where it is ascribed to Wm. B. McBurney instead of to Malone.

12. The tune accompanies still another printing of Malone's "Croppy Boy," in Herbert Rooney, *The Pigott Album of Irish Songs* (Dublin: n.d.), pp. 12, 13. This Pigott version is in 6/8 time, but otherwise close to Mrs. Corkery's. It stands under suspicion of having perhaps been tampered with—to make it closer to the old melody—because it is entitled "Cailin Og a Stor," a name reflecting some of the efforts of previous annotators to interpret "Callino Casturame." See O'Sullivan, *op. cit.* Anything about the history and occurrences of this tune set forth in W. H. Grattan Flood, *A History of Irish Music* (Dublin: 1913), may be safely disregarded.

13. Ordinary sets referred to as "The Jay Bird" are in Ira W. Ford, *Traditional Music of America* (New York: 1940), p. 96, and *The American Veteran Fifer*, rev. ed. by Henry Fillmore (Cincinnati: 1927), p. 18.

14. Table VII: By "Museum" I mean, of course, James Johnson, *The Scots Musical Museum*, 6 vols. (Edinburgh: 1787–1803), in which the tune numbering is continuous through the volumes, from 1 to 600. Table VII, No. II, is "Daddy Shot a Bear," played on the violin by Hiram H. White, Greene Co., Pa.—a representative form of "The Jay Bird" as commonly known in that region in past years.

15. Sets are in Edward Jones, *Musical and Poetical Relicks* (1794), p. 165; Bingley, *Sixty of the Most Admired Welsh Airs*, p. 31.

16. Table VIII: Only the first strain is given in the case of each example. In Richard Roberts' *Cambrian Harmony* (Dublin: 1820), p. 12, is another air called "Pen Rhaw" which seems different from those named in note 15. However, it may

simply be a case of the same air's having been disguised by ornate harping. A roughly similar musical trend between it and the others is seen if we let two bars of the Roberts tune correspond with one of Chappell or the Welsh sets cited in note 15.

17. Table IX: Beside the 1781 set noted here, the air occurs in Edward Jones, *The Bardic Museum* (London: 1802), p. 88, and John Thomas, *The Cambrian Minstrel* (1845), p. 61. All are very similar.

18. The identity of the two airs (which is obvious anyway) had been previously noted by Edward Bunting in *The Ancient Music of Ireland* (Dublin: 1840), p. 98.

19. John Abell gave his Stationer's Hall concert in 1716; see *Grove's Dictionary of Music and Musicians*, 3d ed., I, 7. Tune and words are repeated in the second edition of *The Merry Musician* (1730), pp. 327–28.

20. My copy of Bingley has a (bookseller's) binding marked "c. 1810." However, W. S. Gwynn Williams, *Welsh National Music and Dance* (London: 1932), p. 144, gives 1803 as the date of publication.

21. Unless an air in *Souterliedekens* (1540), which bears a general resemblance throughout, is an earlier version or forerunner. See the edition of *Souterliedekens* by Elisabeth Mincoff-Marriage ('S-Gravenhage: 1922), p. 282, No. 154.

22. Table XI: No. III is "God's dear Son without beginning," in the second edition of Davies Gilbert's *Some Ancient Christmas Carols* (London: 1823), music facing p. 20. In a note in *Journal of the Folk Song Society*, IV, 9, 10, Miss L. E. Broadwood tried to show that the tunes "Hyd y Ffrwynen," "The Duke of Norfolk" (the *Bailiff's Daughter* air) and "God Rest You Merry" are all closely related.

23. Table XII: No. III is an unnamed reel taken down from the fiddling of Levi Hall (then aged 77) in Connellsville, Pa., Aug. 9, 1944. Hall learned the tune from one Worth Bryner, an older Fayette Co. fiddler.

24. For an account of Stenhouse's annotations to the items in the *Scots Musical Museum*, see John Glen, *Early Scottish Melodies*, pp. 6 ff. My copy of Stenhouse's *Illustrations of the Lyric Poetry and Music of Scotland* was published in Edinburgh in 1853. Glen and Stenhouse both deal with the *Museum* items in numerical order.

25. By "Stanford-Petrie" I mean Sir Charles V. Stanford, ed., *The Complete Petrie Collection of Ancient Irish Music* (London: 1902, 1932).

26. For sets see Oswald, *Caledonian Pocket Companion*, VII (London: 1755), 1— a variant of the old set illustrated by Table XIII, No. I; P. W. Joyce, *Old Irish Folk Music and Songs* (London: 1909), p. 280, No. 516; Stanford-Petrie, No. 850; Francis O'Neill, *O'Neill's Irish Music* (Chicago: n.d.), No. 126.

27. Table XIII: No. I is in DM 1707 as "The Mask," a longways dance. No. II is an unnamed cotillion tune taken down from the violin playing of John Meighen (then in his 80's) at Wind Ridge (Jacktown), Greene Co., Pa., in the early 1930's. Some sets (see note 26) are closer to the old DM tune in the second part than Meighen's is; but the later-published versions always end high, like Meighen's, and not low, as in "The Mask."

28. An air in John Playford's *Musicks Hand-Maid* (1678), called "Montross'es March," is distinct from the one considered in these notes. See J. Stafford Smith, *Musica Antiqua* II (London: 1812), p. 178. The old "Scotish March" that we are discussing appears in *ibid.*, p. 175, and there is also a copy of the same set (i.e. from Playford, 1678) in Stenhouse's *Illustrations* as part of the note to *Museum* No. 439.

29. Table XIV: No. I is from Playford (see note 28); No. II is from Oswald's *Caledonian Pocket Companion* and is called "The Highlanders March." No. III is the "Fifers' March," taken down from the fife playing of James B. Taylor, Spraggtown, Greene Co., Pa. No. IV is the "Fife Tune," taken down from the violin playing of William L. Shape, Waynesburg, Greene Co., Pa. No. V is "March," as played on the violin by George G. Strosnider, near Waynesburg, Greene Co., Pa. To judge from the 6/4 setting-down of the old Playford version, the tune must in early times have been played pretty briskly. That is the way Oswald directs his version (in table) to be played, and the way W. L. Shape played his Pennsylvania set. On the other hand, most fifers and other players in Pennsylvania render the tune with deliberation and dignity. It is truly a stately and stirring piece when the fife-and-drum bands perform it, and one cannot be surprised at its long popularity. Oswald, in the first volume of his *Caledonian Pocket Companion*, p. 8, has a slow and fairly ornate setting called "A Rock and a wi Pickle Tow."

30. See, for instance, Stanford-Petrie, No. 220; Francis O'Neill, *Music of Ireland* (Chicago: 1903), No. 771, and also a derivative, No. 820; Herbert Hughes, *Songs of Uladh* (Belfast: 1904), p. 15, "The Wee Pickle Tow"; Katherine E. Thomas, *The Real Personages of Mother Goose* (Boston: 1930), p. 41; and what looks like a simplified version, "Did you see the black rogue" in Bunting, *The Ancient Music of Ireland* (1840), pp. 4, 5.

31. Oswald himself printed a slow 3/4 version before publishing the one with variations: i.e. in *Caledonian Pocket Companion*, I, 9.

32. Table XV: No. 1 is taken from Stenhouse's *Illustrations* already referred to. No. II is the "Giga" version presumably fashioned by Oswald, and discussed above. No. III is "Scotch come over the Border," as played on the violin by William L. Shape, Waynesburg, Greene Co., Pa. Shape learned the tune from John O'Boyle, an old-fashioned peddler and good folk musician. O'Boyle used to lodge with Shape when selling in the latter's neighborhood, and the two men would play for whole nights together, learning each other's tunes. Shape always played this tune with great dignity and measured pace, once more making it a moderately slow air, instead of a quick jig. Other sets are in *W. Blackman's Country Dances for 1827* (London: 1827), p. 1, "All the blue bonnets are over the border," and F. O'Neill, *Music of Ireland*, No. 1064, as "Blue Bonnets Jig."

33. Nicholas Bennett of Glanyrafon, *Alawon fy Ngwlad* (lays of my land), 2 vols. (Newtown: "Express and Times" Office, 1896).

34. This tune is quite different from the one also called "The Irish Trot" in DM 1650 (45), but was likewise a very popular melody. Another Welsh set of this tune, from an 18th-century MS, is printed by W. S. Gwynn Williams, *Welsh National Music and Dance*, p. 133, as "The Galloping Nag, Round O."

35. I.e., Miss M. Jane Williams of Aberpergwm, *Ancient National Airs of Gwent and Morganwg* (Llandovery: 1844); the so-called "Irish Trot" appears here (p. 24) as "Ffoles Llantrisant" (the merry girl of Llantrisant).

36. Chappell, noticing still another occurrence of this air—in his oft-cited note *a* on p. 64— says that it is " 'Jolly Bacchus' with a little admixture of 'In my cottage near a wood.' " As a matter of fact, there is no admixture: the Welsh tunes are straight "Jolly Bacchus," as in the ballad operas. What apparently led Chappell to make this remark is the strong resemblance and evident relationship between the two melodies which he thus links by reference. Both are alike in melodic

trend and in rhythm; each has the allure of a gavotte, and can readily be barred as one (in fact, the French collections usually bar "In my cottage" thus). The heyday of popularity for "Jolly Bacchus" was seemingly the early 18th century; for "In my cottage," it was the late 18th–early 19th. In short, almost everything about the two airs seems to indicate that "In my cottage" is a more recent development or derivative of "Jolly Bacchus" and that the latter is of French origin. However, I have not found unmistakable sets of "Jolly Bacchus" in French collections. On the other hand, "In my cottage" has long been an inseparable part of French popular music, with such titles as "La bonne aventure, O gué," and "Dedans mon petit réduit." See *La Clé du Caveau,* 3d ed. (1820's?), No. 302. Furthermore, "In my cottage" is well known among American fiddlers who perpetuate the British tradition; and in Pennsylvania the tune has even had rhymes in Pennsylvania Dutch set to it. If it is actually a descendant of "Jolly Bacchus," then that tune has been until lately very much alive in American instrumental folk music.

37. E.g., in John Thomas, *The Cambrian Minstrel* (1845), p. 25; John Parry, *The Welsh Harper,* II (London: 1848), p. 100.

W. Edson Richmond

INDIANA UNIVERSITY

BLOOMINGTON, INDIANA

Some Norwegian Contribu-
tions to a Danish Ballad

Just as Professor Child's mag-
nificent edition of the English and Scottish popular ballads con-
trolled the pattern which the study of folksong was to assume in
the United States for nearly the following fifty years, so also
Professor Svend Grundtvig's *Danmarks gamle Folkeviser* con-
trolled the pattern of study in Scandinavia. Because of their excellence and scope, both editions had inhibiting influences: in
America and the British Isles, Professor Child's volumes led to
the conclusion that everything worth collecting had been collected; in Scandinavia, Professor Grundtvig's volumes gave the
equally false impression that the corpus of Danish ballads and the
corpus of Scandinavian ballads in general were nearly identical,
that to study Danish balladry was to study the balladry of Scandinavia. Though neither scholar adhered personally to these false

conclusions or was ever guilty of making an explicit statement to such effect, it was inevitable that less knowing scholars should read these conclusions into the collections, and, indeed, such inferences were foreseen by Grundtvig's contemporary, Christian Molbech, who forwarded his fear of them when he objected to Grundtvig's published plans.[1]

These inhibitions were not easily overcome. The renaissance of ballad scholarship in America did not begin until the late 1920's, but its effects are well known; the renaissance of Scandinavian ballad scholarship has only recently begun, and with it has come the realization that each district of Scandinavia has made its own significant contribution to the balladry of the area as a whole. Enjoying—or perhaps one should say suffering from —some of the same geographical and economic peculiarities as the American Southern Appalachians, the valleys of Norway have been especially fruitful in their contributions. Had the late Professor of Folklore and Director of the Norsk Folkeminnesamling in Oslo, Knut Liestøl, been able to continue his work for one or two more years, we would now have a definitive edition of Norwegian ballads. Professor Liestøl's death, however, must leave us content with his interesting but popular edition, *Norske Folkevisor,*[2] and the hope that the definitive edition upon which he was working at the time of his death will find a worthy successor. If it does, the ballads and folksongs of Norway will take their rightful place alongside those of Denmark.

It is not the purpose of this paper, however, to point out the excellence and the significance of the many songs which Norway contributed to Scandinavian tradition; it is, rather, to show by the example of one song, itself Danish in origin, the peculiar contribution made by Norwegians to a Danish song which took root in their country.

In 1891 Professor Moltke Moe, whose efforts were to establish the Norsk Folkeminnesamling as one of the world's foremost folklore archives, collected from one of his best informants, Hæge Bjønnemyr of Mo in Telemark, the only Norwegian text of *Fredrik den andre i Ditmersken,* the song which Grundtvig calls the "youngest-of-all Danish historical ballads."[3] Although it is plainly Danish in its dialect and obviously fragmentary in its structure, this text, which has never before been printed, is of no little significance for the study of Scandinavian balladry, for it cleverly and effectively elaborates two motifs, stated but otherwise neglected in the Danish texts, in such a way as to make them important elements in the development of the narrative. Such an elaboration of motifs is not uncommon in Norwegian texts and indicates the vitality of the Norwegian tradition; one sees here, in effect, the process of re-creation to fit the taste of the community to which the song has been transported.

Professor Moe's unique Norwegian text of this song is prefaced in the manuscript with Hæge Bjønnemyr's recognition of the fragmentary nature of her text, "Dæ æ noko langt uti, detta, du," and the text itself follows immediately without title. Despite Hæge's obvious Telemål, which is reflected in Professor Moe's spellings, the Danish origin of the song shines through.

1. Kong Frēdrik fram ivi bóri sprangg,
    dei sӱllbode knivane ó sliró rann,
    å dér sto på kong Frēdriks navn.

    —Dei Dyttmarskens herrar dei huva sitt livi forlóra.

2. "Kjære lille pige, vil du vera meg huld
    å ville du skaffe meg lykt a ljus?"

3. "Kom følg med mig til min faders hus,
    så skal du nok fange både lykt a ljus."

4. "Kjære lille pige, vil du ra meg ra,
    hoss eg kann då sleppe ótó Dyttmarsk iår?"

5. "Du réngskór dine hestar, snur hākane fram,
    så ri'e du så fritt igjænóm Dyttmarskens land."

6. Han satte den lille pige for brede bór
    å sjav'e sette han seg for årin i ro.

7. Dei sende etter hāna ei kollutte kū
    dei batt nå mæ hæna båt rókk a strӱ.

8. "Når den kollūtte kui hev no spunni dæ stry,
   då skò kong Fredrik vinne den by.

9. Når den kollutte kua hev nå vòvi å spunni,
   då skò kong Frēdrik Dyttmarsk vinne!"

10. Dei venta av sónna, men han kom av nõra,
    men då bleiv alt deires forlóra.[4]

Six Danish texts of this song have already been printed in
Danmarks gamle Folkeviser (III, 674–80, No. 175, A–D; 931–
33, E–F). Of these, four texts, variants B, C, E, and F, were collected from oral tradition in the middle of the nineteenth century; variant A (since reprinted in Professor H. Grüner Nielsen's
Danske Folkeviser[5] in a normalized text) was found originally
in Anna Krabbe's MS; and D was first printed in Peder Resen's
Kong Friderik den 2dens Krønike,[6] and later reprinted with
minor variations in Syv's Viserbok.[7] As would be expected, the
Norwegian text is closest to the Danish texts collected in the
1860's, especially to DgF E, but it also has peculiarities found in
DgF C, on the one hand, and in DgF D, on the other hand, as
well as one motif not found in any of the other texts. One must
conclude, therefore, that with the possible exception of DgF A
(which may represent its own tradition) each of the texts is but
a facet of a fairly widespread tradition and that each is relatively
independent of all of the others but probably developed from a
single archetype.

In all probability, however, even in its Danish tradition,
Fredrik den andre i Ditmersken is not an independent song. It
is, rather, linked by its refrain to an entirely different ballad
which deals with yet another Danish king's invasion of Ditmarsken: *Kong Hans i Ditmarsken* (1500), DgF 169. This song,
which is no more than a Danish translation of one or more songs
from Ditmarsken, treats of the defeat of King Hans by the men
of Ditmarsken in 1500, even going so far as to suggest falsely that
King Hans lost his life in the battle. As a refrain it has the line:
De danske hoffmendt terres liiff er alt forlorrett. In an ironic
and taunting manner it tells the story of King Hans' unwise decision to invade Ditmarsken despite the advice of a young girl

whose father had made a similar mistake and died in Ditmarsken as a result. The refrain functions as an ironic, moral tag, artistically emphasizing the point of each stanza. Just as the refrain of *Kong Hans i Ditmarsken* points up the narrative, so does the following refrain employed in *Frederik den anden i Ditmersken:*

DANISH

A. *Di dytmerske herrer deris liff er alt for-loren*
B.F. *Nu haver de Dytmærskens Herrer deres Land forloret*
C. *De ditmarsker Herrer de havde deres Løn forloren*
D. *De Dytmerske Herrer de hafve deris Ljff forlaaret*
E. *De Ditmarskens Herrer deres Land er forloren*

NORWEGIAN

A. *Dei Dyttmarskens herrar dei huva sitt livi forlóra*

Taken together with the fact that King Frederik II was momentarily successful in his invasion of Ditmarsken in May and June, 1559, this refrain, contradicting as exactly as it does the refrain to *Kong Hans i Ditmarsken,* suggests that our song was created as a reply to the earlier and taunting song from Ditmarsken; this suggestion is lent support by Frederik's ironic farewell as he escapes from Ditmarsken in DgF B, C, E, and F and the moralizing stanzas which conclude DgF D.

The plot of our song, however, is not at all like the plot of *Kong Hans i Ditmarsken;* it is a separate, though dependent, creation. Aside from the refrain, the two songs have only two things in common: (1) each king receives advice from a young girl; (2) each song deals with a Danish invasion of Ditmarsken. Neither of these elements, however, is borrowed from the earlier ballad. The advice which King Hans receives from the girl is simply to avoid invading Ditmarsken, whereas Frederik is shown how to evade his enemies. King Hans' invasion is completely unsuccessful; whereas *Fredrik den andre i Ditmersken* deals with preparations for what was to be a successful invasion. The song resulting from King Hans' unsuccessful invasion, in other words, brought about a reply in the form of a song about King Frederik's successful invasion, and the ironic nature of this reply is emphasized not only by the perversion of the refrain of the earlier song but also by introducing a similar set of characters— but no attempt is made to slavishly parallel the narrative of the earlier ballad.

All of the texts of *Fredrik den andre i Ditmersken* tell the same story in much the same way. The Danish texts begin with a description of King Frederik II disguising himself as a rich merchant and attempting to spy out conditions in Ditmarsken. His disguise is penetrated,[8] however, and flight becomes a necessity. The introductory stanzas dealing with espionage have been lost from the Norwegian text, which begins with the implied recognition of Frederik when someone sees his name on his knife. The song then continues:

Frederik requests aid from a little girl who gives him both momentary asylum in her father's house and advice about how to escape from Ditmarsken: he must shoe his horse backwards and file off the hakes and thus ride away. Frederik follows the girl's advice, and, in addition, takes her with him. The men of Ditmarsken send after them a hornless cow to which they have bound a spinning wheel and some straw; with this is sent the taunt that Frederik can hope to successfully conquer Ditmarsken when he has taught the cow to spin and weave. The song concludes with the statement that although they expected Frederik to return from the south, he came from the north and "the men of Ditmarsken their lives they lost."

The Danish texts all elaborate upon this story to some degree, adding a ferryman (DgF A, C, D, E) or fisherman (DgF B, F) who refuses to aid the fugitive pair for fear of the town mayor and because he recognizes Frederik; as a result, Frederik is forced to row himself to safety.[9] The content of our stanza six—"Han satte den lille pige for brede bór / å sjav'e sette han seg for årin i ro"— plainly shows that the motif of the ferryman was once a part of our song; but this motif has been lost, and only the memorable fact that the king did his own rowing remains. In addition, all of the Danish texts except D conclude with Frederik rewarding the girl with gifts of castles, estates, and a rich nobleman as a husband;[10] indeed, B, C, E, and F have Frederik express the wish that the girl were noble so that he himself might marry her! Whether or not this once appeared in our text is impossible to say.

Our Norwegian text, however, is not without additions of its own which plainly show its relative independence of the already published texts. Of the six texts published in DgF, only D employs the motif of the cow and the spinning wheel; and here it appears not as an actual event but merely as a simile in a taunt shouted at the escaping Frederik by the men of Ditmarsken:

> 26. Oc førend de skulle hafve Dytmersk inde,
>   Kunde de vel lære en Ko at spinde.

Three stanzas, however, are employed in the Norwegian text to describe the dispatching of the cow as an actual, dramatic event:

> 7. Dei sende etter hāna ei kollutte kũ
>   dei batt nå mæ hæna båt rókk å strȳ.
>
> 8. "Når den kollũtte kui hev no spunni dæ stry
>   då skò kong Fredrik vinne den by.
>
> 9. Når den kollutte kua hev nå vòvi å spunni,
>   då skò kong Frēdrik Dyttmarsk vinne!"

That the song gains in dramatic effectiveness by this elaboration is obvious, and it is perhaps a vindication of popular taste that the episode has been retained in our otherwise fragmentary version.

Even more effective is the handling in the Norwegian text of the trick employed by Frederik and the girl to evade their pursuers. In DgF B, C, and F, Frederik and the girl bind clothes around the horse's hooves so that the trail will be difficult to follow:

> DgF B8:   Liden Kirsten hun var saa snild og saa tro,
>   hun bandt sine Tørklæder om Hestens Fod.
>
> DgF C14:   "Du sadle din Hest og være ikke for sen,
>   og bind dine Klæder om Hestens Ben!"

DgF F10: Den Pige sanken sammen de Tørklæder smaa,
          saa bandt hun dennem om Hestens Fod.

In DgF E, however, as in our Norwegian text, instead of being
muffled, the horse's hooves are shod backwards, and the hakes
are filed off:

DgF E13: "De skor Deres Hest, vender Hagerne frem!
          saa kan De nok vandre Ditmarsken igjennem."

Norw. A5: "Du réngskór dine hestar, snur hākane fram,
           så ri'e du så fritt igjænóm Dyttmarskens land."

Nothing further is said about this in any of the Danish texts; one
moves directly to the ferryman motif and is left to the conclusion
that the ruse was at least momentarily successful. In the Norwegian text, however, the ruse is so successful that the men of
Ditmarsken assume that Frederik rode to the south instead of
to the north and home to Denmark and thus are completely surprised and easily conquered when he returns from the north
instead:

10: Dei venta av sónna, men han kom av nŏra,
     men då bleiv alt deires forlóra.

The obvious fallacies involved in the trick (no tracks would be
leading southward, no one would be long fooled by a horse shod
backwards even if the hakes were filed off, etc.) do not obviate
the fact that our text has cleverly made use of a motif found early
in the song to lead directly to a conclusion which knits the whole
song compactly together. This elaboration of otherwise insignificant or commonplace motifs to a point of dramatic importance within a ballad can be said to be the Norwegian contribution to the song. Contributions of this type are not unusual in
Norway, especially in Telemark, and they can be seen in *Junker
Strange hentar Dagmor* and *Stig liten fell* as well as in many
other places.

    It seems unlikely that this song has any basis in fact other than

Frederik's actual invasion of Ditmarsken in 1559 and the Danish desire to reply to the taunts implicit in *Kong Hans i Ditmarsken*. Certain Danish legends and traditions, however, deal with the same subject matter. The girl captured popular imagination, of course, because of her daring and her sudden acquisition of riches; consequently, she, her family, and the lands she was given have been variously identified. According to the singer of DgF B, the castle given to the girl by Frederik was Mørup in Fjenneslev-Sogn between Ringsted and Sorø. On the other hand, the singer of DgF C maintained that the Haffnerske family in Møn was descended from the ennobled girl. Still other legends attach the girl to King Hans rather than to Frederik II and insist (1) that her name was Mette and (2) that he built her a castle in Bredsted-amt north of the Eider River and called it Mettenwarf. These traditions are discussed fully by Grundtvig (DgF III, pp. 675–76), who reaches no conclusion but suggests that all of the legends belong originally to Frederik rather than to King Hans and implies that there may be some truth in them.

So much smoke implies some fire, but in this case the fire may not be any more than the song itself which, after all, in its oldest text is only fifty years younger than Frederik's invasion of Ditmarsken. That a king should disguise himself, undertake his own espionage, and subsequently receive aid from a peasant girl whom he ennobles as a reward seems much more likely to be the product of a romantic imagination than of history itself.

Notes

1. Christian Molbech, "Kritiske Bemærkninger og Resultater angaaende den Grundtvigske Udgave, Material-Samling, og Kilde-Samling af gamle danske Folke-viser," *Historisk-biographiske Samlinger* (Copenhagen: 1849), Vol. II.

2. Knut Liestøl, *Norske Folkevisor* (Kristiania [Oslo]: 1920–24), 3 vols.

3. Svend Grundtvig, *Danmarks gamle Folkeviser* (Copenhagen: 1853 ff.), III, 674. Hereafter *Danmarks gamle Folkeviser* will be referred to simply as DgF followed by a volume number.

4. This text was collected by Professor Moltke Moe from Hæge Bjønnemyr, who, according to a manuscript note, got it in turn from Jórónn, her mother. The

song was collected in Mo, Telemark, in the winter of 1891; two copies of the text exist in the manuscript collection of the Norsk Folkeminnesamling: Professor Liestøl's clean copy, No. 195, and the original, M Moe 25, pp. 292–93.

In accord with Professor Moe's customary attention to linguistic matters, a note in his hand queries Hæge's historical and geographical knowledge: "Jeg syntes i begyndelsen [og er endnu ikke sikker på om jeg har hørt feil] at hun sagde Dødsmark = Døttmark i steden for Dyttmarsken." In 8^1 *kua* is written above *kui,* and the word *no* is inserted; in the clean copy in the same line the word *da* is written in and crossed out, and the word *no* is inserted above it. This is apparently merely an error of the copyist.

5. H. Grüner Nielsen, *Danske Folkeviser* (Copenhagen: 1927), II, 161–63; notes on pp. 267–68.

6. Peder Resen, *Kong Friderik den 2dens Krønike* (Copenhagen: 1680), p. 367.

7. A. S. Vedel and Peder Syv, *200 Viser om Konger Kemper oc Andre* (Copenhagen: 1787), Part IV, pp. 576–77.

8. The specific means of recognition is unmentioned in DgF A and D; in DgF B, C, and E, he is recognized, as in the Norwegian text, because he has carelessly exposed his knife and fork to view; in DgF F he is simply recognized by two sailors who claim to have seen him in his homeland.

9. In DgF B this motif is doubly employed: the king and the girl are first refused exit from the city by the gatekeeper, but he is persuaded to let them go when they produce the mayor's brothers and sisters as hostages. The king and the girl then proceed to the shore where they meet a fisherman and the episode is repeated, except that here, as in the other Danish variants, bribes and force are employed.

10. DgF A: "hus och jord." B: "en Mand saa rar,/ med Slottet och Fæstet, saa godt som det staar." C: "et Grevskab udaf mit eget Land." E: "en Greve saa bold, / med ham skal du nyde al Ære og Told/ Af de Ditmarskens Herrer." F: "et Grevskab god."

Francis Lee Utley

THE OHIO STATE UNIVERSITY

COLUMBUS, OHIO

Abraham Lincoln's When Adam Was Created

Elizabeth Crawford, wife of the man who lent Abraham Lincoln the famous copy of Parson Weems's *Life of Washington,* was a helpful old lady who gave William Herndon some of his most useful information about Lincoln's early life in Indiana. But when she attributed to Lincoln a variant of the wedding song "When Adam Was Created," she raised questions which have vexed most Lincoln biographers and several students of folksong. My purpose is to study the antecedents of this song, which show that both theme and song itself were much older than Lincoln. Such a study may have two values beyond scotching the ascription: it will illustrate the persistence of the song and the transmutation of a conceit from the Orient to modern America, and it may point the way to a more critical use of documents for folksong investigation.[1]

The conceit or formula is a bit of now popular exegesis on the Bible which explains that Eve was created not out of Adam's foot, lest she be inferior, nor out of his head, lest she be superior, but out of his rib, so that she might be a helpmate for him. This is the core of the Lincoln song, which Mrs. Crawford reports as follows:[2]

> when Adam was created / he dwelt in edons shade
> as moses has recorded / and soon A bride was made
> ten thousand times ten thousand
> of creatures swarmed around
> before A bride was formed
> and yet no mate was found
> the lord then was not willing
> the man should be alone
> but caused A sleep Apon him
> and took from him A bone
> and closed the flesh in sted thare of
> and then he took the same
> and of it made A woman
> and braut her to the man
>
> then adam he rejoiced
> to see his loving bride
> A part of his one body
> the product of his side
>
> this woman was not taken
> from adams feet we see
> so he must not abuse her
> the meaning seemes to be
>
> this woman was not taken
> from adams head we know
> to show she must not rule him
> tis evidently so
> this woman she was taken
> from under adams arm

> so she must be protected
> from injures and harm

Mrs. Crawford, unlike some of the later biographers, is fairly cautious in her ascription. She says

well now I will give you A part or all of A song that abraham lincoln use to sing cauld it adam and eaves wedding song this song was sung at abrahams sisters wedding [April 26, 1826] I do not know A linkern composed this song or not the first that I ever heard of it was the linkern family sung it I rather think that A L composed it him self but I am not certain I know that he was in the habit of makeing songs and singing of them I do not wish to rite any thing but the truth.

Herndon, reproducing her testimony with a "corrected" copy of the song, was less cautious, for under his hand her words became "at the wedding the Lincoln family sang a song composed in honor of the event by Abe himself. . . . The author and composer called it 'Adam and Eve's Wedding Song.' "[3] This flat statement has been repeated with little qualification by such authorities as Albert Beveridge, Nicolay and Hay, and Carl Sandburg. A few cavils have been entered, the most notable of them by John Iglehart, whose mother knew the song and who concludes that she learned it from her British compatriots.[4] He fails to produce her version, however, and since she was born only nine years before the wedding, his hearsay evidence does not clinch the point. George Pullen Jackson has also raised some serious doubts from his vantage point as a student of the fasola tradition of "white spirituals."[5]

A fairly complete context can now be provided of the song complex to which the "Lincoln" version belongs. The Index of Folksong Variants at the end of this study shows some twenty-seven or more occurrences of the head, foot, and rib formula in folksong, twelve of them belonging to the "American" version (A), and fifteen to the "English" version (E).

The earliest occurrences of E are in broadsides or chapbooks of the eighteenth century. One of them is a slip-ballad (E3):

[ia] Both sexes give ear to my fancy
While in praise of dear woman I sing
Confin'd not to moll, nell, or nancy,
But mates from the beggar to the king.

[ib] Old Adam then first was created,
And lord of the universe round;
His happiness was not completed,
Until that a helpmate was found.

[iia] He'd all things for food that was wanting,
Which gives such content through our lives
He'd horses and foxes for hunting,
That many love more than their wives

[iib] He'd a garden so planted by nature,
Man cannot produce in this life,
But yet the all-wise great Creator,
Still saw that he wanted a Wife.

[iiia] Then Adam was laid in a slumber,
And there he lost part of his side,
And when he awoke with wonder,
Beheld his most beautiful bride,

[iiib] In transports he gazed upon her,
His happiness now was compleat,
And praised the bountiful donor,
Who thus had bestowed him a mate.

[iva] She was not took out of his head, sir,
To reign and triumph o'er man,
Nor was she took out of his feet, sir,
By man to be trampl'd upon:

[ivb] But she was took out of his side, sir,
His equal and partner to be,
But as they're united in one, sir,
The man is the top of the tree.

[va] Then let not the fair be despised,
      By Man, as she's part of himself,
      For Woman by Adam was prized,
      More than the whole globe full of wealth

[vb] The Man without Woman's a Beggar,
      Suppose the whole world he possest;
      But the Beggar who's got a good Woman,
      With more than the world he is blest.

This tripping anapestic version has no tune in the early variants, but later variants have been collected with a tune unquestionably from eighteenth-century theatrical sources. In the nineteenth century it became a folksong, orally transmitted, in Devon, Cornwall, Somerset, Leeds, and Wiltshire; and a single version travelled to Massachusetts, where it became one of the Allen family songs sung at their reunions in Medfield, Massachusetts.

This product of Augustan gallantry, which might well have been sung at entertainments by a tuneful actor dressed as a beggar, is quite distinct from the American version to which the Lincoln variant belongs. The American version is clearly from a religious milieu. The fullest text we have was sent to Helen Hartness Flanders some time before February, 1934, by Mrs. Elvira Forman Willey of Bradford, Vermont (A1). Its unique heading is of special interest:

Lines Addressed to William Doolittle and Ruth Enterprise on Their Bridal Day, by Rev C Makepeace, January 10, 1748

[ia] When Adam was created, he dwelt in Eden's shade
      As Moses has related before his bride was made,
[ib] Ten thousand times ten thousand of creatures dwelt around,
      Before his bride was formed and yet no mate he found.

[iia] He had no conversation and seemed as if alone
       Till to his consternation he found he'd lost a bone.
[iib] Great was his elevation to see her by his side
       Great was his exaltation to find she was his bride.

[iiia] He spoke as if in a rapture, I know from whence ye came
   From my left side extracted and woman is thy name,
[iiib] So Adam was rejoiced to see his lovely bride,
   A part of his own body, the product of his side.

[iva] The woman was not taken from Adam's head we know,
   Therefore she must not rule him, seems evidently so;
[ivb] The woman was not taken from Adama's [sic] head we see,
   So he must not abuse her, the meaning seems to be.

[va] For as she was extracted from under Adam's arm,
   So she must be protected, from injury and harm,
[vb] The woman was extracted from near to Adam's heart,
   By which we are directed that they must never part.

[via] Likewise that he should love her and praise her as his friend,
   Prize nothing else above her till life itself shall end.
[vib] This seems to be one reason why man should love his bride,
   A part of his own body, the product of his side.

[viia] And now most noble bridegroom, to you I turn aside,
   To you a loyal consort and to your lovely bride;
[viib] As I have been invited to write a line or two,
   I hope 'twill not be slighted, what I attempt to do.

[viiia] 'Tis by a secret contract, you now are man and wife,
   See that you both endeavor to lead a Godly life,
[viiib] The book that's called the Bible, be sure you don't neglect,
   In every scene of action, it will you both direct

[ixa] There's counsel for the bridegroom, there's counsel for the
      bride,
   Let not that sacred volume be ever laid aside,
[ixb] The bridegroom is commanded that he should love his bride,
   To love her as a Christian and for his house provide.

[xa] The bride she is commanded her husband to obey,
   In everything that's lawful until her dying day,
[xb] Avoiding all contention, nor sow the seeds of strife,
   These are the solemn duties, both of the man and wife.

Mrs. Willey knew the Lincoln variant, and said that her variant was sung "at the marriage of William Farman and Isabel Brown by Mrs. Elvira Farman, April 25th, 1861 and written by her, from memory, at the age of 78 years in 1888."

The early date in the title of A1 is enticing, though it could well be a misprint. All efforts to trace the Doolittle wedding, which is not specifically localized, have been unavailing. Makepeace and William Doolittle are common enough names in New England, but "Enterprise" is conspicuous by its complete absence in the ample genealogical registers of that area. This leads one to suspect that the characters in the archetypical wedding are themselves archetypes. Can it be that a ministerial "makepeace" was needed to restore the balance of equality between a "do-little" William and an enterprising Ruth? Modest as was the original Ruth, paragon of wives, Boaz may once in a while have had his doubts about his gleaning into marriage. A fictitious title, then, would cast doubt on the date. Yet this version is the most complete, and it contains within it marks of written composition: "As I have been invited to write a line or two." These words of the author, either the Rev. C. Makepeace or the mute inglorious Milton whose *persona* he is, were not transmitted to the later American variants. Yet, of these ten iambic hexameter "long" quatrains with internal rime, which are the equivalent of twenty trimeter quatrains in many variants, only three of the trimeter quatrains, vi*a*, vii*b*, and viii*a*, are not attested in some form elsewhere. A glance at them will show that they are exactly the kind of lines which would fall out in an oral version. This tends to diminish the suspicion that some author drew his long variant from the fasola hymnbooks and added three quatrains of his own. Whatever the date and locality, then, the Willey variant looks like an authentic beginning for the tradition.

There is another early New England version (A2), contributed by Mrs. John C. Colby, of Grafton, New Hampshire, whose grandmother, born in Vershire, May 5, 1804, said it was sung at weddings when she was young. This puts it close to the date of the Sarah Lincoln wedding in 1826. John Iglehart's mother, as we have seen, knew a variant in Indiana some time around 1830, and it has been recorded orally from North Carolina, Maine, and Vermont in recent years. But its most flourishing life has been in the fasola or shape-note hymnbooks of the Primitive Baptists, so exhaustively studied by George Pullen Jackson. There it appears in three forms: with a tune ascribed to Z. Chambless of Georgia in the *Sacred Harp* of 1844, with another ascribed to Henry F. Chandler of Hart County, Georgia, in the *Social Harp* of 1855, and with still another ascribed to Elder E. Dumas of Georgia in later editions of the *Sacred Harp* (A5, A6, and A7). Though the musical settings of these variants appear all to stem from the South, Jackson has shown that the folk-hymn tradition began in New England,[6] and thus a bridge to the Willey variant (A1) is easy to surmise.

Hence there is not the slightest doubt, if Mrs. Crawford is accurate in her memory of the text and the occasion, that Lincoln borrowed it from an old tradition. The Willey and the fasola variants all provide a genuine development of the formula, with head, heart, arm, and feet contributing to the sentimental moral. Lincoln may have sung them all complete, but Mrs. Crawford's text has lost the crucial "heart," which was the tropological sign that man and wife should never separate. But the distorted Lincoln fragment contains one stanza, poorly constructed, which perhaps owes something of its character to the gangling Indiana youth:

> and closed the flesh in sted thare of
> and then he took the same
> and of it made A woman
> and braut her to the man.

This is completely absent from other variants, and it has a ring about it which recalls other mischievous Biblical parodies in which Lincoln is supposed to have had a hand.[7] Even the bad rime may reflect a Kentucky accent. Apart from that stanza, however, we must forego in the poem a search for the antecedents of the prose style of the *Gettysburg Address*. Though the first record of the fasola variants in print dates from 1844, it may have existed in oral circulation before that time. Lincoln knew the fasola tradition, and is reported to have sung from the *Missouri Harmony* with Ann Rutledge.[8] His father, moreover, joined the Primitive Baptist church at Pigeon Creek in 1823.[9] Thus there is nothing to impugn Mrs. Crawford's testimony that Lincoln might have known the song and sung it, perhaps with a crude added verse or two, at his sister's wedding.

What is the relationship between the English and the American versions? The tunes give us little help, nor would they be likely to, since their rhythms, anapestic and iambic, respectively, are strikingly divergent. The two English tunes are related, E13 being an "evened-off" variant of E9-10. The three American tunes (A5 = A9; A6; A7) are independent, and some of them have parallels in folksong. But there is no genetic connection between the English and American groups. The texts, however, have been grouped together by such students as Jackson without qualification, and it is hard not to believe that some remote connection exists—in spite of the fact that they share only one phrase of any length, the iambic "When Adam was created," which begins every American variant, and the anapestic English "When Adam first was created," which begins three English variants (E4, E13, E15). Devotees of first-line cataloguing can be misled by these coincidental first lines into assuming more identity between the two versions than strict comparison permits. But, since the one English variant in America (E4) does begin "When Adam was first created," it is possible to assume that the "Rev C Makepeace" reworked a headless English variant. The title, "Creation," in E4 and the first fasola variant (A5) may also be significant, though of course it could have been arrived at independently in each case.

There may be other slight echoes of the English version in the American texts. E3, ib2 ("Until that a help-mate was found") may have suggested A1, ib2 ("and yet no mate [A8 help-meet] he found"). E3, iiia2 ("And there he lost part of his side") seems to correspond to the doublet in Aiiib and Avib ("A part of his own body, the product of his side"). After the slumber Adam beholds Eve "with wonder" in Eiiia; this natural sentiment may corre-

spond to the somewhat Augustan incremental repetition "Great
was his elevation" and "Great was his exaltation" in A1, ii*b*, which
produces many startling variations in the American oral texts
(alimation, admiration, adoration, and exultation). Similarly
Aiii*a* has Adam speak "in a rapture" and Eiii*b* has him gaze in
eighteenth-century "transports." Finally and most important we
have the central formula of head, feet, and side in E sentimen-
talized into head, feet, arm, and heart in A. So, though these
verbal echoes may be independent developments of an independent use of the old formula, there is at least no dominating
argument against a slight kinship between the theatrical English and the religious American version.

The formula itself is old, very old. In 1938 Sister Mariella observed it in Chaucer's *Parson's Tale*:[10]

Now comth how that a man sholde bere hym with his wif, and namely
in two thynges, that is to seyn, in suffraunce and reverence, as shewed
Crist whan he made first womman. / For he ne made hire nat of the
heved of Adam, for she sholde nat clayme to greet lordshipe. / For
ther as the womman hath the maistrie, she maketh to muche desray.
Ther neden none ensamples of this; the experience of day by day
oghte suffise. / Also, certes, God ne made nat womman of the foot of
Adam, for she ne sholde nat been holden to lowe; for she kan nat
paciently suffre. But God made womman of the ryb of Adam, for
womman sholde be felawe unto man.

The Parson continues in the words of St. Paul to the effect that
man should love his wife as Christ loves "hooly chirche," for
which he died. Though there are touches of Chaucerian irony
in this version of the otherwise gallant remark, we need not commit ourselves to Sister Mariella's contention that, since it is not
in Peraldus, Chaucer added it to make the Parson participate in
the Marriage Group debate. The sources of the *Tale* are too un-
certain still for any such assurance,[11] and the formula itself was
a commonplace.

The first assured Western source is in the *Sententiae* of Peter
Lombard, composed in 1150–52:[12]

Cum autem his de causis facta sit mulier de viro, non de qualibet parte corporis viri, sed de latere ejus formata est, ut ostenderetur quia in consortium creabatur dilectionis, ne forte si fuisset de capite facta, viro ad dominationem videretur praeferenda; aut si de pedibus, ad serviturem subjicienda. Quia igitur viro nec domina, nec ancilla parabatur, sed socia; nec de capite, nec de pedibus, sed de latere fuerat producenda, ut juxta se ponendam cognosceret, quam de suo latere sumptam didicisset.

Because of the extraordinary popularity of the *Sententiae* this may well be considered as the most seminal version of the formula. Peter's exact words are found in a sermon of St. Martin of León (1150–1203?),[13] and a briefer form of the formula is found in the *De Matrimonia* of Peter's fellow-Parisian Robert de Sorbon, founder of the Sorbonne and the Petite Sorbonne, who died in 1274.[14] In the same century it had already crept into the vernacular of the Anglo-Norman *La Lumière as lais* (1267–68) of Pierre de Peckham[15] and of a French conte by Jouham de la Chapele de Blois.[16] Another source almost as seminal as Peter Lombard is St. Thomas Aquinas, who says in his *Summa Theologica* (1265–71):[17]

It was right for woman to be made from a rib of man. First, to signify the social union of man and woman, for the woman should neither use authority over man, and so she was not made of his head; nor was it right for her to be subject to man's contempt as his slave, and so she was not made from his feet. Secondly, for the sacramental signification; for from the side of Christ sleeping on the Cross the Sacraments flowed—namely, blood and water—on which the Church was established.

In the early fourteenth century an account turns up in a Dutch version of the popular encyclopedic *Book of Sidrac*[18] and in the Irish *Leabhar Breac*.[19] Chaucer's version was probably preceded by that of Gower's *Mirour de l'Omme* (before 1381?).[20] In the fifteenth century we find it in a Northern or Lowland Scots sermon,[21] in the *Doctrinal of Sapyence*[22] (Caxton's translation of a work by E. de Roye) and in Henry Parker's *Dives and Pauper*.[23]

François de Villon adapts it to his gallant French Renaissance debate in favor of women, *Le Fort Inexpugnable de l'Honneur du Sexe Féminin* (1550).[24] The scholarly Jesuit commentator Benedict Pereira, whose exposition of Genesis was composed between 1589 and 1598, tends to echo Peter Lombard, though he demonstrates his new era by adding certain new explanations which connect the rib with woman's physiology.[25] In a lecture of about 1844 the Prussianist Frenchman Frédéric de Rougemont gave the old theme a new and racy slant: God "took no piece of the head—woman would have had too much intelligence; he took no piece of the legs—woman would have been too much on the move; he took a piece near the heart, that woman should be all love."[26]

In our own time the formula has been recorded from folk prose as well as from our folksongs. A version which well may derive from the songs has been related to me by Professor James N. Tidwell, born in Runnels County, Texas, as a typical ministerial joke among Southern Baptists: "Eve was not made from part of Adam's head because she would have been above him, nor from a part of his feet because she would have been below him, but she was made from a rib taken from under his arm, and she's been trying to get back there ever since." The Catholic tradition likewise has penetrated folktale, for the so-called "tale-less" Quiché of Chichicastenango (Guatemala) say that

Jesus asked the first apostle what they should do about getting a woman for Adam. The reply was that they should cut some flesh from Adam's palm. But Our Lord Jesus said this would not do because then the man would hit the woman with his hand. He asked the second apostle, who advised cutting the flesh from the sole of Adam's foot. . . . Jesus said no, because then Adam would kick her. The third advised that they should take it from Adam's brain and head. No, replied Jesus again, for then the woman would order Adam around. The fourth apostle suggested that they cut a hole in Adam's left chest—the hole to be cut in the shape of the vagina—and take pieces of the heart, lungs, spleen, etc., together with the flesh cut out, to make the woman. It should all be cut out of the left side, because if it were from the right side the woman would be higher and could command the man; the piece of heart should be taken so that the man would have a "good heart" for the woman [i.e., love her and not fight with her].[27]

The earliest certain reference in the West, then, is datable around 1150 in Peter Lombard. The formula has been ascribed to St. Augustine, fountainhead of Western exegesis, but this appears to be an error based on a gloss common to Lombard and Aquinas.[28] An exhaustive search through Augustine produces no sign of the formula, though we remain stimulated by such a promise as the following: "But from the fact that woman was made for him from his side, it was plainly meant that we should learn how dear the bond between man and wife should be. . . . Why God made woman out of man's side, and what this first prodigy prefigured, I shall, with God's help, tell in another place."[29] Perhaps this promise is fulfilled in a later book of the *City of God*, where Augustine explains that "the manner of creation prefigured, as has been said, Christ and the Church,"[30] a technically "allegorical" explanation repeated in Aquinas. Elsewhere Augustine explains that the present domination of man over woman did not exist before the Fall, but is a part of woman's curse.[31] The Quiché left side gives way to the right or spiritual side, which to Augustine signifies that the union of man and woman should be primarily spiritual and not carnal. Man is the head, he continues, but woman was made out of the flesh of man and not of the earth, which is a profound mystery.[32] We need not be surprised at any turn the exegesis may take, since the Christian social structure from the time of St. Paul revolved around the metaphor of the human body.[33] But apparently the fertile-minded Augustine, whose vigorous assaults on the "dark places" of the Bible produced at every point no hard-fixed allegory, but the richest fruits of interpretation, avoided every occasion on which he might have cited our formula.

To find its roots we must take one further backward step, to the East. The rabbis, like the Church Fathers, "sought to confirm from Scripture their solutions of their own doubts,"[34] and it is natural that their attention should turn to the problems of

Adam's rib, and God's purpose in making woman as she is or seems to be. One of the earliest of the great Midrashic commentaries on the Bible is *Bereshith [Genesis] Rabbah,* built around a kernel of oral lore in the third century A.D., and more or less (though not finally) fixed in written form in the sixth century. Rabbi Joshua of Siknin cites his teacher Rabbi Levi, "master of traditional interpretation," for the following tradition:

[God said] "I will not create her from [Adam's] head, lest she be swelled-headed; nor from the eye, lest she be a coquette; nor from the ear, lest she be an eavesdropper; nor from the mouth, lest she be a gossip; nor from the heart, lest she be prone to jealousy; nor from the hand, lest she be light-fingered; nor from the foot, lest she be a gadabout; but from the modest part of man, for even when he stands naked, that part is covered." And as he created each limb He ordered her, "Be a modest woman."

Yet, the passage continues, she is "swelled-headed" and coquettish like Isaiah's daughters of Zion, she is an eavesdropper like Sarah listening at the door of the tent, she is jealous and light-fingered like Rachel, who envied Leah and stole the teraphim, and a gadabout like Dinah.[35] *Debarim Rabbah,* a commentary on Deuteronomy compiled about A.D. 900, cites the same authorities for an adapted comment on Miriam's slander of Moses. Here the eye has become a sign of pride, the head and heart disappear, and Eve is manufactured from Adam's "most private limb, the thigh," instead of the rib. Eve is now the proud one, Leah the gadabout, and Miriam is the loose-tongued slanderer.[36] Other versions are found in some four other Midrashic collections, which need not be detailed.[37] The theme is found with interesting changes in the Syriac *Book of the Bee* (ca. 1222), composed by a Nestorian Bishop, Solomon al-Basrah:[38]

God did not make Eve of earth, that she might not be considered something alien to Adam in nature; and he did not take her from Adam's fore parts, that she might not uplift herself against him; nor from his hind parts, that she might not be accounted despicable; nor from his right side, that she might not have pre-eminence over him;

nor from his head, that she might not seek authority over him; nor from his feet, that she might not be trodden down and scorned in the eyes of her husband; but [he took her] from his left side, for the side is the place which unites and joins both front and back.

A similar passage appears in the *Ausar Raze* of Bar Hebraeus, born in Melitene in 1226, converted from Judaism to Jacobite Christianity, and renowned as a student of many Oriental languages as well as of Greek.[39]

There is nothing to determine how the tradition passed from its Hebrew to its Christian form. Were there sure exemplars from early Christianity, we might assume early borrowing by the Fathers from Judaism, since this kind of borrowing was common enough.[40] Bar Hebraeus might have been a natural channel via the crusades, but the *Sententiae* of Peter Lombard long antedates him. A Spaniard like St. Martin of León might be close to Hebrew sources, but he clearly derived the tradition from Peter, and so it may well be that Peter got it from some contemporary Hebrew scholar of France, which had harbored the great Rashi (Solomon bar Isaac) half a century before in Troyes (1040–1105).[41]

This then is the history of this culturally revealing formula, which begins in misogyny and ends in sentimental defense of women. It is clear that strict friendship between culture groups is not a necessary condition of borrowing. The incongruities are apparent if we consider merely how the Primitive Baptists who keep the folksong version alive today would regard its ironical metamorphoses. They would be equally shocked, we presume, by the sponsorship of Jews, Catholics, playhouses, and that "damyankee" Abraham Lincoln. Yet they climax our breath-taking leap over the centuries, full of traps for the unwary, whether he be anthropologist, bibliographer, historian of literature, folklorist, or just plain son of Adam.

INDEX OF FOLKSONG VARIANTS

Unless otherwise noted all English variants begin "Both sexes give ear to my fancy"; all American variants with "When Adam was created." As in the discussion E3 and A1 are chosen as the standards for stanza numeration, since they are the most expanded variants. E and A refer to the version, the Arabic numeral following to the variant, small roman plus *a* or *b* to the number of the stanza and half-stanza, Arabic numeral following to the line in the half-stanza. Thus E2, ii*b* 2 means the second line in the second half-stanza of the standard version as it appears in the "Old Adam" variant.

ENGLISH VERSION

(E1 [*ca.* 1740?]. "The Honest Man's Favourite," No. 3 in *The Lady's Evening Book of Pleasure, Or, Musical Entertainment: Being a Choice Collection . . . of Love Songs, Sung every Season at the Play-Houses, Public Gardens, and other Places of Diversion, in and about the City of London, &c.* . . . Printed at (No. 30) Cow-Lane, West Smithfield [n.d.]. S. Baring-Gould, *Songs of the West* (5th ed.; London: 1913), p. 27, dates this version "about 1740," but the British Museum *Catalogue* dates it "1775?." The Museum's apparently unique copy is the tenth item in a bound collection of similar chap-books called *Eleemosynary Emporium* (shelfmark 11621. e. 2), made, according to Baring-Gould, by "Mr J. Bell about 1812." A note by J. O. H., presumably James Halliwell-Phillips, indicates that the volume was bound in 1847. i*ab*-v*ab* (5 stanzas).

(E2) [XVIII C.]. No. 10 in *Old Adam. Garland. Containing several excellent New Songs.* . . . [woodcut] Lic[e]nsed and Enter'd according to order. [n.p., n.d.], p. 2. This volume is from the Heber Collection of Penny Garlands (Harvard College Library 25252.6); No. 1497 in *Catalogue of English and American Chap-Books and Broadside Ballads in Harvard College Library* (Cambridge, Mass.: 1905). i*ab*-v*ab* (5 stanzas).

(E3 [XVIII C.]. *The Honest Man's Favourite. A New Song* (n.p., n.d.; woodcut of a king's head at top, and of a man-faced dog at bottom). This is a slip-ballad in the former Harvard College Library Collection, 25242.5.7. This collection, seen by H. M. Belden in the winter of 1916–17, was later broken up and sent to Professor Kittredge for study, and presumably has been returned to Houghton Library, but it is uncatalogued and could not be located on a recent search. Professor Belden, who cites it in his *Ballads and Songs* (Columbia, Mo.: 1940), p. 431 (in connection with two unrelated Adam and Eve songs), was kind enough to provide me with a copy from his notes. *iab-vab* (5 stanzas). Typographically the best of the XVIII C. variants and hence used here as the basic illustration.

(E4) ["about 1800"]. "Creation," in William W. Newell, "Early American Ballads," *JAF*, XII (1899), 250-51. He obtained his copy from Mrs. Emily Allen of Massachusetts, who gives the approximate date. It also appears as one of twelve songs in the fourteen-page pamphlet, "Allen Family Songbook," compiled by Rosa S. Allen with music by Joseph A. Allen in 1899, which I have not seen (Phillips Barry, "Some Traditional Songs," *JAF*, XVIII [1905], 59). Though it begins, "When Adam was first created," it is clearly the British text. *ib/-iva/vb/va* (9 quatrains).

(E5) [XVIII C.?]. "Old Adam," in James Henry Dixon, *Ancient Poems, Ballads, and Songs of the Peasantry of England* (London: 1846), XVII, 230. Dixon knew variants in his boyhood (see E6), but he took this from "an ancient printed copy" provided by Mr. S. Swindells, a printer of Manchester, who "had great difficulty in meeting with" the copy since it had been long out of print. Despite the title, it is not identical with E2, though it may be XVIII C. *ia/ib/iib/-vb* (9 quatrains, omitting 2a).

(E6) [about 1815?]. *Unrecorded.* Dixon says the song "used, in his boyish days, to be very popular with aged people resident in the North of England." Dixon lived from 1803 to 1876 (see *A Supplement to Allibone's Critical Dictionary* [Philadelphia: 1891]).

(E7) [1840–1900]. In Angelina Parker, "Oxfordshire Village Folklore (1840–1900), *Folk-Lore*, XXIV (1913), 82. Hard to date closely. Her mother was born in the village of Barnard Gate and had a memory which reached back to about 1840. But she obtained the song from her grandfather, who sang it "when he was over seventy." Her informant delighted to use it to torment his womenfolk, and the twisting of line *ivb1* to "and how she was bound to obey, sir" helped his purpose. There may be contamination with "Ye Lords of creation, men you are called," another Adam and Eve song found in Belden, *Ballads and Songs*, p. 432. *ib/iva/ivb* only (3 quatrains). E7 begins, "When Adam was first created."

(E8) [before 1857]. In Robert Bell, *Ancient Poems, Ballads, and Songs of the Peasantry of England* (London: 1856, 1857), p. 231, a revision of Dixon's collection. Bell conflates Dixon's stall ballad "from the recital of Mr. Effingham Wilson, who was familiar with the song in his youth." The result is i*a*/-*vb* (10 quatrains essentially identical with the XVIII C. versions.

(E9–10) [before 1889–92]. In Baring-Gould, H. Fleetwood Sheppard, and F. W. Bussell, *Songs of the West: Folk Songs of Devon and Cornwall* (5th ed.; London: 1913), p. 204. This version appears in the earlier editions, which I have not seen (Margaret Dean-Smith, *A Guide to English Folk Song Collections* [Liverpool: 1954], p. 115); the earliest appeared in 1881–92. E9 is a conflation of the variants of two singers, John Richards of Lamerton, Devon, and E10 of J. Benney, Menheniot, Cornwall. i*ab*/ii*ba*/iii*ab*-v*ab* (5 stanzas). Baring-Gould's *Tune* is attributed to Dr. Arne, since it appears as the setting for the song "In Hurry Posthaste for a License" in *The Tragedy of Tragedies, or Tom Thumb* (1734). An earlier form is in Johann Sebastian Bach's "Es nehme zehn-tausend Ducaten," in the comic cantata *Mer habn en neue Oberkeet;* a later form in "Farewell, Ye Green Fields and Sweet Groves," in *Vocal Music, or the Songster's Companion* (2nd ed., 1772). From the latter it was taken over for a pious parody by John Newton in the *Olney Hymns,* now well known as "How tedious and tasteless the hours" or *Greenfield.* See *Original Sacred Harp* (Denson revision; Haleyville, Ala.: 1936), No. 127. For further notes on the fasola tradition see George Pullen Jackson, *Spiritual Folk-Songs of Early America* (New York [1937]), No. 60, and his *Another Sheaf of White Spirituals* (Gainesville, Fla.: 1952), p. 221. Baring-Gould also cites the folksong "The Gallant Hussar" and a scrap written down by Felix Mendelssohn.

(E11) [1889–92 or before]. On p. 27 of his notes Baring-Gould mentions a version recorded by "Miss L. Broadwood . . . from the singing of a baker at Cuckfield, Sussex." I have been unable to find it in any of her printed collections. A nonsense rime, "Adam and Eve could never believe," appears in Lucy E. Broadwood and J. A. Fuller Maitland, *English County Songs* (London: 1893); see Dean-Smith, *A Guide to English Folk Song Collections,* p. 47.

(E12) [1891 or before]. Frank Kidson, *Traditional Tunes: A Collection of Ballad Airs Chiefly Obtained in Yorkshire & the South of Scotland* (Oxford: 1891), p. 153. Tune and text from the singing of "Mr. John Briggs, of Leeds." The tune is a smoothed-out version of E9-10. i*biia*/ii*biiia*/iv*ab* (3 stanzas).

(E13) [1891 or before]. Kidson, *op. cit.,* p. 154, says that "other versions of the song are met with among country singers." I have been unable to check his *Folk Songs from the North Countrie* (London:

1927), to see whether his variant there is E12 or another. See Dean-Smith, *op. cit.*, p. 47.

(E14) [1905 or before]. Baring-Gould also speaks of a version recorded by "Mr. Sharp in Somerset." Since it does not appear in any of Cecil Sharp's Somerset collections, it may have been communicated to Baring-Gould for the 1905 revision of *Songs of the West,* to which Sharp gave musical supervision (Dean-Smith, p. 31).

(E15) [1923 or earlier]. "Old Adam" in Alfred Williams, *Folk-Songs of the Upper Thames* (London: 1923), p. 215. Williams heard it "at Highworth, where it was sung by an old blacksmith, of Seven-hampton [Wiltshire], named Barrett." *ib-vb* (9 quatrains), beginning "When Adam he first was created."

AMERICAN VERSION

(A1) [1748?]. "Lines Addressed to William Doolittle and Ruth En-terprise on Their Bridal Day, by Rev C Makepeace, January 10, 1748," from a newspaper cutting *(Springfield Republican?)* dated Feb. 4, 1934, reprinted in the same month in the *Bangor Daily News.* The two cuttings are in a scrapbook, "New England Folk-Songs," compiled by Phillips Barry and now in the Harvard College Library (27256.31.14.5). The lines were contributed to Helen Hartness Flan-ders by Mrs. Elvira Willey of Bradford, Vermont, who knew of the Lincoln variant and who says that her variant was sung "at the mar-riage of William Farman and Isabel Brown by Mrs. Elvira Farman, April 25th, 1861, and written by her, from memory, at the age of 78 years in 1888." Fanny Eckstorm adds some comments in the *Bangor Daily News* cutting: "Fragments of it are common in Maine, but I have never before seen such a perfect text." Its possibly fictitious title is discussed above. *iab–xab* (10 stanzas, each consisting of 2 short quatrains printed as long-lined couplets).

(A2) [about 1820?]. From a newspaper cutting, apparently from the *Boston Evening Transcript,* in the same Barry scrapbook as A1. Ap-parently it is dated October 22, 1933, since it is referred to under this date in the A1 cutting. It was contributed to Mrs. Flanders by Mrs. John C. Colby of Grafton, New Hampshire, who says, "I was born in West Fairlee, Vt., April 20, 1860. On account of my mother's death I lived with my grandmother who was born in Vershire, May 5, 1804. Grandma told me this was sung at weddings when she was young." Miss Marguerite Olney, Curator of the Helen Hartness Flanders Ballad Collection at Middlebury College, wrote me in 1947 that "we have collected it at least six times, either in manuscript form or in its tune. . . . An interesting fact about our recoveries is that they have all been collected within a radius of sixty miles." Note that the variations "she was taken" and "she was extracted" of A1 (iv*ab* and v*ab*) have become an incremental repetition, four times repeated, of "she was taken," a probable sign of oral transmission. i*a*/ii*b*/iii*a*/iv*a*/iv*b*/ v*a*/v*b*/ix*a*/viii*b* (9 quatrains), much disarranged (lines transposed in ii*b*; iv*a* contaminated with v*b*, and iv*b* with iv*a*).

(A3) [1826 or before]. "Adam and Eve's Wedding Song," recorded and tentatively ascribed to Abraham Lincoln by Mrs. Elizabeth Crawford in a letter of May 3, 1866, to William Herndon. The original letter is among the Herndon-Weik collectanea in the Library of Congress, of which I have a photostat kindly provided through the good offices of Mr. St. George L. Sioussat, Curator of Manuscripts. The Huntington Library possesses a copy of the letter by Ward Lamon, and I owe thanks to Miss Norma Cuthbert of that library for aid in tracing the original. A3 appears frequently in biographies of Lincoln and collections of his work (with Herndon's "corrections"): William Herndon, *Life of Lincoln* (Cleveland: 1938 [1888]), p. 43; Ward H. Lamon, *The Life of Abraham Lincoln* (Boston: 1872), p. 61; John G. Nicolay and John Hay, *Complete Works of Abraham Lincoln* (Harrogate, Tenn.: 1894), I, 288; Carl Sandburg, *Abraham Lincoln: The Prairie Years* (New York: 1926), I, 53; *Lincoln the Poet*, compiled by the Poet Hunter (2nd ed.; New Orleans: 1941), p. 26; Charles G. Vannest, *Lincoln the Hoosier* (St. Louis, Mo.: 1928), p. 127; Sister Mariella, "The Parson's Tale and the Marriage Group," in *MLN*, LIII (1938), 255; Roy P. Basler et al., *The Collected Works of Abraham Lincoln* (New Brunswick, N. J.: 1952–53), VIII, 430; for further remarks see J. R. Perry, "The Poetry of Lincoln," *North American Review*, 193 (1911), 213; Albert Beveridge, *Abraham Lincoln, 1809-1858*, I, 84; George Pullen Jackson, *Down-East Spirituals and Others* (New York: 1939), p. 77. i*a*/i*b*/ii*a*/new quatrain/iii*b*/ iv*b*/iv*a*/v*a* (8 quatrains).

(A4) [about 1830?]. *Unrecorded*. See John E. Iglehart, "Correspondence between Lincoln Historians and This Society," *Proceedings of the Southeastern Indiana Historical Society . . . Indiana Historical Commission Bulletin*, No. 18 (Oct., 1923), 63–88. Iglehart's main thesis (also held by Ida Tarbell) is that Lincoln was much influenced by British settlers in Gentryville, Indiana, and he is therefore sceptical about Lincoln's authorship. "I remember hearing my mother recite the entire poem, so frequently that there is even now at the age of nearly seventy-five not an unfamiliar line in the poem." His mother was born in Somerham, Huntingdonshire, in 1817, and came to this country, where she may have learned it from the young folks of British extraction in Mark Wheeler's family. (Her mother had married Mark Wheeler upon coming to Indiana.) Unfortunately Iglehart gives no version for comparison, so his mother may have sung the Lincoln variant. Charles Vannest, *Lincoln the Hoosier*, pp. 126–28, accepts Iglehart's arguments.

(A5) [1844]. "Creation," *The Sacred Harp*, compiled by B. F. White and E. J. King (Philadelphia: 1844), p. 115. I have been unable to consult this first edition of one of the most important fasola hymnbooks. Professor Wayland D. Hand of UCLA, which now possesses George Pullen Jackson's collection of such books, has kindly informed me that the 1859 edition has a pencilled note by Jackson which indicates that the 1859 tune, there ascribed to "Z. Chambless" of Georgia, is also in the 1844 edition. Jackson in a private communication to me confirms the opinion that this is the earliest recorded version of the *Tune*. I have not seen the tune, but apparently it is related to that of Sharp–Karpeles (A9). iab (2 quatrains only, with tune extending to make a long quatrain like the arrangement in A1).

(A6) [1854.] "Wedlock," *The Social Harp*, compiled by John G. McCurry (Philadelphia: 1855), and later reprints. Attributed to McCurry's contemporary, Henry F. Chandler, of Hart County, Georgia. For text and *tune* see George Pullen Jackson, *White Spirituals in the Southern Uplands* (Chapel Hill: 1933), p. 198; John A. and Alan Lomax, *American Ballads and Folk Songs* (New York: 1935), p. 567; Jackson, *Spiritual Folk-Songs*, p. 41; Olin Downes and Ellie Siegmeister, *A Treasury of American Song* (New York: 1940), p. 100. Jackson relates the tune to that of "The Little Family" (*White Spirituals*, p. 196) and to a tune recorded for "Joe Bowers" in John Harrington Cox, *Folk-Songs of the South* (Cambridge, Mass.: 1925), p. 527 (the last seems remotely related, if at all). Jackson also gives references to "Johnny German" in Sharp-Karpeles, II, 256; to "I Rode My Little Horse" in Baring-Gould, *Songs of the West*, No. 101; and to "The Auld House" in *Lyric Gems of Scotland;* and in *Musical Quarterly*, XXII (1936), 166, he suggests that Stephen Foster's "Virginia Belle" leans melodically on the tune. iab (2 quatrains, arranged with the tune as one long quatrain).

(A7) [1869] "Edmonds," *The Sacred Harp* (1869), p. 115. This is a new *tune,* called "original" and ascribed to Elder E. Dumas; its name is in honor of Elder Troup Edmonds, who aided in the 1869 revision. This variant remains in Dr. R. D. Blackshear's Panama City, Florida, edition of 1902; in the *Original Sacred Harp* of 1911, compiled by Joe S. James and printed in Atlanta, Georgia; and in the *Original Sacred Harp* of 1936, revised by Denson and printed in Haleyville, Alabama. Jackson used the 1911 edition for his text and tune in *Spiritual Folk-Songs,* p. 74; see also *Down-East Spirituals,* p. 77. Carl Carmer heard it as "Edmunds" at Sand Mountain Church, Alabama, along with a sermon about "the solemn duties of every man and wife" (*Stars Fell on Alabama* [New York: 1934], pp. 56–57). In a letter Jackson says that he is quite sure the song does not turn up in other fasola collections except in the innumerable reprints of *Social Harp* and *Sacred Harp* (which, typically, becomes *Original Sacred Harp* in 1911). Jackson continues, "The song was a little offside, anyway. It is practically never sung in Sacred Harp circles today, though they allowed it to remain" in the later editions. iab/iiaiva/vbviiib/xa (remodeled) iib/vaivb/ixbxa/xb. The extreme disarrangement of the 13 quatrains perhaps is an indication of oral channels since A1, if that is the original. Quatrain xa is now a doublet, with a remodeled form:

> The woman is commanded to do her husband's will,
> In everything that's lawful, her duty to fulfill.

(A8) [1914 or before] Variant printed in the *Lenoir* [North Carolina] *Times* (or *News?*) by J. L. Nelson, Jr., "as sung from memory by Mrs. Nancy Coffee, aged 84." (The cutting is dated Jan. 27, 1914.) A note by A. C. Sherrill says that Mrs. Coffee "never had any knowledge of letters" and "learned many hymns when she was young by hearing others sing them." Professor Newman I. White sent me a copy when he was editing the Brown Collection; it has since appeared in Henry M. Belden and Arthur Palmer Hudson, *Folk Songs from North Carolina (The Frank C. Brown Collection of North Carolina Folklore),* III (1952), 84. iab/iiab/iiavib/ivab/vab/ixaviiib/viia1 + ixb2 + xb (14 quatrains).

(A9) [1918] Variant sung by Mr. Jasper Robertson at Burnsville, North Carolina, September 29, 1918, and recorded with *tune* by Cecil J. Sharp, *English Folk Songs from the Southern Appalachians,* ed.

Maud Karpeles (London: 1932), II, 272; reprinted in Jackson, *Down-East Spirituals,* p. 76. Jackson relates it to a capstan shanty tune, "The Banks of Newfoundland," recorded in *JFSS,* V, 300. (I have been unable to consult this reference.) It does not correspond to the tune of the same song recorded in Nova Scotia (William Main Doerflinger, *Shantymen and Shantyboys* [New York: 1951], p. 123). *iab/iiab/ivab/ vab/viia*1 + ix*b* + x*b* (10 quatrains). The mixed form of the last long quatrain shows close relationship to A8.

(A10) [1936 or before] "Adam and Eve," contributed by Miss Sadie Johnson of Dehart or Randleman, North Carolina, as sung by her grandmother in 1936. Sent to me by Professor White and in part included in Belden and Hudson, *Folk Songs from North Carolina,* p. 85. *ia/ib/iia/iib/iiia/iva*1 + *ivb*2/*ivb*1 + *iva*2/*vb/va/ixa*1 + ix-*b*2/x*b/viiib.*

(A11) Other Maine "fragments"; see A1.

(A12) Other Vermont variants; see A2.

Notes

1. A first raid on the many problems in this study was made at a meeting of the American Folklore Society in 1945. Since then, I have been helped by several scholars to discover new versions and other essential knowledge. For their assistance to me I owe a grateful acknowledgment to George Pullen Jackson, Newman Ivey White, Henry M. Belden, Marguerite Olney, Archer Taylor, Wayland Hand, and Claude Simpson, Jr., as well as the staffs of the British Museum, the Huntington Library, and the Library of Congress. It is appropriate to offer such a study to a man who has helped us all at times, Stith Thompson, whose great grandmother was a cousin and friend of Nancy Hanks, and whose Indiana associations recall those of the early Lincoln.

2. From a photostat in the Library of Congress (see A3).

3. *Life of Lincoln* (Cleveland: 1938 [1888]), p. 43.

4. See comments on A4.

5. *Down-East Spirituals and Others* (New York: 1939), p. 76. In a letter to me written before his death, in 1953, he said: "I do not feel that we should look on Fasola as coming from Lincoln. . . . If Lincoln had been a minstrel and had had their means of distributing their wares, 'his' version might have spread and become influential. But he wasn't a minstrel. He wasn't, if my impression is correct, even a fairly good singer. . . . The geography of Lincoln's youth would seem to point to his having heard and learned 'Wedlock' words, if not tune, in much the same traditional form as those other southern findings and recordings."

6. Jackson, *Down-East Spirituals,* p. 4.

7. Carl Sandburg, *Abraham Lincoln: The Prairie Years* (New York: 1926), I, 54–56.

8. Sandburg, I, 181–84. (There are many other references to Lincoln's contact with folksong in the volume.) The *Missouri Harmony* is dated 1808 by Sandburg, but Jackson (*White Spirituals in the Southern Uplands* [Chapel Hill: 1933], 24–25, 38–42) dates it 1820. Wayland Hand reports that the volume in the Jackson collection at UCLA does not contain our song.

9. Albert J. Beveridge, *Abraham Lincoln, 1809-1858* (Boston and New York: 1928), I, 71.

10. "The Parson's Tale and the Marriage Group," *MLN*, LIII (1938), 251–56. Besides a folksong or two, she cites St. Martin of León, Robert de Sorbon, and the fifteenth-century sermon. See her request for further parallels in *Notes and Queries*, CLXXI (1936), 119, and Otto F. Babler's citation of two Hebrew parallels, *ibid.*, 229. The passage is from *Parson's Tale* X, 925–29 (Robinson).

11. Germaine Dempster gives no parallel in the citations from Raymond of Pennaforte, Peraldus, Frère Laurent, and the Anglo-Norman *Compileison* in her study of the *Parson's Tale* for W. F. Bryan and Germaine Dempster, *Sources and Analogues of Chaucer's Canterbury Tales* (Chicago: 1941), pp. 723–60.

12. Migne, *PL* CXCII, cols. 687–88 (Book ii, dist. xviii.3). On the date see Dr. Bernhard Geyer, *Die Patristische und Scholastische Philosophie* (Ueberweg's *Grundriss* II), 12th ed., Graz: Akademische Druck, 1951, p. 274. A briefer form appears in the *Abbreviationes* of Lombard's *Sententiae* by Magister Bandini; see Migne, *PL* CXCII, 1046.

13. Migne, *PL* CCVIII, 583. St. Martin borrows more than a column of Migne's fine print from Lombard without acknowledgement, in his *Sermo Septimus in Septuagesima II*. St. Martin visited France in his youth and may have obtained it then. See his life by Athanasius de Lobera in the Bollandist *Acta Sanctorum, Februarii Tomus Secundus* (Paris and Rome: 1864), p. 370. There is nothing corresponding in the *Glossa Ordinaria* (see Migne CXIII, 90), which both might have used. The *Glossa* contents itself with a quotation from St. Gregory the Great announcing that man should rule and woman be ruled.

14. Mariella, p. 252 (from Hauréau). On Robert see Hastings Rashdall, *The Universities of Europe in the Middle Ages*, ed. F. M. Powicke and A. B. Emden, 3 vols. (Oxford: 1936), I, 457, 497, 536–37.

15. Ch. V. Langlois, *La vie en France au Moyen Age* (Paris: 1928), IV, 82; for date see Johan Vising, *Anglo-Norman Language & Literature* (London: 1923), p. 17.

16. *Le Conte Dou Barril*, ed. Robert C. Bates (New Haven: 1932), p. 7.

17. Part I, Third Number, Question 92, Article 3, tr. Anton C. Pegis, *The Basic Writings of Thomas Aquinas*, I, 882–83. On the date of the first part see Geyer, p. 425. The Latin shows no verbal resemblance to Peter Lombard.

18. Johannes Fredericus Josephus van Tol, ed. *Het Boek van Sidrac in de Nederlanden* (Amsterdam: 1936), p. 173. This is based on a thirteenth-century French *Livre*, which I have been unable to consult, but Italian and German versions do not contain the formula.

19. *The Codex Palatino-Vaticanus, No. 830*, ed. and tr. B. MacCarthy (Dublin: 1892), p. 49; for the date of the compilation see Douglas Hyde, *A Literary History of Ireland* (London: 1899), p. 470.

20. *The Complete Works of John Gower,* ed. G. C. Macaulay (Oxford: 1899), I, 203 (for the date see p. xliii).

21. Mariella, p. 253 (from Owst); the MS is Cambridge University Library Gg. vl. [*sic*] 16, fol. 29b.

22. Westminster, 1489 [British Museum IB 55129], fol. 15ʳ.

23. Westminster: Wynkyn de Worde, 1496 [British Museum IB 55194], fol. 04.

24. Lulu M. Richardson, *The Forerunners of Feminism in French Literature* (Baltimore and Paris: 1929), p. 96.

25. R. P. Benedicti Pererii Valentini . . . *Commentariorvm et Disputationvm in Genesim* (Coloniae Agrippinae: 1601), I, 208 (which I have seen in a copy kindly lent me by Professor Arnold Williams). For Pereira's date see Williams, *The Common Expositor* (Chapel Hill: 1948), p. 273.

26. Carl Vogt, *Lectures on Man,* ed. James Hart (London: 1864), p. 3.

27. Sol Tax, "Folk-Tales in Chichicastenango: An Unsolved Puzzle," *JAF,* LXII (1949), 128. (The tales were collected in 1934–40.)

28. See, for instance, Th. H. van de Velde, *Ideal Marriage* (New York: 1930), pp. 48–49. The Aquinas passage I have cited is often glossed with an allusion to Augustine's *De Genesi ad Litteram* x. 26, but this does not refer to the formula. The Lombard text in Migne that I have cited refers to the same commentary, ix.13, but this explains in another fashion the choice of the rib.

29. *De Civitate Dei* xii. 27, tr. Whitney J. Oates, *Basic Writings of Saint Augustine* (New York: 1948), II, 208.

30. xxii. 17; Oates, II, 637. For the sacramental explanation see also Augustine's *De Bono Conjugali* I. i. 1 (Migne, *PL* XL, 373) and *In Joannis Evangelium* ix. 10 (*PL* XXXV, 1463); Hugh of St. Victor's *Summa Sententiarum* iii. 2 (*PL* CLXXII, 92–93); and Rabanus Maurus's *Comentarii in Genesim* i. 14 (*PL* CVII, 484).

31. *De Genesi ad Litteram* xi. 37 (*PL* XXXIV, 450).

32. *De Genesi contra Manichaeos* ii. 12 (*PL* XXXIV, 205). In *De Civitate Dei* xxii. 17 Augustine objects to those who say that this is an anagogical sign that woman, made from a man, shall rise after Judgment as a man. Later defenders (like the Syriac Solomon al-Basrah quoted below) argue that it means that woman is made of cleaner and finer stuff than man. See Frederick J. Furnivall, ed., *Hoccleve's Works: III. The Regement of Princes* (London [EETSES LXXII]: 1897), pp. 184–85; St. Bernardino of Siena in G. G. Coulton, *Life in the Middle Ages* (New York: 1935), I, 222; *Leabhar Breac* in MacCarthy (*Codex*) as cited, p. 49; Richardson, *Forerunners of Feminism,* pp. 18, 37–39, 55–56, 69, 71, 96–98, 117, 135; Alfred Williams, *Folk-Songs of the Upper Thames* (London: 1923), p. 269.

33. I Corinthians xi. 3; Ephesians v. 23; Shakespeare, *The Tempest* I. ii. 469 (see Horace H. Furness, *A New Variorum Edition,* IX [Philadelphia: 1892], 90–91); Charles H. McIlwain, *The Growth of Political Thought in the West* (New York: 1932), p. 321; Augustine, *In Joannis Evangelium* xv. 8 (*PL,* XXXV, 1513). The metaphor is not necessarily Christian; among the Basuto lower wives are called *serete* ("heels"); see Sir James G. Frazer, *Folk-Lore in the Old Testament* (London: 1919), I, 546.

34. Henry O. Taylor, *The Mediaeval Mind* (London: 1930), I, 69.

35. *Midrash Rabbah,* tr. H. Freedman and Maurice Simon, 10 vols. (London: 1939), I, 141. On the date see I, xxviii–xxix, and Hermann L. Strack, *Introduction to the Talmud and Midrash* (Philadelphia: 1945), p. 218. Strack places Rabbi Levi

among the third generation of amoraim (A.D. 320–359). This passage is cited with parallels in Max Grünbaum, *Neue Beiträge zur semitischen Sagenkunde* (Leyden: 1893), pp. 56–59; Oskar Dähnhardt, *Natursagen* (Leipzig: 1907–12), I, 122–23; Louis Ginzberg, *The Legends of the Jews* (Philadelphia: 1912–28), I, 66, and V, 89; Sir E. A. Wallis Budge, *The Book of the Cave of Treasures* (London: 1927), pp. 60–61; S. Baring-Gould, "What Are Women Made Of," *Curiosities of Olden Times* (New York: 1896), pp. 102–18. For the treatment of the theme in recent Yiddish and Hebrew collections see Joseph Gaer, *The Lore of the Old Testament* (Boston: 1951), pp. 44–45, 344.

36. Freedman and Simon, VII, 128–29. For the date see VII, vii.

37. Ginzberg, V, 89, cites *Midrash Tanhuma, Tanhuma Wa-Yesheb, Aboth deRabbi Nathan,* and *Midrash Ha-Gadol.* Some of these, especially the first and the third, may have dates earlier than Rabbi Levi, but this is an area in which I fear to tread.

38. Budge, *Book of the Cave of Treasures,* pp. 14, 60.

39. Budge, p. 60. On Bar Hebraeus see Anton Baumstark, *Die Christlichen Literaturen des Orients* (Leipzig: 1911), I, 51; and for the Syriac tradition see Grünbaum, *Neue Beiträge,* pp. 58–59.

40. See Louis Ginzberg, *Die Haggada bei den Kirchenvätern und in der apokryphischen Litteratur* (Berlin: 1900), *passim.*

41. "Raschi," *Jewish Encyclopedia,* X, 324–28. The accepted period for such contacts was the thirteenth century, but there are evidences of exchanges between Christians and Jews in France before the time of Peter Lombard. See I. Abraham, E. R. Bevan, and Charles Singer, *The Legacy of Israel* (Oxford: 1928), pp. 292–94 and *passim.*

Wayland D. Hand

UNIVERSITY OF CALIFORNIA

AT LOS ANGELES, CALIFORNIA

American Analogues of
the Couvade[1]

        The couvade is known in many parts of the world,[2] including native North America,[3] but among the non-aboriginal American population apparently nothing is known of the couvade proper, and little has been reported of analogous customs and practices that stem from the sympathetic connection between husband and wife during the ordeal of pregnancy and childbirth. The fact that no traces have been found on our shores of the baffling practice of a woman's getting up and working in the fields after childbirth, while the husband complacently takes to his bed with the newborn child, should, far from foreclosing a study of these matters, invite closer examination of related beliefs and practices than has yet been given.[4] These manifestations are of two general kinds, involving the husband in numerous symbolic associations with the pregnant wife and mother as well as inducing in him, *mirabile dictu,* certain physical symptoms of pregnancy itself. Whereas the physical influence of the *enceinte* wife on her husband appears to be limited pretty much to the period of her own morning sickness, the sympathetic connection between the two, as is borne out in assorted folk beliefs and superstitious practices, encompasses the whole period from the time of conception, and before, through travail itself, and extends on into the age of the growing child.[5]

From the ensuing discussion it will be seen that although the American husband does not enjoy a "lying in" period of his own, where he receives the congratulations and largess of his neighbors, as is prescribed in the classical couvade,[6] he, like menfolk elsewhere in the world, is himself not completely free from the physical ordeal and anxieties that attend propagation of the family. It is beyond the purposes of this paper, of course, to try to establish possible connections between a few peripheral American examples of the couvade and the larger body of material from Europe and elsewhere. This task remains for the ethnographer, the medical historian, or, more likely, for the ethnopsychologist equipped with a knowledge both of sympathetic magic and symbolism. Data supplied by anthropologists, folklorists, and other observers, of course, cannot be neglected, for these materials will show the geographical spread of this tradition, if not its historical depth. Unfortunately, all of the American examples are of recent date, and with few exceptions they are lacking in background and connections sufficient to help establish any real tradition in this country, much less to point with full certainty to borrowing from European and other sources.[7]

Throughout the discussion which follows, it will be seen that the clothing of the husband plays an important part symbolically, and in a few cases magically, too, in the whole relationship between man and wife. Even in the period of courtship, hats and shoes figure importantly in popular beliefs and customs, as is borne out by the following two of several such folk notions current in North Carolina: If a girl puts on a boy's hat, it's a sign she wants to kiss him;[8] to make a person love you, take the bow off your hat and wear it in your shoe.[9]

According to an old Alabama belief, placing the husband's shoes under the bed will secure the fertility of his wife.[10] Known throughout the whole country, and frequently told as a joke, is the notion that some women become pregnant at the mere placing of their husbands' trousers over the bedpost.[11] In Alabama it is likewise believed that laying the husband's pocketbook under his wife's pillow will promote fertility.[12] Hats and shoes figure also in the determination of the sex of the unborn child, for if the husband wears either his hat or his boots during coitus, the child will be a boy.[13]

Georgia Negroes believe that the husband should not see his wife stark naked when she is in a family way,[14] and Alabama whites have a taboo against an expectant mother's crawling over her husband in bed.[15] Evidence of the spiritual bond between the father and his unborn child—and a practice also involving the mother—is the belief that if the child kicks its mother and otherwise gives her an uneasy time, it will desist immediately when scolded by the father, thus enabling the mother to go to sleep. Also, in coming home from work, the husband speaks to his unborn child just as he does to its mother.[16] In another prenatal observance, it is prescribed that the pregnant woman should wear her husband's shoes to keep her ankles from swelling.[17]

Fairly widespread throughout the country, though not treated in the literature, is the curious phenomenon of morning sickness, or something closely akin to it, among the husbands of expectant women. My first acquaintance with this vicarious ordeal came recently when a Los Angeles physician communicated to me a case from his practice in Oakland a few years ago. One day a young soldier just back from the South Pacific came in to verify his wife's pregnancy, he said, because on this occasion he did not have the same nausea that he had experienced at the onset of previous pregnancies.[18] This led him to wonder whether he really had sired the expected child. One of my colleagues in the University of California at Los Angeles Medical School also recalls a case of sympathetic nausea in the father. This happened in San Francisco in the 1930's, but the phenomenon is fairly well known to the medical profession.[19] With only a minimum of inquiry I have been able to assemble from oral tradition in various parts of the country examples of morning sickness, or its symptoms, in husbands of pregnant women, and one such example has been recorded for Ontario in folklore literature besides the better known example from the Ozark country cited in Randolph.[20] A young Italian operating a tavern on 6th Avenue in New York could not keep anything on his stomach, lost weight, and was generally in a bad way around 1948, when his wife was expecting. In another instance a young soldier from Detroit who had fought against Japan was too ill to go to work when his wife became pregnant, and he was unsettled for the whole nine months; in fact, he said, his own nausea was the way he knew his wife was pregnant. This was about 1951, according to my informant.[21] Mrs. Aili Johnson, archivist of the Michigan Folklore Society, reported a case involving a friend of about thirty years of age in Cleveland who suffered extremely from nausea during the first three months of his wife's pregnancy, while the wife herself was unaffected.[22] A similar case of morning sickness involving the husband rather than the wife comes from Fairmont, West Virginia, with details of vomiting and everything else. This was no exceptional case with the husband, because it had happened during two or three previous pregnancies. Two other cases in the same area were also reported, but both of these are without significant details.[23] Dr. Rodney Smith of Bloomington, Indiana, who has practiced medicine in Bloomington and in Monroe County for almost sixty years, tells me that such cases have frequently come to his attention over the years; and last summer I learned from a neighbor that a workman on the new Life Science Building at Indiana University was reported to have been unable to keep food on his stomach when it was found that his wife was a week or more overdue in delivering her child. This is in a somewhat different category from most of the cases noted here. About fifteen miles southeast of Bloomington, in Polk Township, there lives one of the few remaining midwives in that part of Indiana. She is Mrs. Jack Grubb, known for miles around as "Melia" Grubb, and she has delivered hundreds of babies over a period of many, many years. Now in her late sixties or early seventies, Mrs. Grubb remembers a man who about twenty-five years ago lived just below the Grubbs down in the hollow. She recalls that he "jest went to nothing and was as pore as he could be. He'd throw up everything he'd eat, and jest wasted away to nothin'." Recalling the case of Mr. D——, her husband, somewhat her senior in years, remarked that the morning sickness had lasted "the whole nine months." In Alabama, if the man is sick during the first three months of the wife's pregnancy, it is believed that the baby will be a boy; and if the wife is sick, that the child will be a girl. It is not clear from the entry whether morning sickness is specifically involved.[24] The connection between the husband and his wife in regard to morning sickness is also seen in four interesting items that are somewhat more primitive than usual. These were obtained from Georgia Negroes: Anything the father has tasted will "lay easier" on the pregnant mother's stomach; have the father take a sip of anything the mother is drinking during pregnancy, and she will not be nauseated; to cure morning sickness, have the husband chew the first nine bites of a pregnant woman's breakfast for her. These dietary rituals also extend to the unborn child, as the following belief shows: The father ought to eat whatever the mother can't eat when she's uneasy in the stomach, for wasting things on the plate means the baby will go hungry some time in its life.[25]

Before coming to a discussion of the beliefs and practices connected with labor and delivery, I should note one other symbolic use of the husband's clothing, in this case apparently with a negative twist. Negro women along the Georgia coast believe that the pregnant wife, to keep her husband from taking as much "night-time interest" as usual, should put her drawers under the mattress on his side of the bed.[26] A similar principle is at work in a folk medical cure from the Pennsylvania mountains, but sex, not pregnancy, is involved in this case: The husband's underpants, while still retaining the body warmth, are wrapped around the wife's neck to cure a sore throat.[27]

Frequently noted in practices related to the couvade, especially among the North American Indians,[28] is the simulation of birth pangs on the part of the father, with all the attendant malaise and the grunting and groaning. The only example of a farcical performance of this kind that has come to my attention from non-Amerind sources is a case that fell under the observation of an old colored midwife on the Georgia coast some time before 1945. Aunt Lilly was her name, and she was about seventy years of age at the time. She attended a pregnant woman whose husband was from "low-born folks," and apparently not too bright. He made a nuisance of himself throughout the whole period of pregnancy, but of medical interest is the fact that shortly after the onset he began to develop all of the symptoms of pregnancy. He had morning sickness, was short of wind, had swollen legs and feet, and assorted aches and pains. His abdomen also began to swell a bit, but it assumed a "pot-bellied" shape— a kind of "hoodoo" shape different from the usual shape of a gravid woman. When the wife was taken down with child, and the old midwife had arrived with all her gear, she was amazed to see the husband down in bed himself, "a-gruntin' and a-groanin'." Aunt Lilly told him to get out of bed and behave, but he paid no attention, until she finally cut a switch and drove him from the bed, setting him to making a fire and heating water. In her notes, which were unavailable either to her or to me, Miss Marie Campbell has set down this whole unusual incident in detail, with the colorful dialogue and all.

Miss Campbell writes that a friend of Vera Strickland, aged Georgia midwife, refused to wait on a certain woman in childbirth because the husband acted so strangely when she attended his wife. She said that he got into the other bed in the same room as his wife and suffered from the same labor pains as she, making much more noise with his groaning and "taking on" than the wife did. The only difference, Vera's friend said, was that there was actually a baby in his wife's bed the next morning, but not in his.

More and more in modern obstetrical practice there is a tendency to keep the husband from the delivery room, but at an earlier day, when most children were born right in the home, husbands were almost invariably on hand at the time of travail to offer aid and comfort. It is hard to say just how often, under such primitive conditions, the husband himself lent a hand to the doctor or the midwife in matters other than heating water and in generally making himself useful in the sick room, but enough popular beliefs and superstitions bearing on the husband's part in the ordeal of birth itself have survived to indicate that he certainly was more than a passive onlooker at the moment the infant arrived. The most active sort of participation in the work of the sick room where a woman was to be confined found the husband cast in the role of the birthing stool itself. In the southern mountains it is believed that labor pains will be considerably reduced if the wife sits astride her husband's knees.[29] Dr. Rodney Smith had heard of this in Monroe County, Indiana, between 1910 and 1915, and this venerable practice was still in vogue among Georgia coast Negroes as recently as 1945.[30] Other close physical contact at the time that the wife is about to deliver is thought to help in easing the pangs of childbirth. In Alabama it is still believed that transference of the pains to the father is assured if he lies beside his wife in labor.[31] According to an old belief in South Carolina, if an expectant mother crosses her husband in bed at the first signs of delivery, he himself will share in bearing the labor pains.[32] Attention has already been called to a similar belief in Illinois in a transfer of the pains even in advance of labor.[33] In a related Alabama folk notion, the husband need only lay his hand on his wife's abdomen just before the baby is born to stop the downward movement of the child for awhile. Also found in Alabama is an exception to the belief that help is afforded by the presence or activity of the father, for it is thought that a woman's misery in labor will increase, not decrease, if her husband enters the room.[34] There is also a strange folk belief relating to the husband's activity at the time of his wife's delivery. I collected it in Los Angeles in 1953, but this superstition stems ultimately from the Philippine Islands: If the husband goes down the ladder of the house head first, this symbolic act will in some strange way ease the wife's pains when she comes to childbed.[35]

As in other phases of the sex relationship, where the symbols of male and female clothing are so prominently employed (viz., hats, shoes, garters, handkerchiefs, etc.), these symbols—or some of them—figure also in beliefs and practices dealing with birth. Unique for the United States, I believe, is a superstition that the Brownes collected in Prattville, Alabama, in 1953: To lessen childbirth pain, put the husband's folded breeches under the wife's back. The prominence of trousers as a symbol of transference of the pains to the husband himself is well known in Ireland, and elsewhere in Europe, and no doubt other examples of this in the United States exist somewhere in the literature; and they can still be turned up in oral tradition.[36] Nowhere in North America do I find the use of shoes to facilitate childbirth, but cases doubtless exist. It would be strange indeed not to find traces of this use of shoes in view of the almost world-wide prominence of footgear in the symbolism of sex and fertility.[37]

To ease the pangs of childbirth the wearing of the husband's hat is prescribed both by white and colored folk in Southern states[38] adjoining Alabama, and this custom is also known in South Carolina,[39] and doubtless elsewhere. Somehow connected with these ancient customs is the practice of burning the father's hat after the child is born.[40] Old Jack Grubb of Polk Township in Monroe County, Indiana, now eighty-four, remembers that as a lad of eight or so he sat in a room where there was a new baby and that he watched in amazement as women from the neighborhood came in, seized the husband's hat, and burned it, amid loud talking and laughter. He said, "They used to burn fellers' hats, or carry them off every once in a while." The unborn child also figures in these hat-and-cap rituals somehow. Randolph notes the taboo against making a cap or other headgear for a baby before it is born and tells of the destruction (by burning, too!) that awaits such handiwork if the taboo is not observed.[41]

After this article was written, Miss Campbell sent me a strange account of ritualistic burning—this time a man's pants, not his hat. I reproduce it here just as Miss Campbell wrote it:

This story comes from Vera Strickland, who lives about halfway between Bowdon and Carrollton, Georgia. She is an aging Negro midwife licensed by the Georgia Department of Public Health Nursing. She has had long years of practice in her profession. She says this happened years ago—she does not remember the date—when she was visiting a relative in a country community where she herself was a stranger. While there, she was called on to deliver the first baby of a young Negro couple. The baby turned out to be twins, and the father, in his pride, dressed himself up in his best clothes and went to tell the great news around the neighborhood. The old grandmother, who huddled in the warmest corner by the fire, muttered her disapproval and spoke some kind of warning to him. Vera, busy with the mother and babies, paid little attention. Some of his friends brought him home that night—gay with a few drinks. In their celebrating, they stripped off his pants and burned them in a bonfire of dry grass and brush in the edge of a cotton field beyond the barn. "He came to the house," said Vera, "in his drawer tail. And then Old Granny Moe told me it was an old-time way to burn a man's pants he had on when the news got around that his first baby 'got borned.' Old Granny said he got so 'birth-proud' he lost his caution and put on his Sunday-best britches." Vera said she did not know of any such custom in her home community.

In the matter of teeth and toothache, the husband is connected, in the folk mind, with both the mother and her child. I have not found examples of "married man's toothache" in the United States, which is a sign that a man's wife is in a family way; but these do exist, I am sure, and further inquiry by field workers should yield at least some scattered allusions to this old notion.[42] A nursery belief in Monroe County, Indiana, provides that placing the father's hat on a teething child will make it teethe hard.[43]

There are various other nursery-room beliefs and practices which involve the father and child, and also the mother, and which are therefore of interest in this general discussion. The mother's milk will come easier if the father of the baby lays it to the mother's breast for the first time.[44] Of folk medical interest is the belief that covering the infant with its father's wedding coat will cure convulsions.[45] To lose its father before it is born causes the baby to have "thrash" without exception.[46] To cure a three-weeks' colic, scrape off the inside of the father's hatband and make a tea of it.[47] A curious parallel exists between sympathetic morning sickness in fathers vis-a-vis their wives, and colic in the father induced by his child. My neighbor, Dr. Paul Herzog, relates such a phenomenon that came to his attention in Kenosha, Wisconsin, about 1944, including the typical symptoms of nausea, cramps, gasping for air, and coughing. One can easily make too much of the father-baby relationship, as many writers, including the great Bachofen, have, with the mother serving as a physical connection between father and child; and besides, for the United States at least, not much has been reported.[48] Of interest, however, is the following account from Illinois involving a father and his posthumous child.[49] "A man . . . in Quincy was killed about two weeks before his wife gave birth to a child. This baby cried continuously, and the mother did not know what to do. Eventually, someone told her how to show the infant a picture of his father and also to let the child handle something that had belonged to him. She did so, and the baby's crying spells ceased immediately. Throughout babyhood and early childhood, this child was always trying to get his father's picture, and later when grown he would frequently tell how his father had played with him; nor could he ever be convinced that he had been posthumously born."

Finally, the student of the couvade and its modern analogues must at all times distinguish between the real vestiges of the ancient custom and modern humorous and mock customs that have developed. One such has already been noted above in the matter of a woman's claiming that all her husband needs to do is to drape his trousers over the bed for her to conceive. Obviously this sort of remark is a form of sophisticated humor, traceable to the repartee of the drawing room and cocktail lounge rather than to the real folklore and customs of birth. The holding of mock baby showers for "expectant fathers" in various parts of the country is well known, of course, and everyone has likewise heard of the great anxiety for the father as the ordeal of his wife's first childbirth approaches.[50] Much of this humorous sentiment has been epitomized in a saying attributed to doctors everywhere: "We haven't lost a father yet." In considering these manifestations, which run the whole gamut from mild ribbing to elaborate burlesques of the whole role of the father in childbirth, one wonders if perhaps the couvade itself as an institution did come into being without some awareness of the whole travesty of a husband's taking the mother's place in childbed. In 1861 Bachofen put forth the view that this reversal of roles in the family occurred at the time that primitive society was moving from a dominant matriarchal system to an emerging system where the role of the father became decisive in family and communal life; and other scholars, including E. B. Tylor, have, with minor dissent, shared Bachofen's opinion.[51] Unless primitive peoples were more uncomprehending than the record of their civilizations shows—and I am talking mainly about the peoples of Europe in early times—who can believe that anyone was deceived by the hoax of a husband in bed with the child instead of its mother? The visitors who came to offer congratulations and gifts to the family because of God's increase must have exchanged knowing smiles, and in all his outward show and splendor the father must to all intents and purposes have gone through with the farce tongue in cheek. Except among more primitive peoples where physiological paternity was not understood, this demonstration did not conceal the real facts of childbirth.[52] On the other hand, one cannot deny that the husband's open display of primacy in the family group had much to do with the dominant role that he later assumed, for perhaps in these matters, as in most others in life, "possession is nine points of the law."

Notes

1. Besides acknowledging in various places in the notes the help that I have received in preparing this paper, I have the pleasure of thanking Marie Campbell and Ray and Olwyn Browne for contributing so generously from their own collectanea for the states of Georgia and Alabama. Herbert and Violetta Halpert have given valuable bibliographical aid, as has Eddie Wilson; and Louise Darling and Robert Lewis of the Biomedical Library at the University of California at Los Angeles are responsible for the rare medical items listed in note 19. Before writing the paper I had the benefit of a long discussion with William Lessa, who supplied me with some important leads.

2. For a general treatment of the couvade, including its geographical spread, see Warren R. Dawson, *The Custom of the Couvade* (Publications of the University of Manchester, No. CXCIV, Ethnological Series, No. 14 [Manchester, 1929]). Kummer, writing in the *Handwörterbuch des deutschen Aberglaubens* (hereafter cited as *HDA*), 10 vols. (Berlin: 1927–42), V, 1573 ff., has summarized various views on the subject, including opinions critical of the usual interpretations. Good surveys are found in H. Ling Roth, "On the Signification of Couvade," *Journal of the Anthropological Institute*, XXII (1893), 204–43 (including a tabular survey, pp. 228–33); and Hugo Kunike, "Das sogenannte 'Männerkindbett,'" *Zeitschrift für Ethnologie*, XLIII (1911), 546–63 (including an excellent bibliography, pp. 560–63). Herbert Halpert has called my attention to L. F. Newman's article, "Some References to the Couvade in Literature," *Folk-Lore*, LIII (1942), 148–57, which contains several medical references of interest in addition to treating literary allusions to the couvade.

3. Dawson, *op. cit.*, pp. 43–55.

4. Violetta Halpert is working on various American manifestations of this problem, and I had the pleasure of talking over with her the outlines of her paper scheduled for early appearance in *Western Folklore*.

5. In this broad treatment I follow Hartland, who points out that "the 'man-childbed' [which is a literal translation of the German *Männerkindbett*] is only one of a large number of observances by the husband intended for the protection and advantage of the child and of the child's mother. "The close relationship between husband and wife," he says, "engenders a mystic sympathy between them so that the acts of one are reflected in the physical condition and success or failure of the other in enterprises of the other: each becomes so long as the relationship endures, as it were, an outlying portion of the other" (E. Sidney Hartland, "The Couvade," in James Hastings, ed., *Encyclopaedia of Religion and Ethics*, 13 vols. (New York and Edinburgh: 1917–27), II, 635. This view has likewise been expressed by Karl Beth *(Religion und Magie bei den Naturvölkern* [2nd ed.; Leipzig: 1927], p. 238, as cited in *HDA*, VIII, 1308).

6. Although the term couvade, by its meaning (Fr. *couver*, "to hatch"), is generally thought to encompass activity on the part of the father only after childbirth, there is no consistent body of opinion on the meaning of the word as it applies to the whole relationship between man and wife in the series of events connected with propagation. Kroeber has written about this dilemma as follows: "With all this gradation, what constitutes the couvade typologically? The most that would be possible to give as a definition is: the participation of the father in the period of rest and recuperation that is physiologically natural for the mother after childbirth. In other words, the idea is expressed that it is his child, too. Superimposed on this is an endless variety of things prohibited and things required, for the good of the child or for the good of the parents, for a few days or a full month. And above all, there is every intergradation from the father's sole role, through a joint one, to the mother's alone. No wonder ethnographers have come to talk about 'classical couvade,' 'semicouvade,' and 'pseudo-couvade,' and the like, without being able to define the couvade forms so that all specific tribal customs fall unqualifiedly into one or the other class. In short, we have no satisfactory typology for the couvade" (A. L. Kroeber, *Anthropology: Race, Languages, Culture, Psychology, Prehistory* [new ed.; New York: 1948], p. 543).

7. On the problem as to whether the couvade has been diffused from a single origin or has had several independent origins, Kroeber is of the opinion that no answer can as yet be given. "It is not a scientific problem," he writes, "because the couvade is not a definable recurrent phenomenon but a variable series of integrating phenomena" (*op. cit.*, p. 543). There is even some doubt as to whether the couvade has survived into the nineteenth century among the Basques, where in all Europe it is thought to have flourished best. On this point, see Rodney Gallop's note, "*Couvade* and the Basques," *Folk-Lore*, XLVII (1936), 310–13, which is a stricture against Dawson's treatment of the subject. See also Gallop's *A Book of the Basques* (London: 1930), pp. 5–6 (note). Heinrich Ploss, a keen student of the couvade, held to the view that a study of immigration to the new world, particularly to South America, would reveal the answer to the wide diffusion of the custom, but his later editor, Renz, looked for the solution in a study of the prehistory of mankind, and of the elemental factors in the custom itself (Heinrich Ploss and B. Renz, *Das Kind in Brauch und Sitte der Völker* [3rd ed.; 2 vols., Leipzig: 1911–12], I, 211).

8. *The Frank C. Brown Collection of North Carolina Folklore* (5 vols., Durham, N. C.: 1952 ff.), V (forthcoming), No. 4218 (including references to other parts of the United States). For various symbolic uses of the hat in love, courtship, and marriage, see *HDA*, IV, 534 ff.

9. *Brown Collection*, No. 4221. For various folk notions about shoes, see Jungbauer's long article on the subject in *HDA*, VII, 1292 ff., particularly cols. 1319–32, and likewise his treatment of "Schuhband" and "Schuhwerfen," cols. 1353–63.

10. Communicated by Ray and Olwyn Browne. The throwing of old shoes at honeymooning couples embodies ancient beliefs in the shoe as a symbol of fertility, but this custom is losing ground in the United States, and its real signification is unknown to those who indulge themselves in this nuptial sport.

11. Miss Marie Campbell has sent me an interesting example of a wife's use of articles of her husband's clothing to insure pregnancy, this by some principle, no doubt, of contagious magic. Miss Campbell quoted Vera Strickland, aged Georgia midwife, as follows: "She said she did know that wearing her husband's pants next to her skin would help a woman get pregnant and that she was glad when blue jeans made especially for girls were put on the market because it was such a risk for unmarried girls to wear a man's pants because it made their 'nature' run high." Aspects of "reverse magic" are seen in an account sent in by the Brownes from Northport, Alabama, where there is a taboo against a woman's putting on a man's trousers because of the fear that she will become sterile.

12. Northport, Alabama (Browne).

13. Edwin M. Fogel, *Beliefs and Superstitions of the Pennsylvania Germans* (Americana Germanica, No. 18, Philadelphia: 1915), No. 1895 (hat); No. 1897 (boots). Cf. *HDA*, VII, 1319 ff.

14. (Campbell).

15. Wehadkee, Alabama (Browne). Cf. Harry Middleton Hyatt, *Folk-Lore from Adams County, Illinois* (New York: 1935), No. 2508: "If a pregnant woman crawls over her husband, he is going to suffer as many pains as she will have." It is not clear from this text whether these pains are to be of the same sort from which she suffers in either her pregnancy or confinement, but despite its obscurity this item will have considerable interest for students of the couvade in America.

16. Georgia Negroes (Campbell).

17. *Ibid.*

18. Professor Edson Richmond recalls a news item in the Columbus, Ohio, *Dispatch* about an American soldier who figured in some marital situation involving some of the features of the couvade. This was between 1943 and 1945, but I have been unable to trace the news story in any way.

19. Writing on "Psychosomatic Medicine" in the July, 1954, number of *Harper's,* Ian Stevenson mentions pseudocyesis, or false pregnancy, and concludes by saying, "Let no man laugh at this strange disorder, for men, too, sometimes imagine themselves pregnant and suffer from vomiting and labor pains, which is, to say the least, even more bizarre" (Vol. 209, No. 1250, p. 37.) This reference was kindly called to my attention by Professor Francis Lee Utley. Medical literature on the subject is more copious than one would expect, but is not easy to come by. In addition to the generous number of medical references given in Newman, "References to the Couvade," p. 157, there is a general survey in George M. Gould and Walter L. Pyle, *Anomalies and Curiosities of Medicine* (Philadelphia: 1897), pp. 79–80. Of more than usual interest in this work is a statement attributed to Sir Francis Bacon to the effect "that certain loving husbands so sympathize with their pregnant wives that they suffer morning-sickness in their own person" (p. 79). See also the following: William Blyth, "Pseudocyesis Simulated in a Male," *British Medical Journal,* II (1943), 137; lesser items are found in *The American Journal of Obstetrics,* XXI (1888), 731 f.; *The Lancet* (London), I (1878), 666, col. 2 (final paragraph of the Allt communication). Barbara and Leslie Newman report the testimony of London nurses as to the fairly frequent occurrence of morning-sickness in husbands ("Some Birth Customs from East Anglia," *Folk-Lore,* L [1939], 179.) Of psychological as well as of medical interest is William N. Evans' article, "Simulated Pregnancy in a Male," *Psychoanalytic Quarterly,* XX (1951), 165–78.

20. H. J. Rose, " 'Couvade' in Ontario," *Folk-Lore,* XXIX (1918), 87: "It is held by some that a pregnant woman may be free from 'morning-sickness' and from other forms of nausea, while the husband suffers from these discomforts instead." There is no mention of magical transference; it merely "happens so"; Vance Randolph tells of a case in the Ozark country where the wife of the man who always had morning sickness when she was pregnant "was much pleased, thinking that her husband's suffering indicated the depth of his affection for her and somehow made her pregnancy easier. 'My man he allus does my pukin' for me,' she told her neighbor proudly" *(Ozark Superstitions* [New York: 1947], p. 195). This account bears out the notion of the close bond between the husband and his wife at a time that is critical for both of them.

21. This item and the previous one were communicated by Glenn Gosling, Los Angeles editor of the University of California Press, who knows of these cases at firsthand.

22. Transference of the malady from the pregnant wife to her husband appears to be the case here. Such magical shifting of disease from one person to another, or to an animal or some other living thing, is often encountered in folk medicine. See the instance cited in note 19, above, and the curious examples cited by Winifred S. Blackman, "Traces of Couvade (?) in England," *Folk-lore,* XXIX (1918), pp. 319–21. She tells of an English sailor on a Mediterranean cruise who suffered from morning sickness, while his pregnant wife back in England was enjoying

excellent health; when he got well again, his wife immediately became ill. In another instance, a Cheshire woman said, "Oh, I am all right, J—— is bearing the little one this time, and he is awfully bad." This elicited a knowing chuckle from neighborhood women, even though the man was so bad he had to give up his work for a time. (Both instances are related on p. 320.) In this connection see also Ella Mary Leather, *The Folk-Lore of Herefordshire* (Hereford and London: 1912), pp. 111 f., where three instances of transference involving the couvade are given. William George Black's standard volume, *Folk-Medicine: A Chapter in the History of Culture* (Publications of the Folk-Lore Society, XII [London: 1883]), contains a fine introduction to the magical transference of disease (chap. II, "Transference of Disease" [pp. 34–46]).

23. Courtesy of Ruth Ann Musick, Fairmont State College, West Virginia.

24. Millport, Alabama (Browne).

25. Campbell.

26. Campbell.

27. Courtesy John G. Kennedy, Topanga, California.

28. Roth, "Signification of Couvade," p. 217, and a summary under Table I, pp. 228 f.

29. Roland D. Carter, "Mountain Superstitions," *Tennessee Folklore Society Bulletin*, X, No. 1 (1944), 6. See O. v. Hovorka and A. Kronfeld, *Vergleichende Volksmedizin* (2 vols., Stuttgart: 1908–9), II, 558, where there is a sketch of an Ohio woman giving birth on her husband's lap; cf. Hermann Heinrich Ploss and Max Bartels, *Das Weib in der Natur und Völkerkunde* (10th ed.; 2 vols., Leipzig: 1913), II, 191–96, esp. 196, where bearing the child in the husband's lap is noted for several countries, and also for Pennsylvania, Virginia, and Ohio; cf. *HDA*, III, 415. This and closely related practices are also treated in the *Brown Collection*, No. 32 (notes).

30. Campbell. This office is performed only at the actual time of delivery, not throughout the period of labor.

31. Northport, Alabama (Browne).

32. E. Horace Fitchett, "Superstitions in South Carolina," *The Crisis*, XLIII (1936), 360.

33. See note 15, above.

34. This item and the previous one are both from Wehadkee, Alabama (Browne).

35. Courtesy of Louise E. Tomas. What common denominators there are between this feat and an Ozark father's sitting on the roof for seven hours in the hope of siring a male child, is, apart from the obvious acrobatics, hard to see, but both reveal the husband in perfervid activity second only to that of the wife herself (Randolph, *op. cit.*, p. 196).

36. A. C. Haddon, "A Batch of Irish Folk-Lore," *Folk-Lore*, IV (1893), 359, No. 4: "In the countries mentioned [Cork and South Connemara] women in childbirth often wear the trousers of the father around the neck, the effect of which is supposed to be a lightening of the pains of labour" (notes of Dr. R. C. Browne). In Ireland a coat or vest is similarly used, *ibid.*, p. 357, No. 4; a more elaborate account is contained in James Mooney's article, "The Medical Mythology of Ireland," *Proceedings of the American Philosophical Society*, XXIV (1887), 146, where it is related how the nurse places the husband's vest on the woman about to be delivered,

reciting some magic words as she goes about the solemn office. Barbara and Leslie Newman mention the symbolic transference of pain from the woman to a man by her wearing his clothes, and also the husband's donning his wife's clothes for the same purpose ("Birth Customs from East Anglia," p. 178). Cf. Vincent Stuckey Lean, *Lean's Collectanea . . .* , (4 vols., Bristol: 1902–4), II, Pt. 1, 97; also Hovorka-Kronfeld, II, 569, where the wedding shirt is prescribed (Ruthenia). In 1591 a lady of some rank, Eufame Macalyane, was brought to trial in Scotland for seeking the aid of a woman to alleviate her pain at the time of childbirth. Listed among other things that had been utilized was her "guidmanis sark," which had been taken off her husband and laid "woumplit vnder" her "bed-feit" (John Graham Dalyell, *The Darker Superstitions of Scotland* [Glasgow: 1835], pp. 130 f.). Cf. *Brown Collection* Nos. 32, 799, where instances of the wife's stepping over her husband and over items of his clothing are cited. An interesting therapeutic use to which the husband's clothing is put in childbirth is seen in a Blue Ridge Mountain custom, where for flooding (excessive bleeding) after childbirth, all that is necessary is for the husband to take off his shirt and bind it around his wife's abdomen (*JAF*, LX [1947], 184, No. 8).

37. In Suabia toward the end of the eighteenth century a woman in labor was fitted out in her husband's slippers to ease the pangs of childbirth, and in Syria, the spouse's shoes are secretly placed under his wife's pillow for the same purpose (*HDA*, VII, 1320).

38. Wehadkee, Alabama [white] (Browne); Georgia Negroes (Campbell). Miss Campbell has treated this in detail in a chapter entitled "The Daddy's Hat" in her *Folks Do Get Born* (New York and Toronto: 1946), pp. 111–18: "After a while I thought of an old saying that if the mother puts on the hat of the daddy of her baby and pulls down on the brim it makes the pains do more work and the baby get borned" (p. 114); cf. also p. 33. Cf. Rodney Gallop, *Portugal: A Book of Folkways* (Cambridge: 1936), p. 85; also *HDA*, IV, 532, where the view is expressed that the act of putting on the hat is supposed to divert the evil powers from the mother at this critical period. Cf. *Brown Collection*, No. 266.

39. Fitchett, *op. cit.*, p. 360.

40. Randolph, *op. cit.*, p. 205. See my note on this subject in *Western Folklore*, XIV (1955), 52–54, where a detailed account is given for North Carolina, together with notes on other occurrences.

41. Randolph, *op. cit.*, p. 199.

42. E. and M. Radford, *Encyclopaedia of Superstitions* (London, n.d. [1947]), pp. 88 f. Barbara and Leslie Newman have noted the prevalence of the belief in the eastern part of England that a husband's teeth are affected by his wife's pregnancy. When the subject of dental service for expectant and nursing mothers came up in a town council meeting in an east-midland town, they note, "one of the aldermen present openly stated that it was the husbands who required the treatment rather than the wives" (*op. cit.*, p. 181). Cf. Dawson, *Custom of Couvade*, p. 13. If I am not mistaken, the Halperts in their work in Kentucky have come across certain beliefs about the fate of the husband's teeth during his wife's pregnancy. The following two beliefs from the Dominican Republic show the intimate connection between the wife's pregnant condition and toothache in her husband: If, upon getting in and out of bed, she should pass over her husband, he will suffer with a toothache which may last till the first pains of labor come to her. A strip of

a pregnant woman's chemise alleviates any man's toothache if the piece of cloth is simply tied around his cheeks with the knot on top of his head (Manuel J. Andrade, *Folk-Lore from the Dominican Republic* [Memoirs of the American Folklore Society, XXIII, 1930], 405).

43. Collected from Jack Grubb, 1954. In *HDA*, IV, 534, there is a reference to a hat used to facilitate teething.

44. Georgia Negroes (Campbell).

45. Madge E. Pickard and R. Carlyle Buley, *The Midwest Pioneer, His Ills, Cures & Doctors* (Crawfordsville, Ind.: 1945), p. 77; cf. Fogel, *Beliefs and Superstitions*, No. 1774; Thomas R. Brendle and Claude W. Unger, *Folk Medicine of the Pennsylvania Germans: The Non-Occult Cures* (Proceedings of the Pennsylvania German Society, XLV [Norristown, Pa.: 1935]), 163.

46. E. G. Rogers, *Early Folk Medical Practices in Tennessee* (Murfreesboro, Tenn.: 1941), p. 37. For the curing of someone of thrush, or "thrash," as it is more colloquially called, by means of a posthumous child, see the *Brown Collection*, Nos. 413 ff.

47. *Brown Collection*, No. 288.

48. There are many assorted beliefs and practices in Europe connecting the father with the child by means of articles of clothing, just as this means is used symbolically to connect husband and wife. See the entries, for example, in *HDA*, IV, 534. The magical use of saliva is noted in County Cork, where the father spits upon the child after birth (*Folk-Lore*, IV [1893], 357, No. 1). A child was protected from the fairies in the British Isles by placing him on an article of the father's wearing apparel (Radford, *op. cit.*, p. 27); cf. also Hastings, II, 638. A fitting symbol of the essential unity of the father, mother, and child is the Alabama Negro custom of planting something for the child before it is born (Campbell). This life-tree token is known elsewhere in the United States, including an example that came under my observation in Los Angeles 10 years ago.

49. Hyatt, No. 10519.

50. Aili K. Johnson has supplied me with two accounts of these mock rituals in Detroit, where office workers are wont to present one of their colleagues "in a delicate condition" with diapers, rattles, commodes, and the like. Between the time of the baby shower for the husband and the time when his wife is taken sick, he daily receives the sympathy and ribbing of his friends, who not only speculate upon his own need for hospitalization but project their worries to the time when he will be pacing the floor at night, warming the bottle, and manipulating other gear of the nursery. I have been told by Joan Ruman that Hollywood has capitalized on the inherent humor in these hospital and nursery situations in a recent comedy entitled "Everything I Have is Yours."

51. See the Introduction and the first chapter in Dawson, *loc. cit.*; also Hastings, II, 636, quoting from J. J. Bachofen's classic *Das Mutterrecht* (2nd ed.; Basel: 1897), p. 255. Further interpretive matter is found in various references given in *HDA*, V, 1573 ff.

52. For an informative article that serves as an introduction to the subject in a far broader area than the one considered in the paper, see Alphonse Riesenfeld, "Ignorance of Physiological Paternity in Melanesia," *Journal of American Folklore*, LXII (1949), 145–55.

Nils Lid

THE UNIVERSITY OF OSLO

OSLO, NORWAY

The Paganism of the Norsemen[1]

*T*he Scandinavians accepted Christianity during the Viking age, about the year one thousand. The literary records of their pagan religion were committed to writing in Christian times, for the most part in Iceland. Outwardly this literature seems to give a beautiful, heroic, and complete picture of an Olympic home of the gods. But when we search the old Norse religion, we soon see that this source material frequently has little to do with the real paganism itself. First and foremost it bears the marks of the late age at which it was committed to writing.

The greatest collection of traditions about the gods we find in Snorri Sturluson's great compilation, the *Younger Edda,* from about the year 1200.[2] Many of the stories thus reproduced by him are assembled into extensive collections of myths and legends.

The individual traits and features must therefore be examined and judged separately.

Thus we find described a long and eventful trip which the god Thor undertook to Utgard-Loki. On this trip Thor fared together with the evil-minded Loki, the swift-footed Thialfi, and Thialfi's sister, Roskva. Among other things it is told that they came one night to a house with a door at one end just as wide as the house itself and that here they took up quarters for the night. At midnight they were awakened by a great roar and an earthquake, and Thor placed himself in the doorway with the hammer ready for defense. In the morning they went out and saw a mighty giant asleep on the ground nearby. It was the giant Skrymir, who asked Thor what he had done with his glove. When Skrymir bent down to pick up his glove, they saw that what they had taken to be a house (i.e., the place where they had spent the night) was nothing else than Skrymir's glove and that the great noise they had heard was but Skrymir's snoring. They now set out together and at night chose a lodging beneath a huge oak, where Skrymir at once fell fast asleep. Something aroused Thor's wrath, and he grabbed his hammer with both his hands and struck Skrymir squarely on the head. Skrymir awoke and asked whether a leaf had not fallen on his head. Thor again struck Skrymir on the head with such force that the hammer sank in up to the very handle. Skrymir asked whether an acorn had fallen on his head or whether the birds had dropped something from up in the tree.

It is easy to see that such traditions have from the very beginning belonged to the common legends about giants. In this case the prototype is a legend about the giant and the ashiepattle, well-known in the popular tradition in many lands, and the same may be asserted regarding the other legends which have been welded together into the great story of the adventures of Thor on his trip to Utgard-Loki. What remains is mainly a contrast between what is termed Utgard and another realm, Midgard, with which we are also conversant from other Norse traditions. Utgard is the home of the trolls, the ill-favored calamitous land, the great desolate realm where nothing is raised or cultivated, in contrast to Midgard, the abode of the people and dwelling place of the race, the home of man, with cultivated fields and holy ground. This view must have been implied in the very fundamental concepts of Norse religion. We also find the same Midgard in Anglo-Saxon, old German, and Gothic sources.

The traditions about the gods which Snorri included in his *Younger Edda* rest to a large extent upon the poems about the deities found in the *Elder* or *Poetic Edda*[3] and upon the productions of the scalds from the Viking Age, primarily sources in poetic form. It is difficult to distinguish and separate what is genuine and actual doctrine and religion from what is merely invention and fabrication. Nevertheless, one may to a certain extent distinguish various stages in this poetic tradition, as the gods must have been presented in a manner which represented the common view during the author's lifetime. As far as the poems about the gods in the *Elder Edda* are concerned, it is safe to say that they were composed at different times in the Viking Age. Various references to the pagan religion are also found in the Icelandic sagas, where one may glean information about the bearing of religion on everyday life. But here also one must take into account the late date at which the materials were committed to writing and the influence of the church, and remember that the references to the pre-Christian religion are the least reliable parts of the sagas.

The most important parts of these narratives about the gods are those which refer to the worship itself—the heathen cult and ceremonials. As for the old paganism, it is not the narratives about the gods but the actual worship of these gods that is of value in the history of religion. This has been the constant element in religion. There must nevertheless always have been a certain correlation between these two forms of tradition, as the cult was the established point on which the myths centered. Throughout this worship the individual god also retained his characteristic traits although one frequently finds him under different names and in other places or at other times.

It is apparent that in all worship of deities the religious cults may persist almost indefinitely, even after the causative background has disappeared. As a classical example a custom which until quite recently prevailed in a certain church in Denmark is commonly mentioned. It was an established practice that, upon entering the church, people would bow at a certain place in the wall. No one knew the reason for this until, upon a renovation of the church, a madonna painting which had been covered with whitewash at the time of the Reformation was found at this point in the wall. It has, moreover, become more and more evident that the pagan cult consisted mainly of ritualistic performances and ceremonials with deistic symbols to preserve prosperity for the people and to secure luck and good fortune for the future. This type of worship had its background in practices which correspond to various European folkways of the present times, especially springtime performances with symbolic representations of growth and productiveness, or mimical vernal pantomimes in which people in allegorical garbs enact the same roles as the symbolic visualizations of growth.[4]

In order to find a basis for our view of the old Norse worship, we must also consider various sources from other parts of the North. The Roman historian Tacitus (in his *Germania,* chap. 40) gives us, as early as about the year A.D. 100 some information regarding the worship of the gods on the southern borders of the North, among the people who lived in the present district of Schleswig-Holstein:

Of these people there is nothing to be said but that at their feasts they worship Nerthus, i.e., Mother Earth. They are of the opinion that she is a partaker of the people's doings, and she drives about among them. On an island on the Great Ocean there is a holy grove in which there is a consecrated wagon, covered with a cloth. The priest is the only person permitted to touch this wagon. He is aware when the goddess wishes to visit her secret dwelling, and he accompanies her with great reverence when she departs in her wagon, drawn by cows. Then there is much gladness, and great feasts are held at the places which she honours with her visits. Then no one goes warfaring, none takes up weapons, all irons are placed under lock and key. Peace and quiet are the only things desired and wished for, until the same priest has escorted the goddess back to her holy

place, whenever she has had enough associations with mortals. There-
upon they wash the wagon and cover, and, believe it or not, the
goddess herself in a secret pond. Thralls are put to doing this work,
whereupon they are promptly swallowed by the pond. From this
rises the secret fear and holy mystery about those things which no
man may know but those who are dedicated to die.

The form of the deity's name here employed is Nerthus, the
most ancient Scandinavian form of the name, which in Old
Norse has become Njord, a masculine deity. It must be a mistake
on the part of Tacitus or his informant when he makes out that
Njord is a goddess. It appears from the description that in this
case two gods were involved and that a human being represented
at least one of them. The name of the Mother-Earth goddess
must approximately correspond to the Norse Jord (Earth) as the
name of a goddess. That Njord in this case must have had as a
representative the "priest" of whom Tacitus speaks appears from
a description of a worship of Frey (Njord's "son"; Freya was his
"sister" and "wife") in Sweden during the last part of the pagan
era, about the year 1000, as recorded in the Icelandic Flatey-book.
The god is here referred to as incarnated in a real human being.
The story deals with the adventures experienced by a Norwegian, Gunnar Helming, as an outlaw in Sweden. He is
sentenced to death at Uppsala but saves his life by acting the
part of the god Frey. It was the belief among the old Swedes that
the image of the god Frey was alive, and it was said that they had
given the god a beautiful maiden who was to be his priestess and
who was called Frey's wife. The god lived with her in actual
matrimony, and, together with him, she ruled over the temple
and all its belongings. In winter Frey in full attire drove around
in the districts accompanied by his priestess. Wherever they went
they were welcome guests. The results of these visits of the god
and his priestess were that "the weather was favorable, and all
the crops of the field thrived in such a manner that no one could
remember the like." Frey and his priestess were an incarnation
of the fruitfulness of nature, and there was great rejoicing among
the people when, after the conjugal relations between Frey (Gun-

nar Helming) and the priestess, it became known that she was
with child.

Although this tradition was committed to writing as a jocular
story several centuries after these happenings, there can be no
doubt that important features in the worship of Frey are involved. The faring about must have taken place late in winter,
when mild weather is a favorable condition for a plentiful crop
during the coming growing season. Like the Njord pageantry in
Tacitus, this going about on the part of Frey and his "wife" falls
in line with the practices of a "bridal couple," adorned in the
spring with growing things, of which one still finds a survival in
the "May bridal couple." Especially at this time of the year, when
everything in nature is awakened into new life, the effects of
creative energy and productive strength, as embodied in ritualistic practices, are felt to have widespread effects, and by means
of rituals the powers of nature are expected to be stimulated to
greater activity and productiveness.

In harmony with this worship of Frey at Uppsala is also the
ritualistic background for the myth found in one of the Edda
poems, in which Frey meets his feminine counterpart (here
called Gerd) in a holy grove, and where the purpose evidently is
also a furthering of the production of the fields. This pair of
deities must have been worshipped in connection with seasonal
festivals. Their images were found on some golden tablets dating
from the early Viking Age, discovered at Jæren in southern Norway. On the best preserved of these the goddess stands with
flowers in her hand. This "goddess" is thus presented as the
priestess of Frey, and we know from the Icelandic literature that
it was a priestess, Gydja, that was associated with the Frey cult
(Freys-Gydja).

From the accounts given by Snorri we also know that the king
at Uppsala must have acted the part of the god Frey and under
his name. Snorri relates that king Frey erected the great temple,
the *hof*, at Uppsala and assigned to it all its income. When King
Frey died, the chief men erected a large barrow in which were
three vents or openings. In secret they carried the dead king into
the barrow, told the populace that the king was still living, and

watched over him for three years. According to Snorri, Frey received his due of the scats in this wise: They passed the scat in through the vents, gold through one, silver through the second, and copper through the third. In so doing they safeguarded the continuance of good crops and peace. It is further stated that Freya continued the sacrifices after her husband, Frey, had died. There can be no doubt that all this points back to a worship of the deceased king and Frey's-priest, a cult enacted in the great barrow at Old Uppsala, the burial place of the great Swedish kings, who had charge of the worship of the gods at the temple at Uppsala. Snorri relates that toward the end of the pagan era it had been the duty of the Swedish king to take charge of the royal sacrifice. A horse was led forth at the folkmoot (the thing) and butchered. The meat was divided among the people for a sacrificial meal, but the blood was to be used for staining red the sacrificial tree (the *blót*-tree).

For comparison one may also note that, according to the historian Saxo Grammaticus[5] (*ca.* 1200) there existed in Denmark a similar worship of the god Frodi (the Danish equivalent of Frey). This god was represented by the king who bore his name. It is recorded that King Frodi was killed by a witch who had transformed herself into a sea cow. Another version has it that he was gored to death by a stag on a hunting trip. It is stated that the Danish kingsmen feared an uprising in the land if it became known that the king was dead. They had the entrails removed from the king's body and substituted salt, and thus preserved the corpse for three years. Saxo states that in this wise they could, with royal authority, collect the customary scats. They carried the dead king about, not as if on a death bed, but in a royal carriage, pretending great concern about the feeble old man, but when the body began to decay, they placed him in a barrow and gave him a royal burial at Vaerebro in Seeland.

Besides this prose narrative, Saxo quoted a poem about the same subject matter, relating that the Danes, wishing that Frodi might live long, carried him about the country long after he was dead. "The sod now covers the king under the open sky in the barren ground." This seems to have been a wailing dirge over the divine King Frodi. In the old Norse Edda poem, "The Grotta Song," there is an introduction relating how King Frodi met his death. It appears from the poem that the giant woman who turned the great quern "Grotti" caused the death of Frodi in much the same way that grain is killed in the quern. The practice of carrying the king about becomes more intelligible when one compares with it the similar journeyings of Njord, as related by Tacitus, and the conception of Frey as a real person, in the story about Gunnar Helming.

It is important to note in this connection that the people held the king responsible for good or ill luck in regard to the crops. Snorri relates in the story of Olaf Tretelgja, one of the kings of the Yngling family,[6] that when crop failure occurred they blamed it on the king, "as the Swedes used always to reckon good or bad crops for or against their kings." The Swedes took it amiss that Olaf was sparing in his sacrifices, and believed the dear times must proceed from this cause. The Swedes therefore gathered together, made an expedition against him, and burnt him in his house, giving him to Odin as a sacrifice for good crops. The same fate had long before befallen another king of the Yngling family, King Domaldi. During a sacrificial offering for good crops the Swedes killed him and sprinkled the altars of the gods with his blood.

Of a similar nature is the tradition about the burial of Halfdan the Black, one of the later kings of the Yngling family (ca. 850). He had throughout his whole reign been most fortunate in respect of good seasons, so much so that upon his death the four districts constituting his kingdom in the east of Norway began quarreling about the possession of his body. At last it was agreed to divide his body into four parts, so that each district might have good crops to expect, each possessing a part of the king's body. Each barrow was called a Halfdan cairn. They believed that the king through his dead body would continue to exert an influence, which from experience they thought was inherent in him while alive. There is a tradition about Icelandic chiefs that their barrows stayed green both summer and winter. One of these chiefs is referred to as Frey's-priest or Freys-godi.

The heathen temple at Uppsala which Snorri mentions was the last great official center of pagan worship in the Scandinavian countries. Through excavations it has been established that the present church is located on the same spot as the old temple. We are fortunate in possessing important information about the temple in the writings of Adam of Bremen, a German writer, dating from about 1070,[7] when the temple was last in use. Here was the foremost of temples, with the images of three gods whom the people worshipped. The most distinguished among them was Thor, who stood in the middle of the temple, flanked by the others. Of Thor it was believed that he ruled over thunder and lightning, wind and weather, growth and fruit. By his side stood Odin, who ruled over battles and warfare. Thor was equipped with his hammer, and Odin appeared in his full war gear. The third god was Frey, who was roughly presented as the god of fertility. It is said that whereas the people worshipped Thor as a protector against sickness and bad seasons and Odin in war, they worshipped Frey as the god of nuptials. It is further stated that adjoining the temple was a sacred grove where it was the custom of the worshippers to suspend the humans and the animals that were brought as offerings at the sacrifices. A contemporary Christian told Adam of Bremen about these gruesome sacrifices, and said that he had counted seventy-two bodies suspended in the sacred grove. There was also a fount into which the heathens were in the habit of casting people as sacrifices. Furthermore, close by the temple stood a mighty tree which was green both summer and winter, and no man knew what kind of tree it was. This must have been the above-mentioned sacrificial tree. It is also related in an Icelandic saga how the Swedes used to stain the sacrificial tree with the blood of the sacrificial victims.

A significant item in the account given by Adam of Bremen[8] is the reference to the worship of human beings as deities. This points directly to the kind of worship we know from the stories about the Uppsala kings and Gunnar Helming. Finally we are told that the songs they used to sing at the sacrifices were so shameful and vulgar that they were not fit for repeating. In Saxo's account of the worship at Uppsala we are likewise informed that the performances were not only gruesome but what he calls indecent.

At the temple, which Adam of Bremen has pictured as a rich and imposing shrine, a large wooden structure with gilt ornaments and spires, we find a combination of ancient nature worship (worship of fountains and trees) and the higher worship of the gods. If we wish to inquire how the sacrificial feast itself, the offering, was conducted, we must again turn to Snorri, to the description which he gives of the sacrificial celebration at which King Hakon the Good was compelled to take part, and where, among other things, he was forced to eat horse flesh. Snorri tells about the sacrifices which Earl Sigurd in central Norway conducted for the kings when they paid him their visits at guest quarters:

It was an old custom that, when there was to be sacrifice, all the freeholders should come to the spot where the temple stood, and carry with them all that they required while the festival of the sacrifice lasted. To this festival all the men brought ale with them; and all kinds of cattle, as well as horses, were slaughtered, and all the blood that came from them was called *hlaut,* and the vessels in which it was collected were called *hlaut*-vessels. *Hlaut*-staves were used, like sprinkling brushes, with which the whole of the altars and the temple walls, both outside and inside, were sprinkled over, and also people were sprinkled with the blood; but the flesh was boiled into savoury meat for those present. The fire was in the middle of the floor of the temple, and over it hung the kettles; and the full goblets were handed around the fire; and he who made the feast—and was a chief—blessed the full goblets, and all the meat of the sacrifices. And first Odin's goblet was emptied for victory and power to his king; thereafter, Niord's and Frey's goblets for a good season and peace. Then it was the custom of many to empty a beaker over which vows were made, and then the guests emptied a goblet, called a remembrance goblet, to the memory of departed relatives.

These sacrifices must have been conducted in temples similar to that which Thoralf Mostrar-skegg had on his farm in western Norway, and which he, as one of the earliest settlers, brought along with him to Iceland. According to the *Eyrbyggja Saga* (chaps. 3, 4), he consulted the god Thor before he departed and took along with him the earth from under the place where Thor had stood in the temple. He cast overboard his high seat pillars on which were carved an image of Thor, and they drifted ashore on a ness in the fiord which he named Broadfirth. The ness was later called Thorsness. He had the temple rebuilt on the ness, from which fact the homestead has been known as *Hof-stadir* (*hof,* i.e., temple; *stad,* place). It was a large structure with a door in the side wall. Within were the high seat pillars, in which were studs, called "studs of the deities." Inside was the shrine—important, holy, and consecrated. At the further end of the temple was an *afhus,* or bay, similar to the choir in present-day churches. In the middle stood a *stalli,* somewhat like an altar, on which lay a solid gold ring weighing twenty ounces. Upon this ring all oaths were sworn, and the temple priest was to wear it on his arm at all gatherings of the people. On the altar was the *hlaut-bolli* (blood-bowl), with a sprinkling brush wherewith to spatter the blood drawn from the sacrificial animals. About the altar the gods were placed, in the *afhus.* It was a common duty to pay taxes for the support of the temple, but it devolved upon the temple priest to look after its maintenance and have charge of the offerings.

That this description of the temple is in the main correct is testified to by present excavations of old temple foundations in Iceland, on farms which from their founding still bear the name of Hofstadir.

Names like Hofstadir and Thorsness are reliable testimonials of ancient worship. And it also appears that such sources are of still greater importance in the old Scandinavian countries, as it is possible to detect from such names various stages in the worship of the deities. According to Professor Magnus Olsen there are in Norway alone about six hundred names of places which point back to heathen worship. Thus we find eighty-five Norwegian farms with the name Hof, which must be definite proof of an established public worship in a temple (*hof*). To each of these temples must have belonged a certain district, corresponding to the Icelandic *godord* or priesthood. There were in Iceland thirty-nine *godord.* At the head of each was a heathen priest or *godi,* who also exercised civil authority. There are also many Norwegian place names which are compounds of names of gods and the word *hof*: Odinshof, Thorshof, Freyshof, Ullinshof, Niardarhof. An older type of place for worship was the *horg,* which is often mentioned in the old literature. In the *Elder Edda* "hof and horg" is used as a fixed formula. In Sweden, where there are also numerous place names that bear witness to ancient worship, are likewise found names of gods compounded with *horg (harg):* Odins-harg, Thors-harg. Another name for a holy place was *ve,* frequently used in compounds with the names of gods, especially in Sweden, where in no less than eighteen cases it has been suffixed to the name of the god Ull alone.

From this system of name formations one may also infer which gods have been worshipped in relation to each other. Thus we find side by side place names which are derivatives of Frey and Freya, which very likely indicate a joint worship of the two as a pair of deities. In other cases the names show that the gods must have been alternated so as to increase the effectiveness of the worship.

The farther back we go the more evident it becomes that the worship was closely associated with natural phenomena, a fact which also appears from the place names. Names which are combinations of names of gods and aspects of nature are very old. Of special importance among these are combinations with *aker* (field) and *vin* (grass land). In combination with these words we find the names of the old gods, Thor, Ull, Ullin, Odin, Niord, and Frigg, the wife of Odin and also of Frey. Another place name which belongs to this group is Skeidaker, found in many places in the eastern part of Norway. The origin of this latter group of names is clarified when one compares them with the many Swedish places named Skedevi (Skeid-ve). These were holy places, "ve," dedicated to the "skeid," corresponding to the "horse-skeid," horsefights and horseback races which were an established institution in Norwegian country districts until about a century ago. But in the olden days these contests and matches were a part of the public worship. The purpose of the horseback races appears from a later tradition, which in Norwegian country districts took the form of "second-day skeid," i.e., horseback races on the second day of Christmas. Such races took place on or around grain lands and were intended to make the fields produce better crops during the following season. We must infer that certain religious ceremonies were conducted in the holy fields, *akers,* which were called Skeid-aker, Odins-aker, Friggiar-aker, etc., in order to secure better crops. And presumably the deity was a partaker in the ceremonials either in the form of an image or as personified by a living person. During their worship of Frey the Swedes at Uppsala conducted dances and performances which Saxo terms weak and unseemly.

There must have been a certain relation between these religious observances and the dedication of horses to the god Frey. The story is told about Hrafnkel Freys-godi in Iceland that he worshipped Frey, built a temple to him, and shared his own property with him. Thus the two "owned" in partnership the stallion Freyfaxi. Hrafnkel threatened to kill anyone who rode this horse without his permission. When a hired boy nevertheless happened to ride the horse, Hrafnkel killed him and was declared an outlaw for doing so. People took the horse and killed him by pushing him over a precipice and in this way "gave him to Frey." The place is still called the Freyfaxi crag. From various sources it appears that the act itself of pushing the horse over the cliff must have belonged to the rite of sacrificing horses. At another place in Iceland mention is also made of a horse by the name of Freyfaxi which was especially apt at horse fights. Frey-horses are also mentioned in the saga of Olaf Tryggva-son in a story relating how that king destroyed an image of Frey in a temple at a certain place in Trondelag, in central Norway. As Tryggva-son's party landed, they saw by the roadside some horses "belonging" to Frey, and they rode these horses to the temple. These must have been dedicated to Frey and must have belonged to a *skeid-ve.* Even in his day Tacitus was relating that the Teutons raised sacred horses in special groves and woods, white horses which were not desecrated by doing any kind of work for men. He also relates how these horses were hitched to a sacred wagon carrying the priest and the chieftain. The horse cult which had as its purpose the increase and furthering of fertility in its widest sense, is also known in a different form from the old Norse story of Volsi (in the Flatey-book). The symbol of fertility (the phallus of a stallion) was worshipped by means of ritualistic performances. This was a worship of the productive strength of the horse, and the symbol itself was personified in a sacrificial formula as a deity of productiveness. A woman was in charge of this cult just as a *gydja* (priestess) was especially associated with the Freyworship.

The religious observances varied greatly throughout the year, being closely associated with seasonal activities. Of special importance was the midwinter or yule sacrifice. According to Snorri this was celebrated for "growth." And it is evident from folk customs that the time from yuletide until the first signs of spring was a period of important sacrificial rites for the promotion of crops throughout the coming season. In the ancient saga of King Heidrek there is clear evidence of sacrifices at that time of the year. According to the description of how Heidrek worshipped Frey, a boar, the biggest obtainable, was to be given to the god. This boar was considered so holy that in all important matters the oaths were sworn upon him, and he was to be sacrificed at an offering. On yule eve he was brought into the hall and placed before the king. The worshippers put their hands on the boar and made their pledges. In another version of the same saga mention is made of a similar sacrifice to Freya at the beginning of February.

This variation in time for the sacrifices to Frey and Freya corresponds to the time for popular practices in the worship of associated male and female spirits connected with these seasons. In the old Norse worship, Frey and Freya were conceived of as a conjugal pair of deities, Frey having been especially associated with the yuletide and Freya with the immediately succeeding period of time. In the Swedish folk traditions Freya is still associated with the same season. It is old Norse tradition that the months following the yuletide had a special bearing on matrimony and the conjugal relations, and the powers worshipped at that period were conceived of as husband and wife. It might be observed at this point that according to Adam of Bremen, one should upon marrying offer sacrifices to Frey, and that all these traditions harmonize closely with what is otherwise known about Frey and Freya.

Frey, as the name of a deity, means originally lord or master, and Freya is a derivative of the same word. The god Frey seems only to have been the older god Niord with a new name. What we otherwise mostly know about Niord, according to the Norse tradition, is that he was the god of prosperity and voyages. But the latter is only secondary. The older place names with the name Niord (genitive Niardar), indicate that he was an Inland god and a god of plenteous crops.

Another Norse god whose name originally meant lord or master is Balder. But about him we know very little. The most important tradition about him is the legend of his death, which was caused by his brother, the blind Hod, who killed him with a mistletoe. There are few reliable place names connected with Balder.

Thor was, of course, one of the most important of the Norse gods. He was much worshipped during the latter part of the pagan era. How this worship was brought to Iceland becomes apparent from, among other things, the description given of the land-taking by Thoralf Mostrarskegg. Thor is pictured as a god with wholly human qualities. He is quick-tempered and violent in his fight against the giants. He fights vigorously with his hammer, Mjolnir, which is described in the sources as a boomerang, returning by itself after being hurled at the enemy. Thor is presented as driving across the heaven with his two he-goats, so that the mountains quake and the earth flames. This is given as the cause of thunder and lightning. He is also presented as a personification of thunder, which is the original meaning of his name. His smiting of the giants on his celestial journey stems from the popular conception that thunder and lightning strike and frighten the trolls.

His wife, a pale figure, is known as Sif in Norse mythology. In

Lapp and Finnish traditions she is called Rauni and must originally have been borrowed from the Norsemen. The name was
originally associated with the name of a tree, Norwegian *raun*
(the mountain ash), and a saying quoted by Snorri refers to the
mountain ash as "the rescue of Thor." The feminine Norse
counterpart of the god of thunder was a personification of the
mountain ash (corresponding to the visual presentations of the
idea of bountiful crops). Thus in Finnish the thunder-god is referred to by a name which characterizes him as an old man, a
conception which is also of Scandinavian origin. In a Norwegian
folksong he is termed Thorekall (*kall,* old man), and known by
this name. He has also been in the course of time included in
Lapp tradition. His connection with the mountain ash points to
a fertility cult, and, according to Adam of Bremen, the god was
worshipped at Uppsala as a god of good crops. In harmony with
this is the fact that in the eastern part of Sweden are place names
like Thorsaker (Thor's field). It is easily seen that a god who
sends thunderstorms and rain would also play a part in making
the soil productive. That the Lapps have acquired their thunder-
god from some such Scandinavian conception is evident from
the fact that for this god they had an altar adorned with green
branches of birch. Besides, the figures on this altar consisted of
a number of representations of Thor's hammer, just as Thor
himself in the temple at Uppsala was equipped with a similar
symbol. And such hammers often figure in the Lapp traditions
about their thunder-god and also in the characters on their con-
juring drums. Furthermore, wooden hammers smeared with
blood and having handles up to two fathoms long were given as
sacrifices to the Lapp god of thunder. Thor's hammer has played
an important role in the old Scandinavian cult, and the Lapps
must have borrowed the hammer symbol together with the worship of the thunder-god. Thors-hammers are referred to in a
narrative about a Viking expedition made to Sweden in 1124
by Magnus, the son of a Danish king. Saxo tells us that from a
shrine in an island Magnus stole "some unusually heavy Thors-
hammers," made of bronze, "and [that] the Swedes still call him

a wolf in the sanctuary, and a thief who robs the gods of their
property." Such hammers have since had much to do with sorcery.

A god who was closely associated with Thor was Ull. It is said
about him in the old Norse tradition that he was Thor's stepson.
Snorri, who relates this, also mentions that he is the god of the
bow and the hunt, the god of the shield, and the god of skiing.
He states that Ull was so expert at using the bow and at skiing
that none could compete with him. Information about him is
also given by Saxo, who tells how he was made king and god
instead of Odin and was given Odin's name. After a period of
ten years, according to Saxo, Ull was deposed and driven off into
Sweden, where, after trying his luck anew, he was killed by the
Danes. Tallying with the information given by Snorri, that Ull
was the god of skiing, is the statement by Saxo that Ull ran across
the ocean on ice skates which he had enchanted by means of ter-
rible songs or incantations. Otherwise not much is recorded
about Ull; but it appears from various sources in the old Norse
literature that he was at one time considered the highest of the
gods. The before-mentioned gold ring which belonged to the
temple and upon which all oaths were sworn was, according to
the Edda poem "Atlakvida," called Ull's ring.

In southern Norway there are a great many place names which
point to the worship of Ull and give an indication of how important the worship of him had been in pagan times. In Norway
it is always some term referring to nature that forms the last
part of the compounds: Ullar-land, Ullar-vik (cove), etc. But in
Sweden the suffix commonly points directly to the worship itself,
as in Ullar-ve (Ull's holy place). Other examples are Ullar-lund
(grove), referring to three localities; Ullar-aker, to two; and
Ullar-tuna (court), to one. And there is evidence that a closer
connection once existed between these places. Thus Ullar-tuna
is a village in Ullar-aker district, just as one also finds in Sweden
Thors-tuna, a village in Thors-aker district. In these cases a cult-
field and a cult-*tun* (the word *tun* originally meant fence or a
fenced-in place) must together have constituted the religious
center of the community. While there is no evidence in Nor-

wegian place names that the suffixes added to Ull refer to the worship of Ull, the suffix is used in this way with another name of the god, Ullin, in such place names as Ullinsaker and Ullinshof. These names are found in a belt of land stretching entirely across Norway. Ullin seems to have been a higher form of the god Ull, since the latter alone has left a mark upon Norwegian place-names, which in the first place refer to nature. Many factors go to prove that the impression one gets from the literary version of the religion is correct: We have here a Norse and Swedish hibernal deity, a representative of the hibernal powers, and it seems that he was worshipped in a special relation to the deities of the spring and the summer, especially Niord and Frey.

To judge from the place names, it appears that in Sweden Ull was worshipped in connection with a goddess called Lodkona or Hern. The latter name is also mentioned by Snorri, who states that Hern is another name for Freya. In all probability the word means flax-woman, referring to a figure originally connected with the raising of flax. In the worship of this goddess the worshippers must have adorned her with the straw of the flax, as the name Lodkona indicates (the hairy or shaggy woman). The names Ull and Ullin are probably to be explained from another common word, *ull* (wool), Ullin thus being the same originally as the common Norwegian *ullen* (woolly). Reference must here be made to the many magic uses of flax and wool and to the use of costumes made of these materials in the masquerades of real people in the seasonal performances for the securing of good crops of flax and wool during the ensuing seasons.

Ty is another obscured god in the old Norse mythology. According to Snorri, Ty was the son of Odin by the daughter of the giant Ymir. Ty was considered a bold and mighty warrior, and men worshipped him when they advanced to the strife because he gave them courage and daring. Ty is the most ancient of the Teutonic gods of war. His name has been found in Old German and in Anglo-Saxon, and he was also the west Teutonic god of war. Later he was evidently obscured by Odin as the foremost god of war. It is apparent from closely related non-Teutonic languages that Ty, like Zeus, originally meant god of heaven.

There were several gods of war, *valtivar* (gods of the battle-field), as they are called by Snorri. Among these Odin was the foremost. In Norse tradition he is the chief of all the gods. He was also the god of poetry, runic arts, and sorcery. It is frequently mentioned that he was worshipped with human sacrifices. It is stated in many sources that men were sacrificed to Odin by being hanged on the gallows and pierced with spears. In the Edda poem "Havamal" it is told that Odin himself hung on the gallows, having wounded himself with spears on the tree whose roots no man knows. This tree—the same as the world tree Yggdrasil—was in fact "the gallows." The context further implies that Odin was represented by a man who, as a mystes, was going through a kind of magico-religious ceremony. The torture and the hanging, both essential elements of the Odin tradition, were means of self-sublimation and initiation into the rites of the "great sorcerer."[9] We may also safely infer that the worship of Odin was involved when, according to Adam of Bremen, human bodies were suspended from the holy tree in the sacrificial grove at Uppsala. We recall that Odin here was the main god. With this description as a clue it has been possible to identify on a woven picture-tapestry from the Oseberg find (dating from the early Viking age) a sacrificial grove with a number of human bodies suspended from the trees.

Place names related to Odin are scattered throughout southern Scandinavia. The most important are found in southeastern Norway and further south through Sweden and Denmark. Names that point directly to the Odin cult are: Odinshof, Odins-harg, Odinsve. In several other places one finds Odinsaker, and there is an interesting group of place names in central Norway, where Odins-vin occurs three times. Names of the last two types, which undoubtedly are the oldest, seem to indicate that originally Odin was a god of plenteous crops. Snorri states that Odin might be worshipped "for growth," and in Swedish, Danish, and north German tradition the name is found in connection with agricultural customs. (In Swedish tradition Odin was associated with Freya). In Norse mythology there is a god called Od, a duplicate of Odin (just as Ull is of Ullin), and we find that Od's female counterpart is also Freya, the goddess of plenteous crops, just as Odin's wives are Jord (Earth) and Frigg, both of whom are, according to their origin, goddesses of fertility.

According to Snorri, it was also Frigg who effected the union of the sexes and brought about the production of offspring. As the goddess of vegetation she was worshipped at Friggjaraker, a place name which occurs twice in Sweden, where also occurs Odinsaker, as in the east of Norway. These are places of worship which point back to very remote ages, perhaps long before the birth of Christ. Here is probably the very starting point for the further development of the worship of Odin and Frigg. As often happens in other religions, the household deity who brought success at home, both in family affairs and labor, was expected to bring the same results in war. The god was therefore taken along in warfare, like any other mascot.

Associated with Odin were the Valkyries, divine beings of a sort, deciding who would be victorious and who would fall in the strife. They were called Odin's maidens. Odin sent them out, coursing through the air, to select for him those who were to die. The Valkyries are a development of the *disir* (plural), a lower class of goddesses who also ruled over fate. In five places in eastern Norway is found the name Disvin, where in prehistoric times there were sacrifices for the *disir* in a field (*vin*). The place names give evidence that the *disir* were worshipped in connection with the older gods, such as Ull and Thor, just as later Hern and Freya were. In this connection one needs to recall the sacrifice to Freya, which took place at the same season of the year as the *dis*-rites (in Sweden, at the beginning of February), as this sacrifice is presented in the tradition relating to King Heidrek. Among the higher gods Freya has been the heir of the *disir*. The *disir* were both the life-giving powers in nature and, at the same time, the personal guardians of each individual.

It is otherwise difficult if not impossible for us to arrive at any definite conclusion as to the exact nature of the personal attitude toward the gods on the part of each individual during the really pagan era. What the sources reveal applies more to the common human beliefs and concepts. We find it difficult to penetrate into the minds of the people to discover the purposes and the compelling motive for the gruesome sacrifices and to understand the organic connection which the individual perceived as existing between the sacrifices and life itself. But the inner bearing and real substance of Scandinavian paganism must have been the intimate relations between religion and human life in its totality.

What is found in the literature about the origin of the world, its destruction, and life after death is, on the other hand, to a large extent the product of individual speculation and has thus never come to be a part of the real paganism.[10] But otherwise the old Scandinavian religion is a very complete, solidly knit system, closely bound up with nature, which could not have taken form in very different latitudes. The names of most of the gods point to the old Teutonic language, but in the case of Ty to the pre-Teutonic tongue. The Scandinavian place names also show that the Teutonic gods have had a long history of development in the north. Probably it will be possible through future research to construct a more complete chronology in regard to cult names and to bring them into harmony with the archaeological chronology. Very likely some names, especially those with the suffixes *aker* and *vin,* will be traced back to the bronze age, which in Scandinavia extended to about 500 B.C.

Notes

1. Manuals with comprehensive references are: P. A. Munch, *Norse Mythology,* rev. Magnus Olsen, tr. S. B. Hustvedt (New York: 1926); W. A. Craigie, *The Religion of Ancient Scandinavia* (London: 1906); Jan de Vries, *Altgermanische Religionsgeschichte* II (Berlin and Leipzig: 1937); "Religionshistorie," by Nils Lid, *Nordisk Kultur,* XXVI (Oslo: 1942).

2. *The Prose Edda,* tr. A. G. Brodeur (New York: 1916).

3. The text was edited by Sophus Bugge, *Norroen fornkvæði* (Kristiania [Oslo]: 1867). There is a metrical translation by H. A Bellows, *The Poetic Edda,* 2nd printing (New York: 1926).

4. Cf. especially researches made by Magnus Olsen, "Hedenske kultminder i norske stedsnavne," *Videnskapsselskapets skrifter,* II (Hist.-filos. klasse 1914, No. 4, Kristiania [Oslo]: 1915), *Farms and Fanes of Ancient Norway* (Instituttet for sammenlignende kulturforskning, Serie A: Forelesninger [Oslo], 1928), and Nils Lid,

Joleband og vegetasjonsguddom, Skrifter utgitt av Det norske videnskaps-Akademi i Oslo, II (Hist.-filos. klasse 1928, No. 4, Oslo, 1928), *Jolesveinar og grøderikdoms-gudar*, same series, (1932), No. 5, Oslo, 1933.

5. Saxonis *Gesta Danorum*, ed. J. Olrik and H. Ræder, *Hauniæ*, MCMXXXI, Lib. 5, Cap. 16.

6. Snorri's account about the kings of the Yngling family in *Heimskringla*, ed. Finnur Jónsson (Copenhagen: 1893–1901).

7. Adam von Bremen, *Hamburgische Kirchengeschichte*, Dritte Auflage, ed. B. Schmeidler, *Scriptores Rerum Germanicarum* (Hannoverae et Lipsiae: 1917), Lib. 4, Cap. 26.

8. *Op. cit.*

9. A. G. van Hamel, "Othinn hanging on a tree," *Acta Philologica Scandinavica*, 7 (1932), pp. 260–88.

10. Cf. the extensive researches by Axel Olrik, "Om Ragnarok," Aarbøger (Copenhagen: 1902), pp. 175 ff., and "Ragnarok-forestillingernes udspring," *Danske Studier* (1913). Also available in a German translation by W. Ranisch, *Ragnarök, Die Sagen vom Weltuntergang* (Berlin and Leipzig: 1922).

Seán Ó Súilleabháin

IRISH FOLKLORE COMMISSION

DUBLIN, IRELAND

The Feast of Saint Martin
in Ireland

The four focal points of the year in ancient Ireland were February 1 (start of the agricultural year and feast-day of Saint Brigid), May 1 (start of summer, increased milk-yield of cows), August 1 (festival of Lúnasa, coinciding with the first fruits of the harvest), and November 1 (Samhain or Hallowe'en, Feast of the Dead). Many traditional customs are still observed in connection with all four.

Another festival of scarcely less importance in Ireland, to judge from the large body of custom, superstition, and legend associated with it, was the Feast of Saint Martin. This occurs in November, and the Church honors the saint in the liturgy of the 11th day of the month. Traditional custom observes the festival both on the vigil of the feast, November 10, and the following day. The identity of the Martin who is popularly honored in so spectacular a way will be referred to later. A rhyme in the Irish language gives the date of the feast:

*Naoi n-oíche agus oíche gan áireamh
Ó Oíche Shamhna go hOíche 'l' Mártain;*

i.e., nine nights and a night unreckoned from Hallowe'en to the Vigil of St. Martin's Day. In English-speaking districts of Ireland it runs as follows:

Nine nights and a night without counting
From the night of the cabbage[1] to the night of the slaughter.[2]

The "slaughter" refers to the traditional practice, still widely observed in Ireland, of sacrificing a bird or animal "to God and Saint Martin" at this time of year. It is, of course, at this period that animals are usually killed to provide the household with meat for the winter, but the shedding of blood for this festival has had a special significance. A copy of the *Tripartite Life of Saint Patrick,* written some five hundred years ago, refers to the saint killing a pig in Martin's honor. There are occasional references in Irish oral tradition to the killing of cows in a similar way in olden times; it was so, too, in the Highlands of Scotland. In the course of time, however, the animal sacrificed was a goat or kid, but more often a sheep or lamb; and even these have now been replaced by fowl—geese, ducks, cocks, hens, and chickens. People who reared their own fowl generally set aside for special attention, so far as feeding and care were concerned, one bird which was dedicated to Martin and due for sacrifice to him when the proper time came. Those who had no fowl of their own bought a bird at the local market for killing, and stories are told of women who walked as far as twenty miles to secure a suitable bird for the purpose. In some parts of the country it was customary for those who had many fowl to give some to their neighbors as presents before Martinmas to enable them to observe the traditional rite. Special markets were also held where purchases of fowl could be made in early November. Birds were often engaged for buying months before the time came. Male birds seem to have been preferred to females for sacrifice.

A secondary source of supply became providentially available when one of a farmer's stock, usually a calf or a heifer, fell ill in the early part of the year. The owner then dedicated the ailing animal to Saint Martin by drawing some blood from its ear, and promising to give the animal to the saint if it recovered. It often did recover, and there are many stories to tell of the evil results which ensued for the farmer who did not carry out his promise or sold the animal. Some accounts say that it was·not absolutely necessary for the farmer to kill the animal when the feast day of the saint next came around—a cock or some such bird might temporarily take its place, but the animal must ultimately be sacrificed at the traditional time, e.g., a cow, when she could no longer produce milk. *"Tá sé geallta do Mhártan"* (He is promised to Martin) was the phrase generally used to refer to such a dedicated animal. In some parts of Ireland it was customary to kill one fowl for each horse owned by the farmer; a man who had three horses would kill three fowl for Saint Martin at the proper time.

As in all such traditional observances, details varied from district to district and from decade to decade. In general, however, the ritual killing of an animal was carried out by the man of the house, by his son, if the father were dead, or by a neighbor who was a skilled butcher. Even women were said to have killed animals when occasion required. The woman of the house usually killed the fowl for Martinmas. This was done at any time between November 1 and November 10, but more often on the Vigil of Martin's Feast. It would not be acceptable to the saint if done after the festival. *"Glacfaidh Mártan roimhe ach ní ghlacfaidh sé ina dhiaidh"* (Martin will accept before his feast but not after it) is the usual saying in this connection. The sacrifice must be made, and at the proper time—*"Níl aon naomh ins na Flaithis is géire ná Mártan"* (no saint in Heaven is more strict than Martin); this is summed up in another phrase also: "the man who will not skin for Martin will have many occasions to skin during the following year."

The sacrificial blood was shed either indoors, outside the house, or in the barn or outhouse. In recent times it has been generally done without any special ritual, but that was not always the case. An account from County Galway describes how the woman of the house stood at the right-hand side of the fire, in the corner of the kitchen, cut the back of the fowl's neck and, when the blood came, made the Sign of the Cross with it on her own forehead, while starting to repeat the Apostles' Creed; after allowing a small pool of the blood to form on the floor in that corner, she walked to the next corner at the foot of the kitchen, repeating the Creed, and allowed some blood to fall on the floor there; then on to the next corner, and back to where she had started—there the fowl died as the Creed was finished. It was usual for the youngest member of the family to accompany the mother while the fowl was being killed, but this was not a rigid practice.

The mother, or father, as the case might be, made the Sign of the Cross on her (his) own forehead with the right thumb, as well as on the forehead of each member of the family, not excepting the baby in the cradle. In some places where the family was grown up, each member made the Sign of the Cross himself with the blood. The Sign of the Cross was also made with the blood on the door, doorpost, above the lintel, or on the threshold; on the bedpost; over the fireplace; on the doors of the outhouses, and on the manger. It was sometimes made on the back of the door of the dwelling house. In some cases, the head of the fowl was thrown over the roof of the house to ward off evil during the ensuing year. All such crosses, even those on the human foreheads, were allowed to remain until they became obliterated. In many districts the blood was supposed to have curative properties for a variety of complaints, and tow or a piece of cloth was dipped in the blood and kept for later application.

Ritual expressions were commonly used while the blood was being shed. Here are some examples, in translation: "I shed this blood in honor of God and Saint Martin to bring us safe from all illnesses and disease during the year"; "I do this in honor of God and Mary, His Mother, and Saint Martin of the Miracles";

"I offer this blood to Martin of the Miracles; may we, and all belonging to us, be seven times better off a year from today"; "I kill this for thy sake, O holy Saint, even though it be worth a hundred pounds, in the hope that it will benefit me." The basic purpose of the sacrifice seemed to be to please the saint and to beg his protection against sickness and evil of various kinds.

The flesh of the animal or bird sacrificed to the saint was eaten by the family soon after the killing had taken place. It was usually partaken of on the vigil of the feast, that is on the night of November 10, or the next day. There was no traditional prohibition against eating the flesh *after* the feast day, provided the killing took place *before* it. In certain places, ritual sips of water were taken by the parents, then by the rest of the family, during the meal. (This drink was known as *an deoch altuithe*—the thanksgiving drink.) A bone of the fowl or animal was occasionally kept to be cast into the midsummer bonfire on June 23. It may be remarked, concerning the eating of the flesh at Martinmas, that this was one of the rare occasions for flesh-eating in Ireland in olden times; it was only toward the end of the last century that meat came to form a regular part of the diet in rural Ireland— prior to that, it was rarely eaten save at a few festivals, like Michaelmas (a goose), Martinmas, and Christmas. This is well exemplified in the saying: *Tá an aimsir dhá chaitheamh go bhfuil subháilce i ndán dúinn, ag teacht na Féil' Mártain, deoch agus greim* (The time is coming when, at the Feast of Saint Martin, we will have drink and a mouthful).

Many stories have as their basis the punishment meted out to those who failed to fulfil the traditional custom of sacrifice. Three examples will suffice by way of illustration: (*a*) A father who has always carried out the custom is sad that his son, who has succeeded him, ridicules it and refuses to observe it; a stranger (Saint Martin) comes to the old man to tell him that he shall have his reward, while the son will suffer for his neglect; the son loses all his stock within the year. (*b*) A poor family sacrifice their cat, when they have nothing else to offer, and become rich during the next year; when Martinmas again comes around, they sacrifice another cat (although they have better to offer) and become as poor as ever. (c) A sick animal, promised to Saint Martin, recovers, but the owner sells it instead of killing it for the saint; the stranger (Saint Martin), who buys it at the fair, fails to turn up to pay for it, though he has taken the animal, which was his due right.

Similarly, a rich reward is given to those who strive to honor the saint in the traditional way. (a) A poor man who lives alone kills his only cow at Martinmas, goes to bed after throwing the skin at the foot of the kitchen, and awakes to find the cow alive as usual. (b) The wife of a man who refuses to honor Saint Martin kills her only child in the saint's honor; the father, not knowing this, returns home and asks that the child be taken from the cradle and placed on his knee; the mother finds the child alive and well in the cradle; a cock appears miraculously at the door, and the husband kills it for the saint; they prosper.

The custom has given rise to a humorous story also. A servant boy who is badly fed in a house where the sacrifice is not made comes in disguise outside the window at night and, pretending that he is Saint Martin, demands his tribute in verse (literal translation):

> Nancy Farrell, are you within?
> I am Saint Martin outside your house;
> Unless you kill the black wether,
> I'll be at your wake a week from tonight!

The frightened woman obeys, and the hungry servant gets his share.

To complete the picture of the sacrifice in Ireland, I wish to point out that replies to a questionnaire on the festival issued some years ago by the Irish Folklore Commission show a curious distribution: the extreme southwest of the country and the northeastern area seem to have no trace of the blood-shedding custom now, nor do the people in those areas remember ever having heard of its being practiced there. The custom is still followed in most other areas or has tended to die out only in recent years.

Apart from the shedding of blood in honor of Saint Martin, Ireland also has a great many traditional legends which associate the saint with mills. A few may be summarized here: (*a*) Saint Martin sees a miller at work on November 11 (the Saint's own feast day) and demands that, in accordance with popular custom, the wheel should cease to turn on that day;[3] the miller refuses to stop the mill, and when the saint insists, throws Martin into the mill, where he is ground to pieces. (*b*) Martin is employed in a mill the owner of which orders his unwilling workmen to work as usual on November 11; Martin refuses, saying that no wheel should turn on that day, and the miller casts him under the wheel and grinds him to death. (*c*) Martin, who is a miller, insists on working his mill on November 11, but instead of getting meal as a result, he finds that sprouting corn issues from between the millstones; he never again uses his mill on that day. (*d*) Martin, who is employed in a mill, is thrown between the wheels when he refuses to work on Sunday. (*e*) A miller refuses to stop work on the saint's feast day, and his mill is swallowed up by the river; from that time forth, his former customers leave their corn on the riverbank each night and find it ground by morning; this goes on until someone steals a portion of the corn from the riverbank by night; the miraculous milling ceases thenceforward. (*f*) Our Saviour, disguised as a poor man, asks Martin, a poor miller, for some food; Martin has none to give but divides his cloak with the poor man[4]; Martin's mill prospers from that day forth.

These legends of Martin's violent death, which are well-known in Ireland, have either given rise to or are based upon the belief that no mill wheel should turn on St. Martin's Day. In many parts of Ireland it was the traditional custom to abstain from milling on that day. Not only should mill wheels not turn, but wheels of all kinds should be still—no spinning was done, no cart was used, even the knitting of socks (which involved the turning of the knitted portion) was set aside for the day. The abstention has now largely fallen into abeyance, but some old people are still loath to depart from ancient custom in this respect.

A third curious aspect of the cult of Saint Martin in Ireland is the legends which attribute to the saint the power of causing miraculous growth and of creating live animals from inanimate matter. These powers are illustrated by the following story, which is, in one form or another, well known in Ireland: A miserly man orders his servant girl to refuse alms to all beggars. During a drought he tries to keep his failing crops alive by sprinkling them with water. While he is thus employed in the field, a stranger (Saint Martin) in the guise of a poor man asks for alms at the house. The servant girl, who is kneading dough for a cake, refuses, giving the correct reason, and expresses regret at being unable to help. The stranger asks for just a small portion of the dough, and when he receives this, he secretly throws it into the middle of the fire and leaves. The girl notices a young green tree growing up from the flames and increasing in size. She runs to her master, and when he witnesses the miracle, he follows the stranger at great speed through briers and bushes, which tear his flesh. On overtaking the stranger, the master asks for forgiveness, which he receives; but he is warned to be more generous in the future. The stranger says he is Saint Martin and then orders the man to cut off the fat portions of his flesh which have been torn and to place them under two inverted vessels, which are to be left undisturbed for a certain time. The girl's curiosity overcoming her, she raises one of the vessels, and mice or rats run out. Surprised, her master raises the other vessel, and out rushes a cat which attacks the mice or rats. Thus came mice, rats, cats, and other animals, too (according to the various versions) into the world. Other variants say that the man threw his cap or mitten after the mice and that it changed into a cat.

Before hazarding an opinion on the possible origin of these aspects of the popular observance of the Feast of Saint Martin in Ireland, I wish to point out that, so far as is known, there is no saint named Martin who was of Irish origin or birth. There has been some conjecture as to which saint of that name is intended, and many think that it is Saint Martin of Tours, who is said to have been related to Saint Patrick, the Irish National Apostle. I suggest that in Ireland the Feast of Saint Martin, on November

11, has been superimposed on a much older pagan festival, which occurred at that time of the year and which had, as one of its main facets, the shedding of sacrificial blood. It has been a common practice of the Christian Church to use a saint's festival for the purpose of Christianizing a pagan one. It is evident that the ritual shedding of blood in the present instance is, of its nature, very old—probably pre-Christian—and had originally nothing to do with appeasing or importuning Saint Martin.

As I have already said, three aspects of this curious festival observance (the sacrificial shedding of blood, the popular association of Saint Martin with the grinding of corn, and the legends which attribute to him miraculous powers of causing growth in plants and of bringing animals into being) make one wonder whether their origin and background are to be sought for within the shores of Ireland at all. I suggest that the legend that Saint Martin was ground to death in a mill (a legend which is not mentioned in the lives of this saint) may be linked up with the story told of how women in Syria in ancient times let down their hair and wept as they ground the corn with querns at the feast of Nisan (April 23), because they feared that the god Tammuz, who had given them the harvest, was being killed between the quern stones and would not be alive next spring to make the new seed grow. Elpidius,[5] a shadowy figure from Mesopotamia, who may have been an early Christian saint and whose cult seems to have developed as did that of Tammuz, was eclipsed by the better-known Saint George, whose feast day is also April 23 and who is popularly said to have been crushed under a great stone (though his biographers say nothing of this in their lives). I make the suggestion here that the popular Irish legend of Saint Martin's violent death in a mill may be a further link in the chain of myth and legend, which I have just mentioned, and that his feast, which occurs around the time of the start of grain-grinding in Ireland, was used to Christianize an ancient festival of thanksgiving and impetration at the end of harvest-time. Saint Martin's supposed powers of miraculously causing plants to grow (even from the middle of a fire) and of creating animals from inanimate matter (portions of human flesh) would fit into the general background of this tentative theory.

Notes

1. Hallowe'en, when the cabbage features prominently in the popular observance of the festival; also referred to, in another variant of this couplet, as "the night of the apple-chewing." (Apples were eaten along with nuts and colcannon on that night.)

2. Also "the night of the bone-chewing," with reference to the eating of meat on that night.

3. This traditional prohibition of wheel-turning also applied to Saint Brigid's Day, Feb. 1. In *Revue des Traditions Populaires*, VI (1891), 201, David Fitzgerald quotes an old English ballad with reference to this point:

> Nel hath left her wool at home,
> The Flanderkin hath stayed his loom,
> No beame doth swinge, nor wheel go round,
> Upon Gurgutum's walled ground.
> Where now an anchorite doth dwell
> To rise and pray at Leonard's bell:
> Martyn hath kicked at Balaam's ass,
> So merrie be old Martilmasse

He also quotes a French couplet from the Vosges in France:

> A la Saint-Martin, bois le vin,
> Et laisse aller l'eau au moulin.

4. Cf. the well-known legend of Martin dividing his cloak with the beggarman in Amiens. This legend is of very rare occurrence in Irish oral tradition.

5. See 'The Name of St. George and Agriculture," by the Rev. E. Burrows, S.J., *The Journal of Theological Studies*, XL (Oct., 1939), 360–65.

Archer Taylor

UNIVERSITY OF CALIFORNIA

BERKELEY, CALIFORNIA

Proverbial Materials in Edward Eggleston, The Hoosier Schoolmaster

The following collection of proverbial materials is a modest addition to the somewhat scanty sources available for the historical study of the proverb in the United States. Although we have several good collections of proverbs current in contemporary oral tradition, we have rather little information about the use of proverbs in the nineteenth century. There are few collections to set beside B. J. Whiting, "Proverbial Sayings from Fisher's River, North Carolina," *Southern Folklore Quarterly,* XI (1947), 174–85, which is based on a collection of stories and sketches published in 1859, or Irene Yates, "A Collection of Proverbs and Proverbial Sayings from South Carolina Literature," *ibid.,* 187–99, which is based on writings of the decade from 1922 to 1932.

Edward Eggleston's famous novel, which was copyrighted in

1871, gives a picture of life in mid-nineteenth-century Indiana. As the following excerpts show, it contains rather little that appears to be strictly local in character, although many of these items are interesting enough for their own sake. The excerpts are from an edition of *The Hoosier Schoolmaster* published at New York in 1913. This edition contains a few historical and explanatory comments by Eggleston on the proverbial materials.

The annotation of the following collection is as brief as possible. Printed books in which I have found parallels are cited in full when first mentioned and are subsequently cited by the author's name or a generally used abbreviation like NED for *A New English Dictionary.* When one of these authorities is cited a second time in the same paragraph, the page reference is not repeated. The number prefixed to the quotations is the number of the page in the previously named edition of *The Hoosier Schoolmaster.* The collection is alphabetized according to the italicized words. These words are not italicized in Eggleston's text.

59: "You see, Mr. Hartsook, my ole man's purty well *along* in the world." 1830 DAE (*Dictionary of American English,* 4 v. [Chicago: 1938–1944]) *along* 1a, and M. M. Mathews, *A Dictionary of Americanisms,* 2 v. (Chicago: 1951) *along* 2, cite "to get along," i.e., to manage, particularly under difficulty or hardship, but do not include this phrase which has here the meaning "to be prosperous." The phrase "to be well along [in years]" has an altogether different meaning.

270: "She . . . turned her *back* on the house of Means forever." *ca.* 1400 NED *back* sb. 24g. L. V. Berrey and M. Van den Bark, *The American Thesaurus of Slang* (New York: 1942), 58.4. This will be subsequently cited as Berrey.

37: "Why, the boys have driv off the last two [schoolmasters], and licked the one afore them like *blazes.*" 1840 Eric Partridge, *A Dictionary of Slang and Colloquial English* (4th ed.; London: 1951), 62. 1845 NED *blazes* 2b. 1849 DAE *blazes.* 1929–34 B. J. Whiting, "The Devil and Hell in Current English Literature," *Harvard Studies and Notes in Philology and Literature,* XX (1938), 244–245. Berrey, 330. 3, cites "Blazes" as a synonym for "Hell."

234: "It was not wise to reject counsel, but all his *blood* was up."

1879 NED *blood* 5. Compare 1631 Burton E. Stevenson, *The Home Book of Proverbs, Maxims, and Familiar Phrases* (New York: 1948), 203:6, and W. G. Smith and Paul Harvey, *The Oxford Dictionary of English Proverbs* (2d ed. Oxford: 1948), 702, which cite "Her Welsh blood is up." This has been reported only from the seventeenth century. It is not clear whether it is a special tradition concerning Welsh temper or is an example of the phrase.

263: "He felt that he was making a clean *breast* of it—at the risk of perdition, with the penitentiary thrown in, if he faltered." 264: "[He] vowed he'd send him to prison if he didn't make a clean *breast*." 1752 NED *breast* 5c. Compare Berrey, 323. 2 (*bosom*).

147: "I don't know how, but they's lots of ways of killing a *cat* besides chokin' her with butter." 1952 B. J. Whiting, "North Carolina Proverbs," in *The Frank C. Brown Collection of North Carolina Folklore*, I (Durham, N. C.: 1952), 382. This collection, which contains valuable notes, is subsequently cited as NC.

239: "No, you didn't answered the witness with a tone and a toss of the head that let the *cat* out." Eggleston has abbreviated the phrase "to let the cat out of the bag." 1796 Stevenson, 285: 6.

222: "But he screwed his *courage* to the sticking place." 1606 Stevenson 437: 6, citing Shakespeare, *Macbeth* I. vii.

153: "But I a'n't a-goin' to be *cut out* by no feller 'thout thrashin' him in an inch of his life." 1600 NED *cut* v. 56 f. 1834 DAE *cut* v. 20 f. Berrey, 13. 2. Partridge, 202 (*cut out of*), marks the phrase "ob.," i.e., obsolescent.

159: "You see my *dander* was up." 1832 DAE *dander* (*began to rise*). 1837–40 NED *dander* sb.[4] (an Americanism). 1851 DAE (*gets his dander up*). Partridge 207, and NED suggest various etymologies. Berrey, 284. 3.

41: "I don't take no sech a *dare*." The phrase "to take a dare" may mean either "to accept a challenge" or "to refuse to accept a challenge," as Eggleston points out in his note. 1876 Stevenson, 486:4; DAE *dare*. 1892 NED *dare* sb. 1.

145: "he'll . . . make us both as 'shamed of ourselves as *dogs* with tin-kittles to their tails."

45. "I'll be *dog-on'd*, said Bill." 95: "Not a *dog-on'd* bit." The spelling reflects Eggleston's suggested etymology, which is discussed in his note. 1851 DAE *dog-gone*; NED *dog-gone*. Partridge, 230, suggests that the word is an American perversion of "God-damned," but NED suggests a different etymology. Euphemisms involving the trans-

position of letters can be cited to support Partridge, but his etymology is not entirely convincing.

206: "He trotted up and down like a *drill-sergeant*."

159: "And I says, ef God sends me to hell he can't make me holler *'nough* nohow." *ca.* 1845 DAE, *holler* v. 2, and Mathews, *holler,* cite only "to holler" in this sense. The locution as in "he made him holler 'enough' " is familiar to me.

57: "She cast at him what are commonly called *sheep's-eyes.*" 1529 *Oxford,* 580; Stevenson, 735: 11; NED *sheep's eye(s).* 1577 Apperson, *English Proverbs and Proverbial Phrases* (London: 1929), 563 *(sheep-ish).* The phrase "to throw (cast) sheep's eyes" is ordinarily used of a man or boy, but for examples used of a woman see 1586 *Oxford.* 1590 Stevenson. 1614 NED *sheep's eye(s),* 1. 1842 NED *sheep's eye(s),* 2. 1852 Stevenson.

245: "I could put my *finger* on them [the thieves]." This signifies "to identify" but not "to identify for the purpose of causing an arrest by the police." The latter meaning seems to be modern in origin. 1889 NED *finger,* sb. 3.

153: "You don't come no *gum games* over me with your saft sodder and all that." Compare 1840 Mathews, *gum game,* citing Bartlett's curious explanation by a reference to the sweet gum tree.

155: "But *I* say, a twix you and me and the *gate-post,* don't you never believe nothing that Mirandy Means says." 1805 *Oxford,* 43 *(post).* 1832 Stevenson, 1838: 1 *(bed-post).* 1838 Apperson, 47 *(general post).* 1839 Apperson *(post).* 1884 DAE *gatepost. ca.* 1920 Stevenson *(gatepost).* 1941 Stevenson *(doorpost).* Berrey, 206. 7 *(bed post, lamp post).* Partridge, 42 *(bed post, door-post, gate-post, gate).*

84: "*Gewhilliky crickets!*" Compare Mathews, *gee* interjection.

71: "Hawkins was a poar Yankee school-master . . . that couldn't tell to save his *gizzard* what we meant by *'low* and by *right smart.*"

39: "You see, it takes *grit* to apply for this school." 1808 DAE *grit,* n.² ("the bully [doats] on *grit*"). 1825 Partridge, 356 ("clear *grit.*"). 1952 NC 418.

109: "It's so pleasant to have one's *hair* stand on end, you know, when one is safe from danger to one's self." Job 4: 15. 1530 Stevenson, 788–89 ("strode upright"). 1600 Stevenson.

47: "I 'low I could whip you in an inch of your life with my left *hand.*" Although acts with the left hand are awkward for most people, the phrase "to do it with one's left hand" means to do something easily.

165: "he thought that perhaps it was not best to 'show his hand,' as he expressed it." 1845 DAE *show,* v. 2. 1879 NED *show* v. 2k. Berrey, 188. 14.

222: "the adage, 'Faint *heart* never won fair lady,' which he had never heard." 1952 NC 42. See Taylor, *California Proverbs.*

121: "Ef it's [oil from a black dog] rendered right, it'll knock the *hindsights* off of any rheumatiz you ever see." 268: "He told his wife that the master had jist knocked the *hindsights* offen that air young lawyer from Lewisburg." 1834 DAE *hindsight;* Mathews, *hindsight.*

164: "People who live in glass *houses* have a horror of people who throw stones." An allusion to the proverb "Those who live in glass houses should not throw stones."

47: "I 'low I could whip you in an *inch* of your life with my left hand." 153: "But I a'n't a-goin' to be cut out by no feller 'thout thrashin' him in an *inch* of his life." The trochaic "within an inch" is more familiar to me. 1726 Stevenson, 1232: 5.

148: "I'll lay you out flat of your back afore you can say *Jack Robinson.*" 1778 Archer Taylor, *Proverbial Comparisons from California,* Folklore Studies 3 (Berkeley: 1954), 66.

166: "his well-seasoned arms were like *iron.*"

85: "He'll beat the whole *kit and tuck* of 'em afore he's through." DAE *kit* 3d and Mathews, *kit* 4, cite only this instance. For other phrases beginning with *kit* see 1952 NC 433 *("kit* and biling"); Berrey, 18.1, 24.4; 380.3.

70: "But *laws!*" Berrey 194.6; 329.2.

161: "You mean, then, that I'm to begin now to put in my best *licks* for Jesus Christ, and that he'll help me?" 1835 Mathews, *lick* 5 ("When you come to put in the scientific *licks"*). 1847 DAE *lick* n.2b ("biggest kind of *licks"*); Stevenson, 1391: 4. Partridge, 480, cites the obsolescent Australian "big *licks,*" which he believes to be an Americanism.

103: "He . . . was not sure that he was the same man who was spelling for dear *life* against Jim Phillips twelve hours before." NED *life* 3c cites the phrase without examples.

76: " 'Walk up to the trough, fodder or no fodder,' as the *man* said to the donkey." A Wellerism. Compare 1836, "A North Alabamian," *A Quarter-Race in Kentucky,* reprinted from *The Spirit of the Times* in W. T. Porter, ed., *Major Thorpe's Scenes in Arkansaw* (Philadelphia [1858]). 24: "I'm a man that always stands up to my fodder, rack or no rack."

82: "He could not throw well enough to make his *mark* in that famous western game of bull-pen." 1854 DAE *mark* n. 5. 1867 Stevenson, 1529: 3; NED *mark* sb. 13b. Berrey, 261.4.

159: "They's plenty not a thousand *miles* away as deserves it [hell]." This locution, which is orally current in such forms as "not a hundred yards away" or "not a hundred miles away" and the like, signifies "here." It does not seem to be recorded in the dictionaries.

86: "Young men . . . were trembling in mortal fear of the *mitten*." 231: "being a disinterested party he could have comforted Bud by explaining Martha's *mitten*." 1838 NED *mitten* 3. 1844 DAE *mitten* 2a; Stevenson, 508: 9 (" to get the *mitten*"). 1847 DAE *mitten* 2b ("to give the *mitten*"); Stevenson, 1600: 5. Compare 1873 Mathews, *mitten* v. Partridge, 524, calls the phrase an Americanism and suggests it may be a corruption of Latin *mittimus.*

37: "They'd fetch you out of doors, sonny, *neck and heels,* afore Christmas." 1740 Stevenson, 1670: 1; Apperson, 439. Berrey, 24. 19. The phrase, which is synonymous with the more familiar "neck and crop," is of rather infrequent occurrence.

72: "she was so dog-on stuck-up that she turned up her *nose* one night at a apple-peelin bekase I tuck a sheet off the bed to splice out the table-cloth." 1579 Stevenson, 1698: 2 ("hold up the *nose*"). 1779 Stevenson, 1695: 1. 1818 NED *nose* 8 ca. Berrey, 228. 2; 292. 2; 352. 2.

207: "Sound as a *nut* on that side!" 263: "But t'other's sound as a *nut.*" 1901 Taylor, *Proverbial Comparisons* 77.

83: "In the minds of all the company the *odds* were in his favor."

139: "Them crack oxen over at Clifty–ah ha'n't a *patchin'* to mine–ah." 1850 Partridge 609 ("but as a *patch* on"), citing Daniel Webster. 1851 DAE *patching* n; Mathews, *patching* n. 1860 NED *patch* sb.[1] 1e.

102: "But, *plague* upon plagues!" 155: "Why, *plague* take it, who said Hanner?" *ca.* 1560 Partridge, 637, citing the interjection as originally colloquial, subsequently Standard English, and now obsolescent. 1595 Stevenson, 2648: 5, citing the Shakespearean "a plague o' both your houses" *(Romeo and Juliet* III.i). Berrey, III.i.

168:"Pete . . . crawled away like a whipped *puppy.*"

222: "reminding himself that 'ef you don't *resk* nothin' you'll never git nothin'.' " Compare the many parallels to the theme cited in Stevenson, 2418: 1 "Nothing venture, nothing have." Early instances are *ca.* 1380 B. J. Whiting, *Chaucer's Use of Proverbs* (Cambridge, Mass.: 1934), 61 ("He which that which nothing undertaketh,

Nothing n'acheveth, be hym looth or deere") and 68 ("For he that naught n'asaieth, naught n'acheveth").

254: "hence Bud, after that distressful Tuesday evening on which Miss Martha had given him the *sack* wished to see Ralph less than any one else." The use of the phrase "to give the sack" in this sense is rare, but note 1847 DAE mitten 2b, a quotation which does not appear under DAE *sack*. For the phrase "to give the sack" in the usual meaning of "to dismiss, discharge" see 1825 Stevenson, 2021: 5.

132: "I'll fight them thieves tell the *sea* goes dry, I will." Compare 1930 John Masefield, *The Everlasting Mercy* (New York: 1930), p. 68: "Who never worked, not he, nor earned, Nor will do till the seas are burned." See also the modern colloquial "When the Atlantic Ocean goes dry." Many occurrences of the theme may go back, directly or indirectly, to Rev. 21: 1. So, for example in Pope's *Messiah* (1712) 11. 105–8:

> The seas shall waste, the skies in smoke decay,
> Rocks fall to dust, and mountains melt away;
> But fix'd his word, his saving pow'r remains;
> Thy realm for ever lasts, thy own Messiah reigns. . . .

Pope may be remembering the Biblical passage. Not all instances of these originate in Revelations. See as examples references to the heavens falling, the Himalayas bursting, the earth splitting, and the sea drying up in the *Mahabharata* III. 23. 130, and a modern Greek dirge for a deceased daughter whose spirit says that she will return "When thou shalt see the ocean dry and in its place a garden (Lucy M. J. Garnett, *Greek Folk Poesy* [2 v., London: 1897], I, 97). For medieval parallels to the use of the theme as a synonym of "forever" see the medieval German "ich wande ez mohten sanfter meres flüte/ Trucken werden danne er scholt ersterben" (K. A. Hahn, ed., *Der jüngere Titurel* [Quedlinburg: 1842], 354, stanza 3583) and "Er sprach: vraw', des mag nicht gesein,/ ez müest' ê trukken sein der Rein" (F. H. von der Hagen, *Gesammtabenteuer*, II [Stuttgart: 1850], 523); and the medieval Latin proverb, "Dum mare siccatur et demon ad astra levatur,/ Tunc prius laycus clero fit fidus amicus" (Jakob Werner, *Lateinische Sprichwörter und Sinnsprüche des Mittelalters*, Sammlung mittellateinischer Texte, 3 [Heidelberg: 1912], 24, D 165, and compare *ibid.*, p. 15, C 176). A passage from Robert Burns's "A Red, Red Rose" will illustrate sufficiently the theme in love poetry:

"And I will luve thee still, my dear,/ Till a' the seas gang dry,/ Till a' the seas gang dry, my dear,/ And the rocks melt wi' the sun!" (*Poetical Works,* J. Logie Robertson, ed. [London: 1904], 318).

155: "I never tuck no *shine* that air way." 1840 DAE *shine* n. 5; Mathews *shine* n. 5 (4); Partridge, 756. Berrey, 353. 5. These authorities cite only the phrase "to take a shine to————."

74: "in hope of the blissful time when somebody should *"set up"* with her of evenings." 1874 DAE *set* v. 10 c; Mathews, *set* v. 2 (c) cites "to set up to ————" in the meaning "to court," but I have not found a record of "to set up with ————" in the dictionaries. The latter but not the former phrase is familiar to me and is still in current use in Indiana.

157: "That's more'n I'd done by a long *shot*." 1848 DAE *shot* 5c; Mathews *shot* b2; Stevenson, 2099: 10. 1888 NED *shot* sb.¹ 9d. The references to a "long shot," in NED *long* a 18, may perhaps be pertinent to an explanation of the phrase but are not examples of the phrase. The phrase appears to be somewhat older than Partridge, 492, indicates.

221: "she must turn the cold *shoulder* to chivalrous, awkward Bud." 1816 NED "cold *shoulder*"; Stevenson, 2101: 11 ("show"). Berrey, 352. 2.

155: "ef you was to say that my sister lied, I'd lick you till yer hide wouldn't hold *shucks*."

147: "He'll come in————*ef* he don't blow us all *sky-high*." 1840 NED *sky-high*. 1952 NC 476. Compare Taylor, *Proverbial Comparisons,* 48 ("as high as the sky").

41: "I'd like to take the *starch* out uv the stuck-up feller." 1868 Mathews "take" v. 2 b (4). Berrey, 304. 4. Partridge, 825, terms the phrase Standard English.

200: "he did not take quite so much *stock* in Dr. Small as his wife did." 1870 DAE *stock* n¹7; Mathews, *stock* n. 5c. 1878 Partridge, 833. Berrey, 165. 4; 289. 6.

144: "Ralph's countenance was cold and hard as *stone*." 150 [his] face . . . as hard as stone." 1847 Taylor *Proverbial Comparisons,* 28 ("cold"). *ca.* 1390 Taylor, *Proverbial Comparisons,* 46 ("hard").

238: "Here Bronson saw that he had caught a *tartar*." 1679 Apperson, 89–90; *Oxford,* 85; Stevenson, 2280–2281: 7. 1725 Partridge, 866.

124: "You cant never *tell*."

155: "Mirandy! *Thunder!* You believed Mirandy." Partridge,

881, says that the exclamation has been current in the last two centuries.

97: "Here, git out! *go to thunder* with you!" 1848 DAE *thunder* 1d; Mathews, *thunder* 2b2.

69: "*Thunder and lightning!* What a manager you *air,* Mr. Hartsook!" 84: *Thunder and lightning!* Partridge, 881, says that the exclamation has been current since the late nineteenth century.

85: "That beats my *time* all holler!" 1869 DAE "beat" v. 3b; Mathews, "beat" v. 3 (2). Berrey, 354. 6; 847. 9. These authorities do not cite the phrase with the addition "all holler."

144: "He was one of them air sort as died in their *tracks,* was Mr. Hartsook." 162: "And he won't run, but he's took up the old flintlock, and says he'll die in his *tracks.*" 1845 Stevenson, 2356: 2; DAE *track* n. II 8.

70: "But laws! don't I remember when he was poarer nor Job's *turkey?*" 1830 Taylor, *Proverbial Comparisons,* 63.